RISING 2.0

RISING 2.0

20 More Women Who Changed India

KIRAN MANRAL

RUPA

Published by
Rupa Publications India Pvt. Ltd 2024
7/16, Ansari Road, Daryaganj
New Delhi 110002

Sales centres:
Bengaluru Chennai Hyderabad
Jaipur Kathmandu Kolkata
Mumbai Prayagraj

P-ISBN: 978-81-969113-8-6
E-ISBN: 978-81-969113-9-3

First impression 2024

10 9 8 7 6 5 4 3 2 1

Printed in India

CONTENTS

INTRODUCTION

This book comes on the heels of *Rising: 30 Women Who Changed India*, a book that also changed me a fair bit as I researched and wrote it. While writing about the lives of those 30 magnificent women who led lives that defied every construct of patriarchy, or, subversively, lived within the boundaries and still managed to leave their mark, I realized how we really do stand on the shoulders of giants who came before us. My generation of women and the young girls who will come after me owe so very much to these women, and often we don't even realize the debt we owe them, leave alone think about repaying that debt by living our lives to the fullest and achieving all our ambitions and dreams.

There are so many more brilliantly blazing lives that were lived before feminism became a word in common parlance. It was feminism that was lived undaunted and unfettered. I wanted to bring forward some more lives of trailblazing women who carved out their own paths, some of whom we have all but forgotten in our relentless march forward to find new inspirations and icons, in this shiny, glittery age of social media influencers and filters. Why should we know these great women then; why should we remember them; what lessons can their lives teach us; and what takeaways can we draw from how they forged through all that came up to block their paths? And most importantly, why do they matter, some of them after almost a century since they were born?

This book features 20 women, right from the pre-Independence era to the current times. Their stories are as different from each other as could be, but what they all have in common is their willingness to go beyond what is prescribed for them, to defy the odds stacked against them and to reach out unapologetically for what they want. There is the story of a politician who rose from being an actress to becoming the chief minister (CM) of a state, loved and feared in equal measure. There is the tale of a chef who broke through the glass ceiling in the culinary world by becoming the first Indian woman chef to be awarded two Michelin stars (the first in 2018 and the second in 2023). Another story is that of a delicate and frail activist from Manipur with a spine of steel, who did not allow a morsel of food into her mouth for 16 long years, while demanding the repeal of the Armed Forces (Special Powers) Act from her state. This fast took her story all around the world. There is the tale of an athlete who stunned the world of sport by coming out with her partner in a society that still views same-sex relationships with prejudiced eyes. Another story is that of a female cricketer who refused to be just called the 'Sachin Tendulkar of women's cricket' in India.

There are many more such inspiring stories of women rising. For instance, the story of a wide-eyed, long-haired girl from small-town Haryana who wanted to touch the stars and went out into space. Another one is of an icon who wrote poems that made the heart sing and gave fiery speeches that aroused people to demand independence from the colonial rule. We get to see the grit of a woman from Chennai who defied caste and religious barriers to marry a foreigner who was much older than her, travelled the world with him and then threw herself into learning and popularizing a dance form that only *devadasis* practised back then, giving it the respectability it commands today. You will also find the tale of a doctor who left an unhappy marriage, went to Singapore and joined the territorial army founded by Netaji Subhas Chandra Bose and fought the British.

Along with these, there are riveting tales we may have not even heard of before. For instance, the story of a woman who studied law even before Independence and became a judge. There is the heart-warming tale of a tribal woman who, with her knowledge of plants and the forests, became the keeper of forests in Karnataka and is now called the goddess of the forests. We also have the story of a firebrand who took her love for martial arts and defence to become such an expert in the field that she went on to become the first civilian trainer for the Indian armed forces. Additionally, the story of a singer who lived a life of such pain that it echoed in every line that she sang, leaving behind a legacy that no singer has yet been able to fill, is sure to inspire us.

There are countless more such stories: a woman who became a lawyer before women were allowed to practice at the Bar, forcing the world to acknowledge her capabilities; a writer who wrote about lesbianism and had to face a trial for obscenity in her work that was iconoclastic in how unabashedly it explored female sexuality; a botanist who left her small town in Kerala and travelled the world to learn and catalogue, before coming back to India to bequeath her wealth of knowledge to the country; a firebrand activist who was instrumental in the revival of Indian arts and crafts in newly independent India; a writer who wrote unabashedly about desire and yearning at a time when women weren't even expected to have a voice, let alone talk about such things; a woman from the heartland of India who was married off young, but by the sheer dint of determination, educated herself and became a fiery reporter, chronicling stories from the hinterland; and a woman thrown out of her marital home with a new born, who then went on to become a mother to hundreds of orphans.

The aim has never been to put these women on pedestals. Pedestals are shaky places, and can be easily dislodged. As with *Rising*, my previous book, my effort has been to chronicle the essence of their lives—with empathy, with objectivity and with as much respect as their monumental achievements deserve. Some lives have been controversial, but within the controversies have been their courage and refusal to be boxed into corners or toe the expected line. The essays are pieced together from information available through articles, books and other reference material and sources. A few have kindly consented for an interview, telling us their journey first-hand. These essays don't aim to be comprehensive; it would be impossible to go in depth in a few thousand words. But these few thousand words should suffice to light a flame of curiosity and interest, to tell young girls and women reading these stories that it is completely alright to find your path and stick to it, even if the world around you dissuades you from stepping out of the carefully delineated boundaries.

Some of their names are familiar to us; we know their lives, we know their journeys. Others are names that hover on the precipice of unfamiliarity. We may have heard of them, but the details of their lives and achievements are blurred. Yet others we may have not heard of at all, but they deserve to be known and lauded. J. Jayalalithaa, Ismat Chughtai, Begum Akhtar, Dutee Chand, Mithali Raj, Kalpana Chawla, Irom Chanu Sharmila, Cornelia Sorabji, Anna Chandy, Rukmini Devi Arundale, Kavita Devi Bundelkhandi, Janaki Ammal, Tulasi Gowda, Seema Rao, Kamala Das, Garima Arora, Sindhutai Sapkal, Captain Lakshmi Sahgal, Sarojini Naidu, Kamaladevi Chattopadhyay—they are all women who have lived very different lives. However, they have all been pathbreakers, intent on creating their own destinies, following whatever passion and purpose called out to them. They did not set out to become pathbreakers; they did not begin their lives thinking they would be iconoclasts.

Life set them along certain paths and they stayed true to the path, no matter what came their way: social censure, widowhood, divorce, failed relationships, systemic barriers, lack of support and more. Whether they were controversial; faced the pressure of public opinion against them; or their families turned their backs on them, they picked themselves up and carried on, seemingly undaunted. And in their determination to forge ahead is where we, the women and young girls of today, must draw our strength. It is the reserve of strength, hidden deep within us, which emerges only when all doors seem to slam shut in our faces. Through their lived experiences, they inspire us to not lose hope; to soldier on; and to know that anything is possible if one is determined enough. They teach us that if we are firm enough to not bend to the world, it may just be possible for the world to bend to us.

In writing about their lives, I can only hope that young girls in schools and colleges (who might read this book) will realize that they truly stand on the shoulders of giants. I hope they realize that these women have struggled so that this generation of young women and girls can stand up tall, and reach for the stars.

1

MITHALI RAJ

THE WILLOW WIELDER

You could blame it all on sleep. An illustrious, decades-long career in women's cricket came about because a six-year-old Mithali Raj refused to wake early, in time for her older brother's cricket coaching class. At the crack of dawn, the family needed to leave together for the coaching, which was close to their home at the St John's Academy, Secunderabad. Her parents would then head to office from there, and the kids to school. Back then, her mother worked with the engineering instruments division at Lawrence and Mayo, and her father worked with Andhra Bank, having joined the bank after retiring from the Indian Air Force. But Mithali just wouldn't wake up on time.

Mithali's refusal to get up in the morning threw a spanner in their plans, and the schedule of the entire family would go for a toss. Her mother, Leela, told *rediff.com* in an interview, 'This girl, she was very lazy in the morning. Morning she loved to sleep. That morning sleep. We shouldn't disturb her and all that. That became a big nuisance for us. We're all early risers. This girl wouldn't get up from her sleep. Even if she did, she'd been in a cranky mood because her sleep had been disturbed.'[1]

Fortunately for her parents, there was one thing that Mithali loved more than sleep—her brother, Mithun. She adored him, and would do anything for him. Her mother would tell Mithali that they needed to go watch Mithun practice, and she would spring up instantly, only to doze off on the back of her father's Jawa bike. She would wake up only when they reached the cricket ground. They would then sit by the boundary of the ground. Mithali would throw the ball back when it came to the boundary, and would spend her time doing her school work. Her father would clean his bike and watch the practice.

Occasionally, the coach, Jyoti Prasad would bowl to the little Mithali, teaching her to catch, giving her a borrowed bat to hit shots. He realized that this little girl had potential—immense potential. After a few months of noticing her skills, he felt that this potential needed to be formally harnessed. He told Mithali's father quite matter-of-factly that instead of concentrating on their son's career in cricket, it would be better if they focussed on their daughter. That remark changed Mithali's life forever. Instead of accompanying her brother to his cricket practice, she now started training in cricket herself. Jyoti Prasad recommended that Mithali should be trained under a National Institute of Sports coach called Sampath Kumar who was said to be a tough taskmaster. Sampath was then the coach for two women's cricket teams in Secunderabad. Tiny Mithali, in her brother's whites and with his discarded cricket bat, went off to train under Coach Kumar.[2]

Sampath recognized Mithali's potential early on, and told her father that he would make Mithali play for the country. Her parents didn't think too much about it. After all, Mithali was so young; she had only just about begun coaching a few months prior. Declaring that she was 'Team India' material and that he would get her there seemed like a brag from the coach at that point. Sachin Tendulkar had debuted for India at 14 and Sampath vowed that he would make Mithali debut for India at the same age. All he asked from her parents was their complete support. He told her parents that if not 14, she would definitely debut with the Indian team by 16. Her parents, though initially sceptical, decided to give it a shot and put their entire focus behind Mithali's training.

And so, Mithali started living the life of a sportsperson, with her day beginning at four in the morning with training that took up almost six hours every day. Sampath focussed on training Mithali to bat for hours in the narrow corridors of the school, making her bat with a stump to ensure she was hitting the ball in the middle. As Mithali mentioned in an interview with *The Cricket Monthly*, 'Sir used to hit me with a stick if the ball touched the walls.'[3]

She gave up learning Bharatanatyam to focus on cricket. While her parents were fully focussed on Mithali's training, not everyone in her family was happy about her learning to play cricket. For instance, her grandmother was appalled by the idea. She was worried about things like who would marry her, what if she got injured and why make a girl play a boy's sport. However, her parents were fully committed to seeing their daughter become a cricketer. They bulked up her diet in keeping with her nutrition requirements. It all paid off in the end. Hours of daily training resulted in her becoming one of the best technical batters in India, who scored a prolific number of runs and, more importantly, scored them with impeccable technique.

Her career started magnificently when she was nine and became the youngest player to be selected to represent the state in the sub-juniors. It was at this point that the enormity of the path they had chosen for their daughter first hit her mother. Sending a cocooned nine-year-old alone with the team to Jalandhar for 10 days made her mother extremely anxious. Those were not times of mobile phones and instant messaging, and the young Mithali sent inland letters to her parents to let them know she had reached safely and was well. The team travelled in unreserved second-class train coaches, there was no air conditioning and the accommodation was basic. However, travelling together as a team was fun for Mithali. She was often with team members and opponents who were at times years older than her. To ensure that she got batting practice that challenged her, her father made her bat against the older boys.

This was the first of a career that was later defined by constant travel away from home, at times for 15 to 20 days at a stretch. By the time she was 13, she had made it into the Andhra Pradesh cricket team. In 1997, when she was only 14, she was named among the probables for the Women's Cricket World Cup, but didn't make the final list at that time.[4]

She finally wore the India cap when she was 16 on 26 June 1999, with an unbeaten 114 against Ireland in her India ODI (One Day International) debut at Milton Keynes, England.[5] She opened the batting for India on that day with another debutant, Reshma Gandhi, and, between the two of them, they batted through the entire 50 overs, both scoring centuries. She was 16 years and 205 days old on that day, making her the youngest woman to score an international century. Her record was broken in October 2021 when Amy Hunter of Ireland scored a century on her sixteenth birthday. Sadly, though, Coach Kumar was no longer around to see his protégé make his prediction come true, as he had passed away in an accident a couple of years before.[6]

Her Test debut was in 2001 against South Africa in Lucknow, where she scored a duck. She soon got over that initial debacle and went on to prove herself with her bat. In her third Test at Taunton in August 2002, in the final test match of the tour, she scored 214 and broke records.[7] This 598-minute knock of 214 in Taunton broke the previously held record of 209 runs. After 2002, in the next four years, she played five Test matches and none in the eight years after that. She was already firmly on her way to becoming the bedrock of batting strength for the Indian women's cricket team.

She went on to become one of the most prolific ODI scorers, playing in 232 matches, with a record 7,805 runs at an average of

50.68. She went on to play 12 Tests and 89 T20Is for the country, scoring 699 and 2,364 runs respectively.[8]

In 2002, she was down with typhoid during the CricInfo Women's World Cup. Some believe that her absence seriously impacted the performance of the team. In 2004, she was entrusted with the captaincy of the Indian women's cricket team, which ran till 2022. In 2005, she was appointed the permanent captain of the Indian women's team and captained India twice at the ICC ODI Women's World Cup finals in 2005 and 2017. She captained the team into their first finals in 2005 South Africa. Sadly, they lost to Australia that year.[9] The next year, in August 2006, she led the Indian team to their first Test and series victory in England. She also won the Asia Cup that year, for the second time in 12 months.

She was the highest run scorer in women's international cricket; the first player to score seven consecutives 50s in ODI matches; and the second woman cricketer worldwide and the first Indian woman cricketer to score 10,000 international runs, reaching the landmark number in her third ODI against South Africa in March 2021. She is rightfully regarded as one of the all-time cricketing greats, who dominated Indian women's cricket for over two decades with her batting prowess as a right-handed opening batter. She would occasionally pitch in for the team as a right-arm leg-break bowler as well.

Interestingly, in a career that spanned 23 years, she only played 12 Test matches. This is, perhaps, telling of the disparity between men's and women's cricket. It was a disparity she was all too aware of. On the eve of the 2017 ODI World Cup, at a press conference, she was asked who her favourite male cricketer was. It was a question that irked her and she had no qualms in making her displeasure heard. Her response has since gone down in the annals of cricket history. She shot back, saying, 'Do you ask the same question to a male cricketer?'[10] Paradoxically, she was called the 'Sachin Tendulkar of Indian women's cricket'.[11]

She is the highest run-scorer in women's international cricket, and in her two-decade-long career she has played for the country across all formats—Test, ODIs and T20 matches as well. She also became the first woman with 200 ODI matches under her cap on 1 February 2019, during India's series against New Zealand. In July 2021, Mithali gained the honour of being the highest run-scorer in women's international cricket, when she surpassed Charlotte Edwards' record of 10,273 runs.[12]

She later gained the distinction of being the first woman to complete 20 years in international cricket. In September 2019, she decided to retire from T20s in order to focus on one-day cricket. Barely three years later, in June 2022, she announced her retirement from the game entirely. She wrote on her social media, 'I set out as a little girl on the journey to wear India blues...the journey was full of highs and some lows. Each event taught me something unique and the last 23 years have been the most fulfilling, challenging and enjoyable years of my life. Like all journeys, this one too must come to an end.'[13]

After the 2017 ODI Women's Cricket World Cup, the women's cricket team shot into the limelight, and it meant that many of the players became known across the country. Mithali Raj, with her ability to express herself well, saw many brand endorsement deals come her way. She saw an unprecedented surge in her social media following, going from a few thousands to millions. Book and film deals about her life were being sought. Mithali Raj, the captain of the India women's cricket team, became a brand overnight.

She was on hoardings and on the cover of fashion magazines like *Vogue*, featured alongside the best of Bollywood and the business world. This success had come after years of struggle on her end and immense sacrifice on her parents' part. Her mother had quit her job to be able to focus full time on Mithali's training. Her father ran the home on a single income and they lived a frugal life, without indulgences like new clothes and celebrations for years, in order to fund Mithali's career, pay her school fees and put food on the table. Back then, there was no support for the women's team from the Board of Control for Cricket in India (BCCI) and Mithali's father had to scout around for funds and sponsorship on his own.

To quote her:

> There were a lot of challenges and a lot of sacrifices were made by the people who invested their time to make me a cricketer. My dad had to go to banks to ask for sponsorship deals. All I know is, whenever there is a need for motivation or inspiration, I just have to look at these people because they have done all they could at a time when they could have easily turned their back on me.[14]

There were other sacrifices she made. As mentioned earlier, Bharatanatyam, which she pursued till she was in Class 8, was one casualty of her passion for cricket. The other casualty was her studies. Though she was a good student and fared well in her boards, she could not focus on her studies through college and had to drop out. But she remains a reader and a learner. In fact, one of the most iconic photograph of hers is that of her reading a book while waiting to bat at the Women's World Cup in 2017. This got her the moniker of 'Captain Cool.'[15]

It was something her mother had ingrained in her. She was taught to not cry on the field, no matter what happens. She remained stoic and composed on the field all through her career, through the highs and lows. However, of course, there was some controversy. It is inevitable that there will be controversies surrounding such a long and illustrious career. Mithali's biggest controversy, perhaps, was her conflict with the India Coach Ramesh Powar in the Caribbean during the 2018 T20 Cup. Things reached a peak during the league phase of the World Cup, when Powar asked Mithali to move down in the batting order. Mithali was excluded from the semi-finals against

England, a vitally important knock-out match that India ended up losing. This unpleasant phase saw a lot of dirty linen being washed in public, with the media having a field day with the fallout between the two. They are said to have reconciled later.[16]

Towards the end of her career, she was not included in the three-team Women's T20 Challenge Tournament. In the BCCI's Senior Women's T20 Trophy, Mithali was part of the Railways team but chose not to play and instead acted as a mentor to the team.[17]

In an interview with *Scroll.in*, Nooshin Al Khadeer, Mithali's teammate and one of her closest friends, said, 'I have seen her from 1999 and for me, I don't see any change apart from the ageing. Her hunger stayed the same throughout. I have also seen a Mithali who has singlehandedly stood in the centre, making sure that India won matches when there was no media coverage, no social media.'[18] She also spoke about an innings where she went to the crease with a knee issue and helped the team put runs on the board and win. To quote her from the same interview:

> People talk about power hitting in the modern cricket... that innings of hers was a killer knock. Mind you, she had ACL issues at that time in her knee. It's not easy for a batter to play with a knee issue and to come up with that knock required a lot of character. You won't even get any footage of that match, we were the deprived ones at that point.[19]

In that match, with a knee that was troubling her, Mithali scored 91 off 104 balls, at a strike rate of 87.50.

To quote authors Karunya Keshav and Sidhanta Patnaik about the Mithali-Jhulan (referred to as 'MilJhul' by fans) partnership in their book *The Fire Burns Blue*,

> Aptly, 'miljhul' means together; nobody else's fate in Indian women's cricket has been as intertwined as that of the two. When the game needed somebody to be the best, to drag

> Indian cricket from the amateur, lackadaisical era of the '90s into the professional period of the 2000s, it was lucky it got MilJhul, two of the most thorough professionals.[20]

Post her retirement, Mithali continues to be involved with and is a fierce advocate for the advancement of women's cricket in India. On 7 December 2022, she posted on her LinkedIn, saying: '"There is nothing more powerful in the world than an idea whose time has come." We are on the verge of stepping into 2023 and the idea, that I believe whose time has come, is the rise of Indian women's cricket.'[21]

The awards Mithali has received are numerous, befitting a career so magnificent. She's been awarded the Wisden 'Leading Woman Cricketer in the World' Award in 2017, the Arjuna Award in 2003, the Padma Shri in 2015 and Major Dhyan Chand Khel Ratna in 2021. She has also been awarded 'The Youth Sports Icon of Excellence' Award, *Vogue* 'Sportsperson of the Year' Award and the *BBC* '100 Women' Award among others.[22]

In a country obsessed with men's cricket, she has had a movie made on her life; *Shabaash Mithu*, with Bollywood actress Taapsee Pannu playing her in the movie. She is perhaps the only female cricketer to have a movie made on her life. After Mary Kom, M.S. Dhoni and Milkha Singh, she is perhaps the only sportsperson to have a movie made on their life in India. She is a role model for those who followed her into the game, like Smriti Mandhana. To quote Mandhana from a 2019 interview to *The Cricket Monthly*,

> The sense of responsibility she has shown over these years. There was a phase of ten years when Indian batting used to depend on her. The fact that she never cribbed about it, and took on that pressure—that's one thing I'd like to have in my head, because it's hard when you know your wicket is important and that if you lose your wicket, the course of the match might change. [...] She's calm and relaxed even

> if there are, say, two or three dot balls. I used to get a bit panicky earlier, but she has always been calm.[23]

Cricket consumed all of her life. She didn't get married. Not that she didn't want to; in fact, when she was in her mid-20s, her parents did try to set up a match for her. However, the expectation from the prospective grooms that her cricket career would be secondary to being a wife and a daughter-in-law seemed to put her off the idea. In an interview with *rediff.com*, her mother spoke about how they did try to find her a life partner when she was around 24. To quote her:

> But the boy, when he would speak to Mithali—there were two-three boys—started questioning her: 'How long will you play cricket?' Or, 'See, I am in the merchant navy, so you will have to see my finances.' One boy told her: 'Hey look, listen, playing cricket is one thing. Next thing, suppose we have babies, I'm not going to do any diaper cleaning. Nothing I'm going to do. Totally you only have to do.' And the third thing he told her: 'I want to ask you, suppose my mommy's sick and you have a tournament, a match to go to. Are you going to go to the match or look after my mummy?'[24]

These kinds of encounters completely put Mithali off the idea of getting married. She despaired that as a woman cricketer, her career would never be taken as seriously as a man playing professional cricket.

Now, post retirement, she remains as passionately committed to the promotion of women's cricket. She has no regrets about retirement. To quote her, 'I'm content with the way my career is shaped, being part of the evolution of women's cricket. I thoroughly enjoyed playing. I'm fine with my retirement and it was the right time to move on. There's no regret.'[25]

With her formidable career she leaves behind big shoes to fill. Now, she can rest on her laurels and watch with pride as women's cricket in India finally seems to be getting its rightful place under the sun.

NOTES

1 Pande Daniel, Vaihayasi, 'My Daughter Mithali Raj,' *rediff.com*, 9 November 2018, http://tinyurl.com/33excb7w. Accessed on 26 December 2023.

2 Ibid.

3 Kishore, Shashank, 'The Sleepy Girl Who Woke up a Generation,' *The Cricket Monthly*, September 2016, http://tinyurl.com/3r9ycebk. Accessed on 28 December 2023.

4 'From a Classical Dancer to India's Women Team Captain, Here's the Story of Mithali Raj!,' *Wings*, 10 February 2023, http://tinyurl.com/5d5n8t2h. Accessed on 28 December 2023.

5 'Mithali Raj,' *ESPNcricinfo*, http://tinyurl.com/454dw466. Accessed on 28 December 2023.

6 Kishore, Shashank, 'The Sleepy Girl Who Woke up a Generation,' *The Cricket Monthly*, September 2016, http://tinyurl.com/3r9ycebk. Accessed on 28 December 2023.

7 'On This Day: Mithali Raj Scores Record-Breaking 214 against England at Taunton in 2002,' *Firstpost*, 17 August 2020, http://tinyurl.com/5n7nn72p. Accessed on 28 December 2023.

8 'Mithali Raj Retirement: 10 Major Records That Highlight the Icon's Incredible 23-Year Long Cricketing Career,' *CricketNext*, 9 June 2022, http://tinyurl.com/26r8jft6. Accessed on 28 December 2023.

9 'Mithali Raj,' *ESPNcricinfo*, http://tinyurl.com/454dw466. Accessed on 28 December 2023.

10 'A Journalist Asked Mithali Raj to Name Her Favourite Male Cricketer. She Gave a Cracking Reply!,' *The Cricket Lounge*, 4 February 2023, http://tinyurl.com/53n8vetx. Accessed on 28 December 2023.

11 ‘Mithali Raj, India’s Female Tendulkar, Becomes the Highest Run-Scorer in the History of ODI Cricket: Facts about the Indian Skipper’, *India Today*, 13 July 2017, http://tinyurl.com/yc5vm9tw. Accessed on 28 December 2023.

12 Tanya, ‘Mithali Raj Becomes First Woman Cricketer to Play 200 ODIs’, *NDTV Sports*, 1 February 2019, http://tinyurl.com/4dsubbmt. Accessed on 28 December 2023; ‘India Captain Mithali Raj Sets New World Record, Overtakes Charlotte Edwards for Most Runs in Women’s Cricket’, *India Today*, 3 July 2021, http://tinyurl.com/dtbx7y3b. Accessed on 4 January 2024.

13 Nalwala, Ali Asgar, ‘Mithali Raj, India Legend, Retires from All Forms of Cricket’, *Olympics.com*, 8 June 2022, http://tinyurl.com/bddtxhmp. Accessed on 28 December 2023.

14 ‘“Sports Teaches You to Move On”: Mithali Raj’, *The Indian Express*, 19 September 2022, http://tinyurl.com/mbpmkc43. Accessed on 28 December 2023.

15 ‘Captain Cool: When Mithali Raj Was Spotted Reading a Book before Her Batting at 2017 World Cup-Watch’, *SportsNow*, 8 June 2022, http://tinyurl.com/56y5rnsp. Accessed on 28 December 2023.

16 ‘Mithali Raj Retires from International Cricket’, *ESPN*, 8 June 2022, http://tinyurl.com/bfd2bku8. Accessed on 28 December 2023.

17 Ibid.

18 Mohanarangan, Vinayakk, ‘Mithali Raj: A Glorious Cricketing Career That Went beyond Just Incredible Numbers’, *Scroll.in*, 9 June 2022, http://tinyurl.com/ycxb2e8a. Accessed on 28 December 2023.

19 Ibid.

20 Keshav, Karunya, and Sidhanta Patnaik, ‘Book Excerpt: When Indian Women’s Cricket Needed Somebody to Be the Best, It Got Mithali and Jhulan’, *Scroll.in*, 5 November 2018, http://tinyurl.com/4ev86wx3. Accessed on 28 December 2023.

21 'Mithali Raj's Post', *LinkedIn*, http://tinyurl.com/274ep8m2. Accessed on 4 January 2024.

22 'Who Is Mithali Raj?', *Business Standard*, http://tinyurl.com/4zjt698r. Accessed on 28 December 2023.

23 Ghosh, Annesha, '"I Never Thought I'd Hear People Say They Felt Threatened to Bowl to Me"', *The Cricket Monthly*, 6 March 2019, http://tinyurl.com/3vyuwyxa. Accessed on 28 December 2023.

24 Pande Daniel, Vaihayasi, 'My Daughter Mithali Raj', *rediff.com*, 9 November 2018, http://tinyurl.com/33excb7w. Accessed on 26 December 2023.

25 'Mithali Raj on Having No Regrets after Retirement from Cricket: It Was the Right Time to Move On', *India Today*, 13 February 2023, http://tinyurl.com/2p7u5s9c. Accessed on 28 December 2023.

2

DUTEE CHAND

SPRINTING OUT

Dutee Chand has many laurels to her name for her performance on the track, but what set her down irrevocably in the annals of history is the fact that she is perhaps the first athlete in India to openly come out as LGBTQIA+. She did so in 2019, barely a year after the Supreme Court of India decriminalized homosexuality. It took a tremendous amount of gumption to do so, but then, Dutee has always been a person who has faced controversy head on. She also didn't shy away from taking on the inevitable media spotlight that ensued.

Let's get the professional credentials out of the way first. Dutee Chand is the first Indian to ever win a gold medal in a 100 m race at an international event; the third Indian woman to ever qualify for the Women's 100 m event at the Summer Olympics; and a two-time Olympian from India. She won silver in 2018 at the Jakarta Asian Games, and in 2019 she won gold at the FISU World University Games (formerly Universiade) with a timing of 11.32 seconds in the 100 m.[1] These are very impressive achievements, made even more impressive when you think about the difficult circumstances she came from and the incredible odds she had to beat to get there.

She was born on 3 February 1996 to Chakradhar and Akhuji Chand, saree weavers from the Chhaka Gopalpur village in the

Jajpur district of Odisha (previously Orissa). The family was extremely poor; in fact, they were below the poverty line. As a traditional weaver, her father spent a month weaving two sarees which earned him a pittance. On this meagre sum, he had to feed his wife and six children. They lived in a single-room tenement. It was survival in its barest form. The only path out from dire poverty for the children was the hope of a permanent job in government organizations. Because education was difficult, this could only come through prowess in sports.

Dutee's older sister, Saraswati Chand, became a national-level runner, with the hope of eventually getting a government job through the sports quota. She encouraged Dutee to take up sports in the same hope. It was their one chance to escape their circumstances. Dutee ran barefoot along the river bank in her village to train because there were no tracks in her village. To quote Dutee:

> During that time, financial strain was huge on us. Children who did well in sports would get free books and their school fee was waived off. My sister got job in police through sports quota. I realised sport was the only way for a better tomorrow. In the beginning there was no coach to guide me. I had no proper shoes or a good diet. I would survive only on rice and vegetables. By the time I turned 10, I won the scholarship to a government-run sports hostel in Bhubaneswar. From there things became better.[2]

Young Dutee showed immense promise and became a national champion in the Under-18 category in 2012, with 11.85 seconds in the 100 m event. In 2013, she got the bronze in the Asian Athletics Championship's 200 m event with a timing of 23.81 seconds. In the same year, she reached the finals of the World Youth Championship. She also became a national champion in the 100 m and 200 m events, with a timing of 11.23 in the 100 m finals and 23.73 in the 200 m at the National Senior

Athletics Championship at Ranchi. Even with this, she was determined to complete her education. The same year she enrolled herself to get a law degree.[3]

She found support from the founder of the Kalinga Institute of Industrial Technology (KIIT), Dr Achyuta Samanta. To quote Dutee:

> I come from a very poor family. So when I completed my 12th grade I was wondering how I could carry on my education along with sports. I was also facing a lack of funds for my training. At that very moment, I was introduced to Dr. Achyuta Samanta. He stood by me like a pillar and offered me to study law at his university for free. Besides, this he has constantly provided me with all sorts of support to train and grow as an athlete. He does the same to date.[4]

The next year she faced a controversy that almost stymied her career. It was in 2014 that the controversy over hyperandrogenism began. She had won two golds at the Asian Junior Athletics Championships in the 200 m and the 4 x 400 m relay. This was in June 2014. She had a timing of 23.74 in the 200 m and was hoping that it would help her qualify for the 2014 Commonwealth Games. However, she was dropped from the contingent at the last moment, with the Athletic Federation of India (AFI) saying that she was ineligible to compete as a female athlete because of hyperandrogenism. This was followed by her being dropped from the Indian contingent for the 2014 Asian Games.[5] This decision of the AFI led to much criticism from intersex activists and advocates. To quote Dutee, 'Suddenly everyone was calling me a boy. It was an incredibly tough period. The only test I knew was dope test, I didn't know what tests they were doing on me that day. Once the news was all over, people started viewing me differently. Many shunted me.'[6]

Chand was found to have hyperandrogenism, a medical condition where her body produces the androgen hormone, testosterone, at higher levels than commonly found in women. The International Association of Athletics Federation (IAAF) had introduced a rule back in 2011, making women with higher testosterone levels ineligible to compete in the women's category. The International Olympic Committee (IOC) had also adopted this rule before the 2012 Olympics in London. Dutee then had few choices: she could quit sports, have her testosterone levels lowered through medical intervention or she could challenge this decision.

She was clear on her stand that she had not done anything unacceptable. This was how her body was made naturally. So, she decided to fight this decision. She found support in Kolkata-based gender activist Payoshni Mitra, who approached the Sports Authority of India (SAI) to take up cudgels for Dutee Chand. The SAI brought together an international group of scientists, former athletes and bioethicists, including Canadian Olympian and author, Bruce Kidd, and medical anthropologist, Katrina Karkazis, from the Stanford Center for Biomedical Ethics to take up Dutee's cause. A Canadian law firm, Davies Ward Phillips & Vineberg LLP, took up her case pro bono.[7]

She appealed to the Court of Arbitration for Sports. Her case led to the suspension of the IAAF policy on hyperandrogenism. The case, *Dutee Chand v. Athletics Federation of India (AFI) & The International Association of Athletics Federations (IAAF)*, was decided in July 2015. According to the ruling, there was a lack of evidence proving that testosterone enhanced the performance of a female athlete and the IAAF was notified to provide evidence of the same. Because of this ruling, Chand's suspension from competing was overruled, allowing her to compete in international meets again. It was a difficult period for her, but she emerged triumphant.

In an interview, the middle-distance runner athlete Santhi Soundarajan, who had faced a similar controversy earlier, extended her support to Dutee, saying:

> They have tested her at the last minute, humiliated her and broken her heart. All sorts of things have been written about her. [...] That things became public, is wrong. Would they have done it if it was their daughter? Who is responsible for her future now? The job and the money are secondary problems. Think about how much she would have suffered. She is not from a wealthy or powerful family; just another ordinary family. Even if she gets help from the state association, can she stay in peace in her village?[8]

To quote Dutee from an interview with *The Indian Express*, 'These four years have been extremely tough for me. The negativity, fear of my career ending prematurely, insensitive comments about my body, I have faced them all. I am extremely relieved that I can run fearlessly again, knowing that now my battle exists only on the track and not off it.'[9]

The change in the hyperandrogenism rule allowed her to resume competing in track events. She then competed in the 2016 Asian Indoor Athletics Championship, in the 60 m category. In the qualifiers itself, she set a new national record at 7.28 seconds, winning bronze in the final with 7.37 seconds. In the women's 100 m sprint in the 2016 Federation Cup National Athletics Championship, she broke a 16-year-old record to win gold but missed the Rio Olympics qualification cut-off of 11.32 seconds by one hundredth of a second. A little later, in June 2016, she clocked 11.30 seconds in the heats and 11.24 seconds in the finals at the XXVI International Meeting G. Kosanov Memorial in Almaty, Kazakhstan, and qualified for the Rio 2016 Olympic Games. This was 30 years after P.T. Usha had taken part in the 1980 Moscow Olympics.[10] Unfortunately, she bowed out at the heats itself, clocking 11.69 seconds. In 2016, she also got appointed as an assistant manager in the Odisha Mining Corporation.[11]

In 2017 she made a powerful comeback, with two bronze medals at the Asian Athletics Championships. At the 2018 Asian Games, she won silver in the women's 100 m with a timing of

11.32, and another silver in the 200 m. This 100 m silver for India came 32 years after P.T. Usha had won it in 1986, and the 200 m silver came 16 years after Saraswati Saha had won gold in 2002 at Busan. Nonetheless, despite the medals, she was still worried about the ongoing legal battle that could snatch this away from her. To quote her at the time, 'My legal team helped me to come back. But nobody could guarantee what will happen in the future. Caster Semenya is still fighting. There is always fear but you need to overcome it.'[12] Dutee even sent an email offering Caster her legal team.[13]

In 2019, she caused another storm. In May 2019, she came out to the world, publicly declaring that she was in a same-sex relationship. She added that the decriminalization of gay sex in 2018 by the Supreme Court of India had encouraged her to speak out about her sexuality. With this brave declaration, she became the first openly queer athlete in India. She had no idea what the word 'lesbian' even meant, or about the LGBTQIA+ community. She had met her partner at a village festival, they had exchanged phone numbers, kept in touch and eventually become close. In an interview with *MansWorld* she said, 'After some months, we realised that we would want to spend the rest of our lives together, and even get married. I never thought about whether it's right or wrong to think like that. Everything felt absolutely normal to me.'[14]

To quote her from an interview with *ESPN*:

> When I was at the sports hostel in Bhubaneswar as a junior, my closest friend was also my roommate. [...] I didn't know what being a lesbian meant. I had never heard of the term either. But when she entered into a relationship with a boy, I felt jealous. I couldn't understand why.[15]

Coming out in public wasn't something she had planned. She was forced to do so when reports about her sexuality came out in the press, with her older sister going to the press about it. About a year before the news became public, she had come out to her mother and older sister and expressed her wish to get married to her partner. She had initially planned to come out after 2020, as she was unsure of how the revelation would affect her professional career. But her sister, who had been until then her mentor, took the revelation badly and went to the press about it when relations between them became estranged. Dutee decided that she would speak up for herself to the media in order to stop the slanderous stories about her and her partner.

The backlash she had to face was debilitating. Her village turned against her, her own sister threatened to disown her from the family. Her partner's family was more accepting. The people in her village who had earlier taken great pride in her achievements accused her of humiliating them. It broke her heart, but she said she wasn't angry with them. They just didn't know differently, she told reporters. It was a tough time for her. To quote her from an interview:

> Everyone knows that I am a straight forward person, so I had no fear in confessing that I happen to love a girl from my village. But small towns and the majority of the population did not take my life decision positively. I had to face a lot of backlash for this. For 15 days I could not leave my house. Even the media was highlighting the issue a lot. Thankfully I received immense support as well and could win over the negativity. To date, our families are not very happy about my love life, but it is what it is.[16]

By this one radical act of speaking out, she became a role model to many in the queer community who, through her actions, found the courage to come out to the world themselves. Fellow gay athletes take inspiration from her, and young same-sex couples in love write to her asking for advice and support. She's become an icon for the LGBTQIA+ community, been on the covers of magazines and spoken in talk shows and panels. She has also received support from the AFI. In the interview with *ESPN* she said:

> Given what I went through with the hyperandrogenism case, I honestly wasn't sure what the regulations were for openly gay sprinters. When the news became public, I got a call from Athletics Federation of India president Adille Sumariwala. He told me not to worry and assured me that my orientation was strictly a personal matter and would have no bearing on my opportunities as an athlete.[17]

Times have also changed since. People have become more accepting of the LGBTQIA+ community. The Supreme Court judgment on Section 344 also led to a change in how society viewed LGBTQIA+ relationships. Dutee herself speaks of the change within the sports fraternity. In an interview she spoke about how former athlete Pinki Pramanik would have to face comments when seen with a girl, and how things have changed since, and that she didn't face the same when she came out.[18]

At the July 2019 Summer Universiade in Napoli, she became the first Indian woman sprinter to bag gold, with a timing of 11.32 seconds in the 100 m. True to form, she tweeted a picture of her gold medal after her win, saying, 'Pull me down, I will come back stronger.'[19] Incidentally, she was also the flag bearer at the opening ceremony of this event. In August 2019, she signed with Puma for a two-year endorsement deal. This deal made her the first athlete or sportsperson from the LGBTQIA+ community in India to bag a significant endorsement.[20]

To quote Dutee, 'From a girl who used to run barefoot around a lake to becoming a sportsperson recognized across the world, it's been a long, hard journey. People now see me for my sport, for my hard work and for what I stand.'[21] In 2020, she was awarded the Arjuna Award—the nation's highest award for a sportsperson—by the then President of India.

In an interview she declared,

> Coming out can be really liberating. I don't regret it. In our country, culture and tradition are often used as tools to suppress people and communities. Resist it. [...] Love is a human right. Only you can decide for yourself who you really are, what kind of life you want to lead and with whom by your side.[22]

On her Instagram, she regularly posts pictures of herself with her partner. While Dutee failed to make it to the finals at Tokyo 2020 in both the 100 m and the 200 m events, she does plan to run until the 2024 Olympics.

She's received many offers to have a biopic made on her. To *India Today* she said, 'My focus is entirely on my sport for the next five years. If it does get made though, I would love if the film is named *Born to Run*.'[23] The name sounds about apt for a woman who ran on, undaunted, through whatever life threw at her, whether poverty or social stigma, and emerged triumphant.

NOTES

1 Twinkle, 'Who Is Dutee Chand? Early Life, Career, Personal Life, Marriage, Achievements & More', *JagranJosh*, 2 December 2022, http://tinyurl.com/4mp4twav. Accessed on 29 December 2023; 'Current Affairs July 2019 - Sports', *tutorialspoint*, http://tinyurl.com/3ksdyn5j. Accessed on 5 January 2024.

2 Tiwari, Pragya, 'Dutee Chand: Running, Her Sole Weapon in Fighting Odds', *Deccan Herald*, 18 September 2019, http://tinyurl.com/355ayu24. Accessed on 29 December 2023.

3 Apoorva, 'Dutee Chand Life Story, Career and Records', *Chase Your Sport*, 30 June 2022, http://tinyurl.com/bdhpjay8. Accessed on 29 December 2023.

4 Tanima, 'Dutee Chand – Meet the Woman behind the Athlete

and the 2020 Arjuna Award Winner', *Life Beyond Numbers*, 29 August 2020, http://tinyurl.com/2vyver4m. Accessed on 29 December 2023.

5 PTI, 'Dutee, Women 4x400m Relay Team Shine on on Final Day', *The Times of India*, 15 July 2014, http://tinyurl.com/46k2n2uw. Accessed on 5 January 2024; Tanima, 'Dutee Chand – Meet the Woman behind the Athlete and the 2020 Arjuna Award Winner', *Life Beyond Numbers*, 29 August 2020, http://tinyurl.com/2vyver4m. Accessed on 29 December 2023.

6 Tiwari, Pragya, 'Dutee Chand: Running, Her Sole Weapon in Fighting Odds', *Deccan Herald*, 18 September 2019, http://tinyurl.com/355ayu24. Accessed on 29 December 2023.

7 Sengupta, Rudraneil, 'Dutee Chand's Extraordinary Journey', *mint*, 2 July 2016, http://tinyurl.com/mrye7rhv. Accessed on 29 December 2023.

8 Josyula, Vijayhardik, 'Dutee Chand: Breaks Hurdles and Taboos against Odds', *Different Truths*, 3 June 2019, http://tinyurl.com/mr2d8vrk. Accessed on 29 December 2023.

9 Amsan, Andrew, 'I Have Offered Caster Semenya My Legal Team: Dutee Chand', *The Indian Express*, 27 April 2018, http://tinyurl.com/5n95bp7v. Accessed on 5 January 2024.

10 PTI, 'Dutee, Women 4x400m Relay Team Shine on on Final Day', *The Times of India*, 15 July 2014, http://tinyurl.com/46k2n2uw. Accessed on 5 January 2024; 'Dutee Chand Qualifies for 100m in Rio Olympics', *The Hindu*, 17 November 2021, http://tinyurl.com/2bxp5h42. Accessed on 5 January 2024.

11 PNS, 'Dutee, Srabani Get Jobs in State PSUs', *The Pioneer*, 24 May 2016, http://tinyurl.com/ysajkt96. Accessed on 29 December 2023.

12 'Dutee Chand Scoops Second Silver, Says Fearful over Future', *Sportstar*, 29 August 2018, http://tinyurl.com/yc7aecew. Accessed on 29 December 2023; 'Asian Games 2018: Dutee Chand Wins Silver in Women's 100m Race', *India Today*,

26 August 2018, http://tinyurl.com/34bbehe8. Accessed on 5 January 2024.

13 Ramavat, Mona, 'Big Strides: Q & A with Dutee Chand,' *India Today*, 8 July 2018, http://tinyurl.com/y5s4sbw3. Accessed on 29 December 2023.

14 Singh, Veenu, 'Olympian Dutee Chand Leads by Example When It Comes to Living One's Truth,' *Man'sWorld*, 23 March 2022, http://tinyurl.com/sb8swvu5. Accessed on 29 December 2023.

15 Ninan, Susan, '"Love Is a Human Right": India Sprinter Dutee Chand Tells Her Coming Out Story,' *ESPN*, 11 October 2021, http://tinyurl.com/5fuhrudd. Accessed on 29 December 2023.

16 Tanima, 'Dutee Chand – Meet the Woman behind the Athlete and the 2020 Arjuna Award Winner,' *Life Beyond Numbers*, 29 August 2020, http://tinyurl.com/3mub5c8n. Accessed on 29 December 2023.

17 Ninan, Susan, '"Love Is a Human Right": India Sprinter Dutee Chand Tells Her Coming Out Story,' *ESPN*, 11 October 2021, http://tinyurl.com/5fuhrudd. Accessed on 29 December 2023.

18 Ibid.

19 IANS, 'Dutee Chand Wins 100m Gold at World University Games,' *India Today*, 10 July 2019, http://tinyurl.com/cu7nrzz8. Accessed on 29 December 2023.

20 Pinto, Viveat Susan, 'Sprinter Dutee Chand Strikes Two-Year Endorsement Deal With Puma,' *Business Standard*, 8 August 2019, http://tinyurl.com/56ve65et. Accessed on 29 December 2023.

21 'Dutee Chand,' *Olympics.com*, http://tinyurl.com/mr37jaax. Accessed on 29 December 2023.

22 Ninan, Susan, '"Love Is a Human Right": India Sprinter Dutee Chand Tells Her Coming Out Story,' *ESPN*, 11 October 2021, http://tinyurl.com/5fuhrudd. Accessed on 29 December 2023.

23 Ramavat, Mona, 'Big Strides: Q & A with Dutee Chand,' *India Today*, 8 July 2018, http://tinyurl.com/y5s4sbw3. Accessed on 29 December 2023.

3

J. JAYALALITHAA

AMMA

On 5 December 2016, an era in Indian politics came to an end. Jayaram Jayalalithaa or J. Jayalalithaa passed away in a Chennai hospital from a cardiac arrest after a protracted illness. She was only 68.[1] The announcement of her death was followed by scenes of unprecedented mourning in Chennai and Tamil Nadu. Many of her followers died by suicide, devastated by her passing. Some reportedly died of cardiac arrest on hearing the news.[2] Revered by her followers and despised by her opponents in equal measure, J. Jayalalithaa was a megalithic presence in the politics of Tamil Nadu. She straddled Tamil Nadu's political landscape like a colossus for decades.

The movie-star-turned-politician, J. Jayalalithaa, had a cult following. Even when she was alive, her followers demonstrated extremes in their loyalty to her—chopping off fingers, drawing portraits of her from their own blood, shaving their heads and even getting her image tattooed on their bodies. When she was jailed on corruption charges, some followers even set themselves on fire in protest. Sceptics may state that these acts were encouraged by her party, that allegedly offered hefty compensation to the families of people who displayed their loyalty through such extreme measures. The families of those who died after Jayalalithaa's death are reported to have received

₹3 lakh as compensation along with assistance in funding the education and weddings of their children.[3]

She inspired fanatical devotion among her followers, as was evident at her funeral. A sea of mourners accompanied her body to the site, where she was buried on the Marina Beach, next to the memorial of Maruthur Gopalan Ramachandran (MGR), her mentor. Her incredible journey into the thrust and parry of electoral politics had actually begun with the funeral of another star-turned-politician, MGR, and it had come full circle with her funeral.

J. Jayalalithaa was an unlikely actress, and an even more unlikely politician. But she went on to be the chief minister (CM) of Tamil Nadu for over 14 years, serving six terms between 1991 and 2016. She was the longest serving secretary general of the All India Anna Dravida Munnetra Kazhagam (AIADMK) party. She was worshipped by the cadre. They called her *Amma* or mother. The other title her followers bestowed upon her was *Puratchi Thalaivi* or the revolutionary leader. It was not uncommon during her time as CM to see senior legislators and ministers prostrate themselves in front of her at public gatherings. The cult following she commanded was incredible, and she did nothing to discourage it. In fact, some would state she quite encouraged it.

Jayalalithaa was born on 24 February 1948 to Jayaram and Vedavalli (also known as Sandhya) at Melukote in Mysore (now Karnataka). She was named Komalavalli at birth after her grandmother. She had one brother, Jayakumar. The family, a Tamil Brahmin one, was illustrious; her paternal grandfather, Narasimhan Rengachary, served as surgeon and court physician to Maharaja Krishna Raja Wadiyar IV of Mysore.[4] Her maternal grandfather, Rangasamy Iyengar, worked with Hindustan Aeronautics Limited. Her mother was one of four siblings.

The young Komalavalli was renamed Jayalalithaa when she was barely one. This then became her formal name. Interestingly, her new name was the combination of the names of the two houses she lived in while in Mysore, 'Jaya' Vilas and 'Lalitha' Vilas. Her father, a lawyer, passed away when she was barely a toddler, and her mother went back to her father's home with both her children in 1950. Times were tough and her mom learnt shorthand and typing in order to support the family. Jayalalithaa's maternal aunt, her mother's younger sister, Padmavalli, had by then moved to Madras (now Chennai) and was working as an air hostess. She was also acting in dramas and films. She insisted that Vedavalli also begin acting in order to support her family. While their mother pursued a film career under the screen name of Sandhya, little Jayalalithaa and her brother were brought up by their maternal grandparents in Bangalore.

Jayalalithaa studied at the Bishop Cotton Girls' School. She often spoke about how she missed her mother while growing up, as she saw her only during the summer vacation for a month or so. Padmavalli got married in 1958, and so Jayalalithaa moved to Madras to be with her mother. She was enrolled in the Sacred Heart Matriculation School and was such an excellent student that she won a government scholarship for further education. She also won the 'Gold State Award' for the first rank in Grade 10 in the entire state. She joined Stella Maris College, Chennai, for her degree; but as fate would have it, she couldn't complete her graduation.

Jayalalithaa was beautiful, with huge doe-shaped eyes, sharp features and a clear complexion. She had all the attributes essential to becoming a leading lady on screen. She was also trained in the performing arts. She was an excellent student, and did not really see a career in the movies as her future, although she had already done a few roles. But her mother coerced her to drop out of college and become an actress.[5]

While in Chennai, she learnt Carnatic music, Western

classical piano, Bharatanatyam, Kuchipudi, Mohiniyattam, Manipuri Raas Leela and Kathak from renowned gurus like K.J. Sarasa and Padma Bhushan Guru Dr Vempati Chinna Satyam. She had her *arangetram* (the debut performance of a dancer, marking the completion of their training and the beginning of their career as a professional dancer) at the Rasika Ranjani Sabha in Mylapore in May 1960, and the chief guest was none other than the noted Tamil cinema icon Sivaji Ganesan.[6] Ganesan was so impressed by her performance that he is reported to have called her a *thanga silai* or golden statue and said that she would one day become a film actress.[7] The moniker stayed with her for years and his words proved to be prophetic. Or perhaps, this was what her mother had already envisaged for Jayalalithaa's career.

The young Jayalalithaa was initiated into the film world as a child actor. It was serendipitous. While visiting her mother during one of her summer vacations, she went to a studio during the shooting of the Kannada film *Sri Shaila Mahathme*. The selected child actor did not show up and the producer and director quickly roped in the young Jayalalithaa to shoot the scene. That serendipitous entry into filmdom was followed by the role of Krishna in a three-minute dance sequence in the Hindi film *Man-Mauji*.

She began acting in dramas and plays along with her mother and her aunt, under the drama troupe 'United Amateur Artistes'. It was in one such small role that she was spotted by Shankar Giri, the son of the former Indian President V.V. Giri. He asked her mother if Jayalalithaa could play a role in his film *Epistle*. Her mother put forth the condition that shooting for the film should not interfere with Jayalalithaa's school, and should happen only on weekends or school holidays. He agreed to her conditions. Jayalalithaa was barely 12 at the time.[8]

Her next offer came for the Kannada movie *Chinnada Gombe*, to be made by the Kannada filmmaker B.R. Panthulu. He, too, promised her mother to finish the shooting in two months so that it wouldn't affect her studies. The film was shot in six weeks and became a blockbuster when it was released in 1964. At the time, Jayalalithaa was set to join Stella Maris College and her ambition was to study law. However, this film totally changed the trajectory of her life. In 1964, she played a sales girl in a play titled *Undersecretary* where she was paired with Cho Ramaswamy. This performance bagged her the role of the leading lady in a play called *Malathy*. The movies shot during her vacation became hits, and producers and directors lined up with offers. These offers were tempting because her mother was in massive debt and she urged Jayalalithaa to sign these projects to rid them of their financial woes.

She debuted in Tamil cinema as the lead in *Vennira Aadai*, and in Telugu cinema in *Manushulu Mamathulu*. In 1968, she did a Hindi film opposite Dharmendra called *Izzat*. Her most popular on-screen pairing, though, was with MGR, with whom she did 28 movies between 1965 and 1973. Jayalalithaa soon became an established star. In 1966, she had 11 hit releases in a single year. She became the regular leading lady for the production house Devar Film Factory in 1966. She acted opposite Jaishankar in Tamil movies and opposite N.T. Rama Rao in Telugu movies, apart from others like Ravichandran, Sivakumar and Sivaji Ganesan, to name a few. A movie she did in 1972 with Sivaji Ganesan, titled *Pattikada Pattanama*, won the National Film Award in 1973 for 'Best Feature Film in Tamil'. Her movie *Deiva Magan* with Sivaji Ganesan was the first Tamil movie submitted by India for an Academy Award for 'Best Foreign Language Film'.

In 1973, she did a Malayalam movie titled *Jesus*. By 1974, she had already acted in 100 movies. She courted controversy too, but never shied away from taking it head on. This personality trait only became more pronounced in her career as a politician. In 1972, she was to perform in Mysore but had to cancel at the last minute. Political parties jumped into the fray, stoking up controversy, saying that despite being a Kannadiga she had dared to cancel the Dussehra performance. She retorted through an interview in the magazine *Vikatan*, saying that she was a Tamilian. This created a furore. Activists stormed the studio she was shooting in and demanded that she withdraw her statement of being a Tamilian girl. Displaying the indefatigable courage that went on to define her as a leader, she remained unshaken even as the mob surrounded her.[9]

Such was her popularity that even the titles of the films indicated that it was woman-centric. She set a record for the maximum number of silver-jubilee hits in her career as a heroine in Tamil cinema. Out of the 92 Tamil movies she made, 85 were silver-jubilee hits, and all her 28 Telugu films were silver-jubilee hits as well. From 1965 to 1980, she was the highest paid Indian actress. She was among the first female superstars of Tamil cinema. Her performances, too, were lauded. Her work in *Chandhrodhayam*, *Adimai Penna* and *Engirundho Vandhaal* won her Filmfare Special Awards. *Pattikada Pattanama* and *Suryagandhi* got her the Filmfare Best Actress Award. Not content with winning awards and ruling the silver screen, she also wrote columns, short stories and a serialized memoir of her life in the Tamil weekly *Kumudam*. It was around 1980 that she decided to stop signing any more movies.

Around the same time, she had a reunion with MGR. The relationship between her and MGR was very authoritarian. She became more and more dependent on him after her mother passed away. It was around this time that she warmed up to the idea of getting into politics, and driving this decision was MGR. To quote her, 'He was a very warm and caring kind of a person. And after Mother died, he replaced her in my life. He was everything to me. He was mother, father, brother, friend, philosopher, guide. Everything. He sort of took over my life.'[10] She often said that both her careers came into being by other people urging her to pursue it—her acting career because of her mother and her political career because of MGR.

MGR was an icon in Tamil cinema and had a fan following that worshipped him. He entered politics, using his popularity as a film star to his advantage, and soon rose to become the CM of Tamil Nadu. Jayalalithaa joined the party he founded, the AIADMK, in 1982. She was quoted at the time saying, 'Everything about him [MGR] is wonderful, his charisma, his personality, everything. I joined the AIADMK partly because it is MGR's party, also I was impressed by their various schemes and their implementations. By making villages self-sufficient, a big influx into the urban areas was stalled.'[11]

She became the AIADMK propaganda secretary, and soon was elected to the Rajya Sabha. In politics, where gender and caste assumed immense proportions, she was outspoken enough to say that she was proud to be an upper-caste Brahmin woman and a Hindu. This was radical because the political environment at that time was to decry religion and the caste system. However, the coterie surrounding MGR ensured she was kept away from him. Jayalalithaa was well-spoken and fluent in multiple languages. In fact, when she was in the Rajya Sabha, Prime Minister (PM) Indira Gandhi and Khushwant Singh, a member of the Rajya Sabha then, were impressed by the clarity of her diction and the elegance of her speech. In fact, she was first sent to the Rajya Sabha by MGR because she was fluent in English, thanks to her convent education, and also fluent in Hindi.

However, all was not well, as soon there was a rift between her and her mentor. To quote Solai from Vaasanthi's book:

> MGR now wanted Jayalalithaa to meet Indira Gandhi. Solai, who had also been sent to Delhi by MGR to be with Jayalalithaa, describes the meeting: 'Congress was in alliance with the DMK. Our proposal was that Congress must have an alliance with the AIADMK. Jayalalithaa was told to impress this point on the PM. Jayalalithaa was given only ten minutes but they spoke for thirty minutes. [...]

> But after the meeting with Indira Gandhi, Jayalalithaa did not at once report on it to MGR, as she should have done since she had been deputed by him [...] This behaviour of hers, taking him for granted, sent out a wrong signal to MGR.[12]

In 1984, MGR suffered a stroke. His wife, Janaki, and the family refused to let Jayalalithaa visit him in hospital. On hearing that PM Indira Gandhi had visited MGR, she is quoted to have said, 'She would surely have taken me to see him if I had met her before.' In her desperation to see her mentor, she wrote to the PM, a letter 'drenched with tears,' and begged for her help. She was instructed to wait for the doctor's permission to visit him, but MGR was taken to the US by his medical team and his wife Janaki, and Jayalalithaa did not get the opportunity to see him.[13]

It was after MGR's death in 1987, during his funeral, that she faced unprecedented public humiliation. She was not allowed to see his body when she went to his home. Nonetheless, she stood for over 16 hours, like a statue in vigil, next to his body while it lay in state at Rajaji Hall.[14]

At the funeral, even as the soldiers accompanying the gun carriage carrying his body tried to help her up, she was pushed off ruthlessly by those loyal to MGR's wife Janaki. She was even abused and called a prostitute. Hurt, she went back home in her Contessa, not accompanying the gun carriage to the cremation. Her willpower during those hours is the stuff of legends. She had, through her actions and her commitment to her mentor, firmly established herself as the chosen heir to MGR's legacy—a fact that MGR's widow Janaki found unacceptable. MGR's death in 1987 became a flashpoint between his widow and Jayalalithaa, with both claiming to be his political heirs.

The AIADMK split into two factions after this, one that followed Janaki Ramachandran and the second which threw their weight behind Jayalalithaa. In January, Janaki was made the CM, but soon, after some mayhem, President's Rule was declared in Tamil Nadu. In 1989, Jayalalithaa contested the elections from the Bodinayakkanur constituency and won. Her journey into electoral politics had now begun. She was the leader of the Opposition in the house, with M. Karunanidhi heading the DMK government.

Her faction won 27 seats and she became the first woman leader of the Opposition in the Tamil Nadu Legislative Assembly. She was also the first Indian actress to become the Opposition leader in a legislative assembly in India. In her post-election press conference, Jayalalithaa declared, 'I am the leader of this party, and it is my utterances alone that are to be considered, not irresponsible statements made by others in the party.'[15]

In February 1989, both factions of the AIADMK merged and she became the unanimous choice for the post of the general secretary of the party. In March 1989, the Tamil Nadu Assembly witnessed scenes of violence between the DMK and AIADMK. In the melee that ensued, Karunanidhi fell to the floor and the *pallu* of Jayalalithaa's saree was torn. As she left the House trembling with rage from the humiliation, she vowed not to return until she became the CM.[16] She was mocked by many who wondered how a woman, and a Brahmin to boot, could ever aspire to this. This incident, nonetheless, won her a lot of public sympathy.

And she did what she had vowed. She returned to the House as CM when she won the elections. In 1991, the sympathy wave after Rajiv Gandhi's assassination benefitted the coalition. The alliance won 225 of 234 seats contested; she became the youngest CM of Tamil Nadu and served her full term from 24 June 1991 to 12 May 1996.[17]

Throughout her political career, she lived at her Poes Garden bungalow—the plot for which was bought by her and her mother in 1967—with an approximate area of 24,000 sq. ft. However, her mother died before the house-warming ceremony of the bungalow when she was barely 47, and never got the chance to live in it. Jayalalithaa named the bungalow 'Veda Nilayam' after her mother Vedavalli. She had a lavish house-warming with dinner and a veena recital by the classical musician Chitti Babu. Her brother, Jayakumar, had his wedding at the residence, and he and his family lived with her till 1978.[18] They had a falling out when Jayalalithaa adopted her confidante Sasikala's son, Sudhakaran. Her brother, Jayakumar, passed away in 1995. She formally adopted Sudhakaran in 1995 and then publicly disowned him in 1996 over charges of corruption.

The over-the-top lavishness displayed at Sudhakaran's wedding with Sivaji Ganesan's granddaughter in 1995 was partly responsible for Jayalalithaa's downfall in the 1996 elections. In fact, so lavish was the wedding that it found mention in the Guinness Book of World Records in two categories: for the most guests at a wedding and the largest wedding banquet. The scale of the wedding was incredible, with a 2-km-long *baraat* pathway, 10 dining halls with a capacity of 25,000 guests each and a 75,000 sq. ft pandal. There were huge cut outs of Jayalalithaa everywhere and the décor was lavish, with the wedding pandal resembling a palace. The VIP invitations contained a silver plate, a silk saree and a silk dhoti. There were over a thousand such invitations. The scale of the wedding incurred the wrath of the electorate and was possibly responsible for her party losing all 39 seats in the Lok Sabha in the 1996 elections. Later, though, Jayalalithaa told an inquiry that the expenses for the wedding were paid by the bride's family.[19]

A raid on her premises, after the corruption allegations in 1996, had the police declare that they had seized large quantities of diamond-studded gold jewellery, more than 10,000 sarees and 750 pairs of shoes. Her excesses led to her being called the 'Imelda Marcos' of India. The DMK government then filed a number of corruption cases against her. The Colour TV scam accused her of receiving kickbacks of around ₹10 crore. The amount was supposed to have been routed to a relative of her confidante Sasikala. She was acquitted of this case by the trial court and the High Court upheld this acquittal in 2000. It was while the case was going on in 1996 that she disowned Sudhakaran. To accusations that Sasikala functioned as a de facto power centre of the government, Jayalalithaa retorted in 1996, 'Sasikala never functioned as extra constitutional power centre. Calling her de facto chief minister is nonsense. She is not interested in politics and I have no intention to bring her into politics.'[20]

The influence of Sasikala on her was all encompassing, down to ministerial decisions and land deals in the state. According to sources, Sasikala had brought over 40 people from her village Mannargudi to be part of the staff at Jayalalithaa's home. At one point, every single staff member, right from the driver to the cook, was from Mannargudi. The coterie was unkindly called the 'Mannargudi mafia' by some. According to reports, this group was debarred from Poes Garden in 2011, when tests showed traces of arsenic in Jayalalithaa's blood. That was when Sasikala fell out of favour with Jayalalithaa.[21] However, the fallout between the two was short-lived.

Jayalalithaa was known for her formidable protests, like the 80-hour fast she undertook demanding the release of the waters of the Kaveri in July 1993. She ended the fast only when a Cabinet Minister, Union Water Resources Minister V.C. Shukla, personally came down from Delhi to meet her and the CM of Karnataka to resolve the issue. Some called it gimmicky, but the fact remained that it did boost her popularity among the citizens of the state.[22]

She was, to the citizens, a CM who put into place many welfare schemes that earned their loyalty. Among them, the Cradle Baby Scheme allowed mothers to anonymously give their newborn baby girls up to be adopted. This was introduced in 1992, in response to the rampant female infanticide and foeticide prevalent in the state at the time. Recognizing women's hesitancy to walk into a police station and deal with policemen, she introduced police stations with all-women police personnel, introduced 30 per cent quota for women in police recruitments and established 57 all-women police stations. She also launched all-women libraries, stores, banks and co-operative establishments in a bid to empower the women of the state. She was mercurial in her decisions though. In 1999, her sudden decision to withdraw support to the BJP government, led by Atal Bihar Vajpayee, led to the fall of the government.

There were controversies and allegations of corruption that surrounded Jayalalithaa. She could not contest the 2001 elections because of the TANSI land case. Two companies in which Jayalalithaa and Sasikala had holdings were accused of purchasing lands owned by the Tamil Nadu Small Industries Corporation (TANSI), in 1992, at an undervalued rate. Despite this, her party won a majority and she was appointed CM as a non-elected member of the state assembly on 14 May 2001. The cases, nonetheless, had her disqualified from holding the position of CM and O. Panneerselvam was put in her place.[23] She was acquitted of all charges by the Madras High Court on 4 December 2001 and, subsequently, the Supreme Court upheld the order of Madras High Court on 24 November 2003, on grounds of lack of evidence.

With the acquittal of the cases against her, she came back as CM after contesting a mid-term poll from the Andipatti constituency where the sitting MLA gave up his seat. She was ruthless against her political opponents once she was back in power. She was also intent on the welfare of the people. She launched the Rainwater Harvesting Scheme in 2001 to improve the ground water levels in the state—a scheme that was soon taken up by other states as well as the central government. She brought about the Veeranam Project to help a water-deprived Chennai get adequate water supplies.

She set up India's first company of female police commandos in Tamil Nadu in 2003, making them undergo the same training as male commandos. She banned the sale of all lotteries in the state in 2003. She created a special task force to capture and eliminate Veerappan in the forests of Karnataka. To quote her on this task force, 'My only brief to them was capture Veerappan dead or alive. After that I never interfered. I left them to work out their own strategies and this paid off.'[24]

Her relief efforts post the 26 December 2004 tsunami that hit Tamil Nadu were noteworthy. She divided the ₹153.37 crore relief package into a general one and another specifically for the fishermen affected by the tsunami. Families received a compensation of ₹1 lakh for every member they lost to the tsunami, and a dhoti, a saree, two bedsheets, 60 kg of rice, 3 l of kerosene, ₹1,000 in cash for groceries, ₹1,000 for utensils and ₹2,000 for temporary accommodation. The relief package for the fisherman also included an extra ₹65 crore to cover the costs for gill nets and boats.[25]

The Assembly elections in 2006 saw her party getting defeated in the hustings, and she resigned as the CM. The AIADMK won just 61 of the 234 seats, and the Opposition won only 96 of the 234 and formed a coalition government. She was elected as leader of the Opposition. She was back as CM in 2011, with a landslide victory. She herself won from Srirangam. She put into place a range of populist schemes that endeared her to the people. She introduced a range of 'Amma'-branded daily-needs goods, subsidized for the common man.

A radical scheme she announced was a pension scheme for transgenders, where transgenders over the age of 40 could get a monthly pension of ₹1,000. She promoted education opportunities for transgenders and employment opportunities as well. Students in rural areas were given laptops. Families falling below the poverty line were given four goats and a cow, mixer grinders, fans for all households, free school uniforms, school bags, notebooks, geometry boxes and cycles. A very popular scheme that she launched was the marriage-assistance scheme where girls received 4 g of gold for their weddings, and cash of ₹50,000 for undergraduate or diploma-qualified girls. The state went from power deficits to power surplus in her term. Another very popular scheme was the Amma Canteen, which offered subsidized cooked food to the poor. The Amma baby care kit offered to every new mother who had their children in government hospitals had 16 baby care products.[26]

Among the key achievements during her tenure were the ruling to increase the storage level in the Mullaperiyar Dam by the Supreme Court in 2014, and the final award of the Cauvery Water Disputes Tribunal by the Union government in 2013. In August 2014, she was re-elected to the post of the general secretary of the AIADMK, making her the longest serving general secretary of the party.

The same year, she was convicted in a disproportionate assets case, removing her from the office of CM. She was sentenced to four years in jail and fined ₹100 crore. The case had been filed back in 1996 by Subramanian Swamy after an income tax report on her. Sasikala as well as her family members, including the disowned foster son, were also convicted and sentenced to jail. O. Panneerselvam became CM in her stead. She was acquitted by a special bench of the Karnataka High Court in 2015. With the acquittal, Jayalalithaa was once again CM of Tamil Nadu, after being re-elected in a by-election from the Radhakrishnan Nagar constituency in a landslide victory.

She introduced the Amma Master Health Check Up Plan for the underprivileged section to get check-ups in government hospitals, and the Amma Arogya Plan for tests at primary healthcare centres. A very popular scheme she introduced was the free bus ride for senior citizens. During her terms there were many big-ticket investments in the state. She stormed ahead with more populist measures. These included writing off outstanding crop loans by cooperative banks to almost 17 lakh farmers, giving 100 units of free electricity to households,

200 units of free electricity to handloom weavers and 750 units of free electricity to powerloom weavers. She cracked down on liquor shops, closing over 500 and reducing the timings of others. She established the first 1,000 MW nuclear power plant at Kudankulam. This worked towards making Tamil Nadu a power surplus state. Another popular measure she undertook was increasing the pension for freedom fighters and their families.

There is no doubt that she was a towering personality. Despite the numerous allegations against her, her supporters worshipped her blindly. Some even called her *Adi Parashakti,* the eternal goddess. The Amma brand, carefully nurtured over the years, reached cult frenzy. The state saw posters of Jayalalithaa as a goddess. Her temper was the stuff of legends. One anecdotal recounting speaks of her beating up her auditor.

She also had ambitions of playing a more dominant role in national politics according to reports leading up to the 2014 general elections, though she herself never said so. In the second half of her political career she veered away from the ostentation that marked her earlier years. She remodelled herself to resemble a benevolent mother figure. She eschewed the lavishness of the silks and diamonds and chose to wear plain colours like green, blue and maroon as suggested by astrologers. An allergic skin condition, reportedly atopic dermatitis, also had her change her wardrobe to capes and long-sleeved blouses to hide the flare ups.

Her last public appearance before being hospitalized was the inauguration of two Chennai Metro lines via video. On 22 September 2016, she was admitted to Apollo Hospitals in Chennai, for acute dehydration and pulmonary infection. She had multiple illnesses to begin with—vertigo, diabetes, and cardiac, respiratory, digestive, thyroid and nerve-related problems—as well as a skin condition for which she had been prescribed steroids. She was barely conscious when she was in the hospital, but when she was conscious, she had a mind of her own and would not be dictated.

Even while doctors at the hospital were trying to stabilize her, she would consume sweets. Her cook would come to the hospital and cook her food to her preference, under the supervision of the team of doctors treating her.

According to an article, when Dr Richard Beale (the London-based intensive care expert who was flown in to treat her) was told by the team of doctors at Apollo that she wasn't following the treatment, he told her, 'You might be the boss of this whole state, but I am the boss of this hospital. You should listen to what I say.' At the time, Jayalalithaa, who could not speak because of her pulmonary infection, gestured back to him, implying, 'You are not the boss, I am the boss.'[27]

She refused to go abroad for her treatment. Perhaps, memories of what had happened with MGR when he went to the US for his treatment haunted her. O. Panneerselvam took over her duties as CM. She was also said to have septicaemia and pulmonary infection, which were both cured, but she was reportedly re-admitted to the ICU on 5 December 2016, after a massive cardiac arrest.

The hospital announced that she was critical and on life support. They announced her death shortly after. She was only 68. She was kept in state at her residence in Poes Garden until the evening of 6 December 2016, and then buried at the northern end of the Marina Beach in Chennai, close to the MGR memorial, in keeping with her wishes. The memorial for her was shaped like a phoenix, perhaps an appropriate metaphor given how she rose over and over from what her opponents considered the end of her political career.

In a patriarchal culture supporting only male politicians in Tamil Nadu, she ruled the political arena for so many years without coming from a political background. This was despite all the efforts from her opponents and controversy surrounding her. It is indeed a commendable achievement. Flamboyant and controversial in life as well as in death, Jayalalithaa continues to be one of those rare female politicians in India—a woman you can love or hate, but never ignore.

NOTES

1 '"Mystery" behind Jayalalithaa's Death: A Recap', *DTNext*, 19 October 2022, http://tinyurl.com/ycys5bss. Accessed on 5 January 2024.

2 'MGR to Jayalalithaa - Why Tamilians Commit Suicides on Leaders' Deaths', *Zee News*, 17 September 2022, http://tinyurl.com/bdduwrez. Accessed on 29 December 2023.

3 Barry, Ellen, and Hari Kumar, 'Suicides Reported in India after Death of Jayalalithaa Jayaram', *The New York Times*, 10 December 2016, http://tinyurl.com/mr6jn4ye. Accessed on 29 December 2023.

4 'Life and Times of Our Golden Stellar J Jayalalithaa', *Live Chennai.com*, http://tinyurl.com/33esbu84. Accessed on 29 December 2023.

5 Karthikeyan, Divya, 'When Amma Was a Schoolgirl: The Girl Who Gave up Her Books for Cinema', *The News Minute*, 6 December 2016, http://tinyurl.com/j72kyxzz. Accessed on 29 December 2023.

6 Veejay Sai, 'Tribute: Jayalalitha's Love for the Classical Arts', *mint*, 9 December 2016, http://tinyurl.com/9tdpbvd9. Accessed on 29 December 2023.

7 'What Stars Who Worked with Jayalalithaa Say!', *ETimes*, http://tinyurl.com/4xnpskpr. Accessed on 29 December 2023.

8 M.L. Narasimham, 'Jayalalithaa: The Queen Bee of Politics', *The Hindu*, 6 December 2016, http://tinyurl.com/v3cdzurc. Accessed on 29 December 2023.

9 Vaasanthi Sundaram, *The Lone Empress: A Portrait of Jayalalithaa*, Penguin Random House India, 2020.

10 Jha, Shefali, 'Jayalalithaa about MGR: He Was Everything to Me, Sort of Took over My Life (Throwback)', *International*

Business Times, 7 May 2020, http://tinyurl.com/3tjxdan2. Accessed on 2 January 2024.

11 Jaychander, Neeti, 'The Life and Times of Dr J Jayalalithaa (1948–2016)', *Femina*, 6 December 2016, http://tinyurl.com/bdfea7x7. Accessed on 30 December 2023.

12 Vasanti, *Amma: Jayalalithaa's Journey from Movie Star to Political Queen*, Juggernaut, 2016; Vaasanthi, 'In Delhi, Jayalalithaa Charmed Indira Gandhi, but in Madras MGR's Trust Was Eroding', *The News Minute*, 28 June 2016, http://tinyurl.com/2r7983xs. Accessed on 29 December 2023.

13 Jaychander, Neeti, 'The Life and Times of Dr J Jayalalithaa (1948 – 2016)', *Femina*, 6 December 2016, http://tinyurl.com/bdfea7x7. Accessed on 30 December 2023.

14 Vaasanthi, '"For 2 Days, Jayalalithaa Stood by MGR's Body. She Did Not Shed a Tear."', *NDTV*, 8 December 2016, http://tinyurl.com/52wxzjm2. Accessed on 29 December 2023; Vaasanthi, 'J Jayalalithaa (1948-2016): The Last Mother', *Open*, 8 December 2016, http://tinyurl.com/2wvkyapu. Accessed on 29 December 2023.

15 Vaasanthi, 'Jaya and Now: A Tale of Two AIADMK Splits and Why the Twain Shall Never Meet', *The New Indian Express*, 2 August 2022, http://tinyurl.com/2386v9e6. Accessed on 29 December 2023.

16 Bhagat, Rasheeda, 'Pepper Spray Pales against past TN Assembly Events', *The Hindu Businessline*, 23 November 2017, http://tinyurl.com/32fcxhz8. Accessed on 29 December 2023.

17 'Jayalalithaa Jayaram Biography', *Elections.in*, http://tinyurl.com/2ne6e53m. Accessed on 29 December 2023.

18 'Regal in Its Splendor: Jayalalithaa's House', *Housing.com*, 26 May 2021, http://tinyurl.com/ycstwx4j. Accessed on 29 December 2023.

19 Shekhar, G.C., 'Jayalalitha's Foster Son Married off amid Extravagance and Controversy', *India Today*, 26 June 2013, http://tinyurl.com/59fwht6w. Accessed on 29 December 2023;

'Profile: Jayaram Jayalalitha', *BBC News*, 5 December 2016, http://tinyurl.com/yckahzme. Accessed on 29 December 2023.

20 Kumar M., Anil, 'Sarees, Shoes Were Mementoes, Claims Jayalalitha', *The Times of India*, 24 November 2011, http://tinyurl.com/2fybw9rw. Accessed on 5 January 2024; Vaasanthi, 'The Post-truth Takeover', *India Today*, 11 February 2017, http://tinyurl.com/msv3yv2v. Accessed on 29 December 2023.

21 'From Video Parlour Owner to Amma's Soul Sister, the Incredible Tale of Sasikala', *SW*, 6 December 2016, http://tinyurl.com/yb4yynzm. Accessed on 5 January 2024; 'The Fascinating Life of J. Jayalalithaa', *National Herald*, 28 June 2017, http://tinyurl.com/yeyehhrr. Accessed on 5 January 2024.

22 Rai, S., and P.M. Swamy, 'Jayalalitha Exploits Tamil Insecurity', *India Today*, 24 July 2013, http://tinyurl.com/bdfyte9z. Accessed on 29 December 2023.

23 '23-Year-Old TANSI Case Has Finally Ended for Jayalalithaa: A Look Back', *The News Minute*, 7 March 2015, http://tinyurl.com/2rrydhd6. Accessed on 29 December 2023.

24 Padalkar, Ravindra, *Ruling Dynasties of Independent India - Volume 2*, Notion Press, 2021.

25 *Tsunami and One Year After*, Relief and Rehabilitation, Cuddalore Collectorate, Cuddalore, 2005, http://tinyurl.com/2ezd2z3d. Accessed on 5 January 2024.

26 'The Many Things Amma Was: List of Schemes Implemented by Jayalalithaa', *The Economic Times*, 6 December 2016, http://tinyurl.com/y854tebz. Accessed on 29 December 2023; 'Profile: Jayaram Jayalalitha', *BBC News*, 5 December 2016, http://tinyurl.com/yckahzme. Accessed on 29 December 2023.

27 Subramanian, Lakshmi, 'How Did Jayalalithaa Die?', *The Week*, 23 March 2019, http://tinyurl.com/mrx8mkfy. Accessed on 29 December 2023.

4

SAROJINI NAIDU

THE NIGHTINGALE OF INDIA

A solemn, pensive face stares at us from grainy black-and-white photographs that document her and her life. Her expression does no justice to the vibrant and fecund mind that lies beyond it. The Nightingale of India, as she was called, Sarojini Naidu was among the important personages in India's struggle for freedom from the British. She was also the first woman president of the Indian National Congress (INC) and the first woman governor of an Indian state. Throughout her life, she dedicated herself completely to the cause of freedom and nationalism.

She came from a family that set great store by education. She was born on 13 February 1879, into a Bengali family settled in Hyderabad. She got the privilege of a well-rounded education in her childhood. Her parents—Aghorenath Chattopadhyay and Varada Sundari Devi—originally came from Brahmagaon Bikrampur, Dhaka. Her father was the founder and administrator of the Hyderabad College (later known as Nizam College) and had a doctorate in science from Edinburgh University.[1] Her mother was a Bengali poet. The oldest of eight siblings, her brother Virendranath Chattopadhyaya became a freedom fighter; another brother, Harindranath Chattopadhyay, ventured into the performing arts, earning repute as a dramatist, poet and actor. The family was highly regarded in Hyderabad and her father was among the earliest members of the INC. The young Sarojini was an exceptionally bright and earnest student. She was barely 12 when she passed the matriculation exam and topped it as well.

She was always a precocious writer and had a flair for languages. In a letter quoted by Arthur Symons in his introduction to her first book of poems, *The Golden Threshold,* we are told how once she was locked in a room filled with books by her father as a punishment. It is said that when she emerged from the room she was a full-blown linguist. Fluent in multiple languages—Urdu, Telugu, English, Bengali and Persian—she was a precocious early literary talent. She had already begun her writing career at a time when most children were focussed on games of childhood. In fact, her father was keen that she become a mathematician or a scientist when she topped the matriculation exam. However, the young Sarojini was clear about what she wanted to do. Her heart was set on pursuing a career in the arts, and her passion was writing poetry.

What made her father change his mind about her career path was reading a poem written by her, titled 'Lady of the Lake'. A long poem of 1,300 lines, reading it convinced him that his daughter was a prodigious talent and that her destiny lay in words and not in numbers and science.[2] She wrote a Persian play titled *Maher Muneer* which was read by the Nizam of Hyderabad. The Nizam was impressed, as he saw the immense promise of the young girl. He awarded her a scholarship to study at King's College, London and then Girton College, Cambridge. From her sheltered life in Hyderabad, the then 17-year-old Sarojini left alone for London from Bombay (now Mumbai), on a steamship in September 1895. It was a radical thing in those times, for a young Indian girl, in her teens, to travel alone to Britain on a scholarship. She was part of the privileged elite, the few young Indians who could study in British universities and gain a Western education.[3]

In England, she became the ward of Elizabeth Manning, the secretary of the National Indian Association. Manning had a further connection to Girton College; her stepmother had been part of the founding of the college.[4] It was in England that she met the famous laureates of her time, like Arthur Simon and Edmund Gosse, who went on to have a huge influence on her work. She was advised to stick with Indian themes in her poetry—the mountains, rivers, temples and the socio-cultural parameters of life in India. This is what set her poetry apart and gave her work a voice of its own.[5] Gosse felt that a false English vein in Naidu's poetry could only be a poor imitation of the Anglo-Saxon Romantic poetic tradition. He wrote to her about the themes she should write about, saying, '[...] What we wished to receive was...some revelation of the heart of India, some sincere penetrating analysis of native passion, of the principles of antique religion and of such mysterious intimations as stirred the soul of the East long before the West had begun to dream that it had a soul.'[6]

It was in Cambridge and London that she got drawn to the suffrage movement, and then to the INC's movement for independence from the British. She threw herself wholeheartedly into the freedom movement, and became an ardent follower of Mahatma Gandhi and his philosophy of *swaraj*. She married Govindarajulu Naidu, a doctor, in 1898, on returning to India. She had met him when she was 17 and had fallen in love with him even before she left for England.[7] At the time, the marriage was quite the scandal, as they were from different castes and communities. However, both their families were extremely supportive of the couple. They went on to have five children and a long and happy marriage. In fact, her daughter, Padmaja Naidu, later joined the Quit India Movement, and eventually became the governor of West Bengal.

When Naidu returned to India in 1898, she was beset with health issues that went on to plague her all her life. While she plunged headfirst into a life in politics, she continued to keep up a correspondence with the poets she had met in England. Whenever she visited England, she would not just attend political meetings and rallies, but also poetry readings and literary salons. Her health issues necessitated that she spent time convalescing in nursing homes in England.

Her political career began in earnest in 1904 with her joining the INC. A powerful influence on her was Gopal Krishna Gokhale, whom she considered her first *guru* in the freedom movement. He had said to her, 'Stand here with me with stars and hills and witness and in their presence consecrate your life and your talent, your song and your speech, your thought and your breath, to the motherland.'[8]

Over the years, she grew to become a renowned and critically acclaimed poet. The span of her work extended from children's poetry to poems on patriotism. Gandhi ji gave her the moniker of 'The Nightingale of India,' because of the lyrical quality of her poems.[9]

There was a strong bond between her and Gandhi ji. Meeting Gandhi ji in 1914 galvanized her with new purpose and mission. She first met him in London while he was having his dinner. She scrunched up her face seeing his food, it is believed, and her expression made Gandhi ji laugh. Of this first meeting, she said:

> A little man with a shaven head, seated on the floor on a black prison blanket, eating a messy meal of squashed tomatoes and olive oil out of a wooden prison bowl. Around this were ranged some battered tins of parched groundnuts and tasteless biscuits of dried plantain flour. I burst instinctively into laughter at the amusing and unexpected vision of a famous leader, whose name has already become a household word in our country. [10]

She graciously declined sharing the meal that Gandhi ji offered her during this meeting.

Gandhi ji often mentioned that he had been influenced by Sarojini's insistence that women should participate in the freedom movement as well. To quote Gandhi ji from a 1932 letter that he wrote to Sarojini:

> It may be that this is my last letter to you. I have always known and treasured your love. I think that I understood you when I first saw you and heard you at the Criterion (in London) in 1914. [...] If I die I shall die in the faith that comrades like you, with whom God has blessed me, will continue the work of the country which is also fully the work of humanity in the same spirit in which it was begun.[11]

Even with her tumultuous participation in the freedom struggle, she continued to maintain her interests in literary circles. She held a regular literary salon in Bombay which was attended by literary talents from across the country. Her poems were written in English, influenced heavily by the Romantic movement in poetry, and they were very lyrical in nature. She used vivid imagery in her writings, which earned her the title of 'Indian Yeats'. As mentioned earlier, she published her very first book of poems in London in 1905. *The Golden Threshold* had a sketch of Sarojini, a teenager then, drawn by John Butler Yeats, the father of William Butler Yeats.[12] Her second book of poems, published in 1912, titled *The Bird of Time*, was more influenced by her nationalistic leanings.

In the book *Sarojini Naidu: An Introduction to Her Life, Work and Poetry*, V.S. Naravane writes about how back in 1905, when Lord Curzon had first announced the infamous Partition of Bengal, Sarojini was fiercely in the front of every protest, marching alongside personalities such as Gopal Krishna Gokhale.[13]

She soon became known for her powerful oratory skills. She focussed on the independence movement and women's issues. She was a strong advocate for women's education. She followed the five-part rhetorical structure of reasoning in her arguments. Her oratory skills first came into the spotlight in 1906, when she addressed the INC and the Indian Social Conference in Calcutta (now Kolkata). The British Indian government awarded her the *Kaisar-i-Hind* Medal for her work in flood relief. She returned this medal in 1919 to protest against the Jallianwala Bagh massacre.A powerful woman who influenced Sarojini was Annie Besant. In 1917, Sarojini accompanied Besant to advocate universal suffrage in front of the Joint Select Committee in London.[14]

She threw herself wholeheartedly into the freedom movement, and through her dedication she became the first Indian woman to serve as the president of the INC. She joined the Satyagraha Movement in 1917, went to London in 1919 as part of the All India Home Rule League and participated in the Non-Cooperation Movement. To quote her:

> As long as I have life, as long as blood flows through this arm of mine, I shall not leave the cause of freedom...I am only a woman, only a poet. But as a woman, I give to you the weapons of faith and courage and the shield of fortitude. And as a poet, I fling out the banner of song and sound, the bugle call to battle. How shall I kindle the flame which shall waken you men from slavery...[15]

In 1916, she fought for the indigo farmers in Champaran; in 1917, she co-founded the Women's Indian Association with Annie Besant; and in 1918, she, along with other feminists, began publishing a magazine called *Stri Dharma* which looked at the news from a feminist perspective. She attended the East African INC in 1924 as the representative of the INC. She also represented India at the International Women's Congress in 1929 in Berlin.[16]

In 1914, she was elected as a fellow of the Royal Society of Literature. Her published poems were printed in a collection in

1928. A more comprehensive collection, including her previously unpublished works, was published in 1961. It was edited by her daughter, Padmaja Naidu. Her speeches were collected and first published in 1918.

During the Dandi March in 1930, at first, Gandhi ji had not allowed women to join him because of the distance they were to cover and the threat of violence and arrest by the authorities. Khurshedben Naoroji, Kamaladevi Chattopadhyay and Sarojini Naidu, among the other women activists of the movement, convinced him that women should be allowed to join the march. Following his arrest on 6 April 1930, Gandhi ji appointed Sarojini to lead the campaign in his absence. However, soon after, she was also arrested along with other Congress leaders like Madan Mohan Malviya and Jawaharlal Nehru. After the Gandhi–Irwin Pact, she took part in the Second Round Table Conference headed by Viceroy Lord Irwin.[17] She was arrested in 1932, and then again in 1942 during the Quit India Movement.

She would take her incarcerations in good spirit, despite her persistent and chronic ill health. Sushila Nayyar has written about how when she arrived at the Aga Khan Palace detention camp, Sarojini offered her a meal of bread and butter. Sarojini would also insist on setting the table for meals; ensure that everyone had a proper meal; bathe and change; and then sit in the balcony to gaze upon the flowers in the garden. She was particular about keeping up a daily routine, as she firmly believed that a fixed routine kept up the morale. In the 21 months of her detention, Sarojini developed a good equation with Gandhi ji, even calling him Mickey Mouse in a tongue-in-cheek manner.[18]

After India gained independence in 1947, she was made the governor of the United Provinces (modern-day Uttar Pradesh), thus becoming the first woman to be appointed governor in independent India.[19]

However, she was not destined to live long in post-Independence India. Upon returning from an official trip to Delhi on 15 February 1949, she fell acutely ill. On 1 March, therapeutic bloodletting was performed after she said that she had a severe headache. She passed away soon after, on 2 March 1949, barely two years after India achieved independence. She had suffered a cardiac arrest at the age of 70. Her last rites were performed on the banks of the Gomti River.[20]

As a tribute to her, an off-campus annexe at the University of Hyderabad is named after her first collection of poetry. It is now the seat of the Sarojini Naidu School of Arts & Communication at the University of Hyderabad. In 1990, Eleanor Helin discovered an asteroid which was named Asteroid (5647) Sarojininaidu in her honour. In 2014, her 135th birth anniversary was celebrated with a Google Doodle. Her birthday is commemorated as Women's Day in India to honour the work she did for the emancipation of women.

Her wit, wisdom and passion for the causes she espoused made her a towering personality of her times—and even afterwards. At a time when the arena of politics was dominated by the men, Sarojini carved a place for herself, and remained there, unshakeable. She was someone for whom the beauty of words and passion of oration mingled, making her a force to be reckoned with even today—decades after her passing.

NOTES

1 'Sarojini Naidu: Indian Writer and Political Leader', *Britannica*, 26 February 2023, http://tinyurl.com/m5knwwat. Accessed on 2 January 2024.

2 Karthika, 'Sarojini Naidu: The Nightingale of India | #Indianwomeninhistory', *Feminism in India*, 22 March 2017, http://tinyurl.com/4wjb3ahz. Accessed on 2 January 2024.

3 Parr, Rosalind, '1 - The Cosmopolitan-Nationalism of Sarojini Naidu', *Cambridge University Press*, 6 August 2021, http://tinyurl.com/3p8xcway. Accessed on 2 January 2024.

4 'Sarojini Naidu,' *The Open University*, http://tinyurl.com/mv4uc8s3. Accessed on 2 January 2024.

5 'Sarojini Naidu Biography,' *Vedantu*, http://tinyurl.com/yckvpa7v. Accessed on 2 January 2024.

6 Hoene, Christin, 'Senses and Sensibilities in Sarojini Naidu's Poetry,' *South Asia: Journal of South Asian Studies*, Vol. 44, No. 5, 2021, pp. 966–82.

7 Alexander, Meena (ed.), *Name Me a Word: Indian Writers Reflect on Writing*, Yale University Press, 2018.

8 Sinha, Vaishnawi, 'How Sarojini Naidu, the Fearless Indian Political Activist, Spent Her Days in Detention Camps during Freedom Struggle,' *India Today*, 19 June 2020, http://tinyurl.com/mryu5xhn. Accessed on 2 January 2024.

9 'Backstory: When Sarojni Naidu, the "Nightingale of India," Called Mahatma Gandhi "Mickey Mouse",' *CNBCTV18*, 13 February 2021, http://tinyurl.com/2adk7b34. Accessed on 2 January 2024.

10 Sinha, Vaishnawi, 'How Sarojini Naidu, the Fearless Indian Political Activist, Spent Her Days in Detention Camps during Freedom Struggle,' *India Today*, 19 June 2020, http://tinyurl.com/mryu5xhn. Accessed on 2 January 2024.

11 'Letter from Gandhiji to Sarojini Naidu, September 17, 1932,' *MKGandhi.org*, http://tinyurl.com/2aerxda3. Accessed on 2 January 2024.

12 Everts, Marijke, 'Sarojini Naidu: India's Renowned Poet and Freedom Fighter,' *europeana*, 13 February 2022, http://tinyurl.com/yembyjt7. Accessed on 2 January 2024.

13 Naravane, V.S., *Sarojini Naidu: An Introduction to Her Life, Work and Poetry*, Orient Longman, 1996.

14 Ray, Sanjana, 'Remembering Sarojini Naidu: A Poet, Patriot, and Emancipator,' *the quint*, 2 March 2022, http://tinyurl.com/fhs6d96s. Accessed on 2 January 2024.

15 Karthika, 'Sarojini Naidu: The Nightingale of India | #Indianwomeninhistory,' *Feminism in India*, 22 March 2017,

http://tinyurl.com/4wjb3ahz. Accessed on 2 January 2024.

16 Seltzer, Joanna, 'Sarojini Naidu: Activist, Leader, Poet, & Caregiver during the Plague,' *Medium*, 13 May 2021, http://tinyurl.com/498cchcv. Accessed on 2 January 2024.

17 Karthika, 'Sarojini Naidu: The Nightingale of India | #Indianwomeninhistory,' *Feminism in India*, 22 March 2017, http://tinyurl.com/4wjb3ahz. Accessed on 2 January 2024.

18 Sinha, Vaishnawi, 'How Sarojini Naidu, the Fearless Indian Political Activist, Spent Her Days in Detention Camps during Freedom Struggle,' *India Today*, 19 June 2020, http://tinyurl.com/mryu5xhn. Accessed on 2 January 2024.

19 'Sarojini Naidu: Indian Writer and Political Leader,' *Britannica*, 26 February 2023, http://tinyurl.com/m5knwwat. Accessed on 2 January 2024.

20 Gaur, A., 'Nightingale of India: Know All about Sarojini Naidu,' *Adda247*, 21 February 2023, http://tinyurl.com/yfvx96sy. Accessed on 2 January 2024.

5

RUKMINI DEVI ARUNDALE

THE DOYENNE OF BHARATANATYAM

The photographs show us a graceful woman, draped elegantly in a flowing saree, her eyes wide yet calm, her body languid and restful—almost as if she were completely unaware of the camera. This is how it must be, one assumes, for a woman accustomed to having everyone's gaze upon her, as a stage performer. For her, the proscenium was nothing but an extension of herself. Rukmini Devi Arundale, a colossus in the world of Indian classical dance, wore her accomplishments lightly and with a sanguine grace that came through in her photographs.

She was much more than just a dancer and choreographer as many think of her today. She was, in fact, the person instrumental in the revival and reinvention of the Indian classical dance form of Bharatanatyam (taking away from it the stigma of being perceived as a dance performed only by *devadasis*), a Theosophist and an animal welfare activist. She was also the first woman in India to be nominated as a member of the Rajya Sabha. She could have also been the president of India, as she was almost nominated by Morarji Desai. This was an offer she turned down to focus on her work in dance and animal welfare.

It wasn't an easy journey by any standards, but are journeys that change how a nation perceives an art ever easy? There were battles to be fought and won, and she took them on indefatigably.

❧

On 29 February 1904, a baby girl was born into a Brahmin family in Madurai, Tamil Nadu. They named her Rukmini. Her father, A. Neelakanta Sastri of Thiruvisanallur, was an engineer with the Public Works Department as well as a respected Sanskrit scholar and follower of Buddha. Her mother, Srimati Seshammal, was from a highly cultured family of Thiruvaiyar, and a music lover.[1] The family moved homes frequently, because of her father's constant transfers owing to his job. In 1901, her father was introduced to the Theosophical Society. His brother, Neelakanta Sri Ram, later went on to become the president of the society. Neelakanta Sastri himself became a follower of Dr Annie Besant, even moving to Madras (now Chennai) after he retired to build a home close to the headquarters of the Theosophical Society in Adyar.[2]

The couple introduced their children to texts like the Valmiki Ramayana, which their father read to them in Sanskrit every evening. The girls were trained in music, and according to her younger sister, Visalakshi, Rukmini was a good student of music. Their home in Adyar was called Buddha Vilas, in keeping with her father's fascination with Buddhist philosophy. Rukmini wrote about her parents, saying, 'I have had the fortune of having the most understanding and loving parents. No discipline was imposed on us, but traditional values and correct behaviour we learnt automatically by watching them... Father was...very forward thinking and disliked many of the narrow prejudices, the caste distinctions, animal sacrifices, etc. which were part of our religion in those days.'[3]

Dr Annie Besant and the Theosophical Society became a part of young Rukmini's life. Barely 14, she signed up to volunteer in the Theosophical Society, and began attending lectures conducted by eminent speakers both from within India and abroad. She also began working with the villagers in the villages near Madras to teach them hygiene and to spread awareness about stopping animal sacrifice.

Theosophical thought went on to have a profound influence on her. She explored concepts not just in philosophy, but also around art and culture, and in what later proved to be seminal in her life—music and dance. She met her future husband, George Arundale, at the Theosophical Society as well. He was much older, a close associate of Annie Besant, and later went on to become the principal of the Central Hindu School, Banaras (now Varanasi).

In 1920, she shocked the conservative society she lived in by marrying George. She was barely 16 and he was 42 at the time, an age gap that was considered scandalous even in those times. She wrote of her husband, saying that he had a great sense of humour. She also spoke of how he always had a group of admirers surrounding him. Her mother used to affectionately call him 'Krishna' and she was 'Yasoda'. Owing to this closeness, her parents were not too opposed when he proposed marriage to Rukmini. Her mother was worried about the public outcry but supported them wholeheartedly. For her mother, only the support of Annie Besant mattered and they had that.[4]

Annie Besant advised her mother to allow the couple to get married, and so on 27 April 1920, George Sydney Arundale and Rukmini Devi were married in a civil ceremony in Bombay (now Mumbai), far away from the hullabaloo their decision had created in the conservative social circles of Madras. Years later, in 1936, she spoke of marriage, saying, 'The real spirit of marriage is an ideal. We must each live according to our own ideal.'[5]

The wedding ceremony was conducted by Alladi Mahadeva Sastri and, by doing so, Rukmini Devi became the first well-known Brahmin lady to break caste by marring a foreigner.

The fallout from this marriage was immense. The rigid Brahmin community in Madras ostracized her and her family. But the support of the Theosophists and the Indian public was strong. The couple integrated back into society in due course.

They lived their lives as they always had. She continued to follow the traditions and customs she was taught and ate the food she had grown up with. He educated her in English, as well as the manners, customs, arts and philosophy of the Western world. The couple lived for a while in Bombay and then moved to Indore, where Maharaja Holkar made George the minister of education in what was then a princely state.[6] The couple eventually returned to Adyar to help Annie Besant with the work of the Theosophical Society. During this time, cultural and social icons like Rabindranath Tagore, Sarojini Naidu and Leopold Stokowski visited the Theosophical Society. J. Krishnamurti, a student of George Arundale, was named World Teacher by the Theosophical Society.

George was a prominent Theosophist. He was also a respected name and a member of the Society for the Promotion of National Education. In 1926, he was made the general secretary of the Australian Section, and in 1928 he was appointed to the same position in India. The couple travelled to the United States (US) for the dedication of the new headquarters building in 1927, and back again in 1929 for the Third World Congress in Chicago as speakers.

Rukmini was appointed the president of the All-India Federation of Young Theosophists in 1923 and as the president of the World Federation of Young Theosophists in 1925. They became members of the American Theosophical Society on 5 September 1929 and were charter members of the Wheaton Olcott Lodge. They were part of the International Theosophical Centre in Naarden, the Netherlands from 1930 to 1934, where George was the head of the society. In 1934, he became the president of the Theosophical Society. Rukmini succeeded him, and remained the head till her death in 1986. Though she was based in India, she ensured she visited the centre at least once a year.

George passed away in 1945. At the time, Rukmini was only 39. She was a member of the General Council, the international governing body of the Theosophical Society, and was on the society's executive committee. She was invited to lecture at conferences and gatherings around the world. In 1952, she was the guest of honour at the annual convention of the Theosophical Society in America, and toured across the US in that same trip. That year, she was also invited to inaugurate the new lodge in Saigon, Vietnam.

In the course of her marriage, her travel with her husband on his extensive lecture tours brought her in contact with Theosophists from around the world. She established friendships with the likes of pathbreaking educationist Maria Montessori and the poet James Cousins. A meeting that changed the course of her life was with the Russian ballerina Anna Pavlova. In 1924, on their trip to England, George and Rukmini had gone to Covent Garden to see a performance by the famous ballerina. Some years later, when they were travelling to Australia, they found that Pavlova was travelling on the same ship as them.[7] This was the start of a great friendship and a cross cultural influence, with Rukmini Devi beginning to learn dance from Cleo Nordi, one of the solo dancers in Pavlova's troupe. To quote her on her friendship with Pavlova:

> Later on in 1929, Dr Arundale was sent on Theosophical work to Singapore, Java and Australia and to my delight I found that Anna Pavlova was travelling on the same route. She was dancing in every city we visited and I took different members of the Society with me when I went to her dance. [...]The entire company was with her as also the hundreds of birds that she kept as pets.[8]

She further wrote about Pavlova, saying, 'She was not beautiful in the ordinary sense but had a great presence on stage and an almost divine grace. That was what made her great. I can never forget her, for she showed me the great possibilities in dance as an art form.'[9]

Pavlova also encouraged Rukmini to rediscover traditional Indian dance forms. This was the start of a lifelong mission for Rukmini, one which resulted in her reinventing the dying tradition of the *Sadhir*, a temple dance in South India performed only by the devadasi community. This dance form was stigmatized because it was considered erotic, and not 'seemly' for women from respectable homes to learn or perform it in public. The turning point in her life and her purpose came in 1933, at the annual conference of the Madras Music Academy, when she saw Sadhir being performed. She was fascinated.

At the time, Brahmin women had no access to the dancers, and she found a *guru* with great effort. She convinced Pandanallur Meenakshi Sundaram Pillai, a respected *nattuvanar* (male Bharatanatyam performer) to be her guru. She became accomplished enough in the dance form in merely two years to give her first public performance in 1935 at the Diamond Jubilee Convention of the Theosophical Society.[10] The event made waves because of Rukmini's talent, but also because of the fact that it was the first of what we now know as a Bharatanatyam performance—a staged public event. This was a radical shift from what was hitherto the norm, wherein the dance was performed in a temple by devadasis. She wrote of the Diamond Jubilee performance, saying that they were expecting only around 200 people but 2,000 had turned up. This performance was instrumental in shattering people's biases towards the dance form. George and Dr Cousins were convinced that this was a spiritual medium.[11]

After the Diamond Jubilee performance, she wanted to dedicate her mission to the Lord and visited the Chidambaram Nataraja Temple. To quote her:

> I wanted to carry the work further and start giving shape to my own ideas on Bharatanatyam. But before starting, I wanted to go to Chidambaram and dedicate myself to the lord of dance, Shiva. [...]Though normally nobody was allowed to dance inside the main prakharam, we went quietly without making much noise. When we reached there Srinivasa Sastri came running to warn us. [...]Somehow, the word had got out about the dance. But having come, I did not want to go back. So, we went in. [...] I somehow got in front of the main shrine and I shouted to my musicians to start singing and playing wherever they stood. [...]The hard-stone floor of the temple was soft to my feet like a bed of flowers. It was a great spiritual experience.[12]

Her decision to take the dance form away from temples has been criticized, but not many know that she had initially argued for the dance to remain within the temples. In fact, the inspiration to keep the statue of Nataraja on the right of the stage for every performance came to her after she had danced in the sanctum of the Chidambaram Nataraja Temple.[13]

Of her Diamond Jubilee performance, C.V. Raman, renowned Indian physicist and Nobel Prize winner, stated, 'Some of you, I hope—for your sakes all of you—must have been thrilled by what you just witnessed... grace brought down from the heights of the Himalayas and put on the earth of this platform.'[14]

Her guru, Pandanallur Meenakshi Sundaram Pillai, was unsure about the choice of venue for her first performance. The annual convention of the Theosophical Society in 1935 was an unusual and bold choice of venue. The performance couldn't be termed an *arangetram* in the traditional sense, but was a small montage of dramas. Her guru sent his son, Chokkalingam Pillai, in order to conduct *nattuvangam* for her performance. Later, Rukmini said, 'Meenakshi Sundaram Pillai was quite relieved with the response to the performance and he continued to teach me. Later, when he wanted to get back to his village, he sent Kattumannar Koil Muthukumara Pillai.'[15]

Thereafter, Rukmini was highly in demand to demonstrate and teach her art. That Rukmini—born a Brahmin, married to a respectable member of Madras society—performed this dance in public sent shock waves through the rather rigid community. These waves did not bother Rukmini; she was intent on creating more waves as she went along. Her passion for dance had now consumed her life, and she devoted herself to the cause of reviving Indian dance forms. She once said about her passion for dance, 'Many people have said many things. I can only say I did not consciously go after dance. It found me.'[16]

She decided to take the work of T. Balasaraswati and other noted dancers from the devadasi community to the proscenium it deserved—public performances. E. Krishna Iyer and Rukmini were instrumental in repositioning it to become the dance style now called Bharatanatyam. They worked with the Pandanallur style of Bharatanatyam, modifying it by removing the elements of *sringaar* and eroticism which were part of it. She turned the dance form into one of devotion by incorporating religious and mythological narratives into it, making it a form of *bhakti* rather than than sringaar. She initiated the dance-drama format that we know it as today. She introduced musical elements, like the violin, for instance; created costumes and jewellery inspired by the sculptures in temples; and introduced set and lighting elements, thus changing the dance form completely.

She took inputs from scholars, classical musicians and artists, creating dance-dramas based on the epics like Valmiki Ramayana and Jayadeva's Geeta Govinda to name a few. Six of the dance-dramas based upon the Ramayana which she created have remained her most noted works even today. To quote her from her demonstration talk at the National Dance Seminar in Delhi, 1958, 'The Devadasis and others who danced, whatever their customs, whatever the circumstances in which they lived, they were people with devotion, they were excellent artistes. Even today, they really are the people from whom we can get the best ideas in Bharatanatyam. I must pay my tribute to them.'[17]

She created a distinct style of Bharatanatyam that focussed on stylized *abhinaya*. It differed from the Vazhavur style, which focussed on *lasya* and sringaar expression, and had comparatively stiffer movements with the use of a smaller range of *adavus*.[18]

She established Kalakshetra, an academy of dance and music, taking inspiration from the Indian *gurukul* system, at Adyar in Chennai, the year after Dr Annie Besant passed away. The name *kalakshetra* itself means a holy place of arts. The name was suggested by Pandit S. Subramania Sastri, who was a respected Sanskrit scholar of the times and a member of the Academy.

At Kalakshetra, Rukmini conceptualized dances that were based on the Ramayana, Kalidasa's *Shakuntalam* and *Kumara Sambhavam*, Jayadeva's *Geeta Govinda* in Sanskrit, several *Kuravanjis* in Tamil, *Bhagavatamelas* in Telugu, as well as more contemporary works like Rabindranath Tagore's *Shyama* in Bengali, focussing on the spiritual learnings from them rather than merely the narratives. She meticulously researched every single detail to ensure that it would achieve a sense of authenticity. This included not just the dance form but also costumes, stage design, language used and the accompanying music. In her extensive career, she went on to produce more than 25 full-length dance-dramas. The students at Kalakshetra were trained in all forms of these arts so that they get a holistic understanding of the dance they were performing. The first graduate from Kalakshetra was Radha Burnier and Sarada Hoffman was the second.

Rukmini was also disturbed by the slow death of traditionally-woven handloom sarees which were being replaced by cheaper Chinese weaves. She was encouraged to set up a natural dyeing and weaving venture by noted textile revivalist, Kamaladevi Chattopadhyay. She set up a centre to revive traditional textiles. She installed looms, started an animal shelter and simultaneously taught dance, art and music. She brought traditional weavers to Kalakshetra in 1944, and the sarees they produced were called Adyar sarees. The school became a gurukul in the true sense of the term. The cows on campus produced enough milk for the consumption of those who lived there. Life on campus was simple—there were simple woven mats for sitting and sleeping on the floor. Rukmini's mother oversaw the kitchen to ensure the food cooked was healthy and nutritious.[19]

Within a few years, by 1947, she had made Kalakshetra a complete institute within the Theosophical Society campus. The last devadasi of the Mylapore Kapaliswara Temple, Mylapore Gowri Ammal, taught dance there to aspiring Bharatanatyam students. The dancer and actress Kumari Kamala (later known as Kamala Lakshman) went there to find nattuvanars who could teach her young daughters the dance form.[20]

The Academy today is a deemed university and has a huge 100-acre campus in Thiruvanmiyur, Chennai, where it was relocated in 1962. Famous students who have emerged from its portal include Radha Burnier, Kamaladevi Chattopadhyay, Sanjukta Panigrahi, Sarada Hoffman, Anjali Mehr, C.V. Chandrasekhar, Yamini Krishnamurthy and Leela Samson.

Rukmini and George were also instrumental in introducing the Montessori Method of education in India. George invited the pioneer of the Montessori Method, Dr Maria Montessori, to start courses in the Besant Theosophical Higher Secondary School in 1939. Later, he went on to establish the Besant Arundale Senior Secondary School, Rukmini Devi College of Fine Arts, The Maria Montessori School for Children, The Craft Education and Research Centre and the U.V. Swaminatha Iyer Library within the Kalakshetra campus. Rukmini Devi was deeply influenced by Maria. To quote her on Maria:

> Madame Montessori as a person when she was nearly eighty-one, was one of the most youthful human beings I had ever come across. One could easily have said that she was eighty years young. It is the same with many others whom I have seen working with children, because being in the company of children has given them a new outlook, a new experience, so that they are eternally alive and youthful in the right sense of the term.[21]

She practised a theosophical approach that integrated arts, animal welfare and vegetarianism. In fact, so strong was her philosophy and approach that she was proposed to be named 'World Mother', much like Jiddu Krishnamurti was proclaimed as 'World Teacher' by Annie Besant and Charles Leadbeater. It was a title she bore with some scepticism. She felt that in India every woman is addressed as *mataji* or *amma* by strangers. This is done to recognize the ideal of the mother in every woman. She was only 21 at the time and establishing a league for motherhood did not quite excite her. She is quoted to have said to C. Jinarajadasa, 'If I start an organization it will go dead if it is only my ideas instead of an inspired thing. I can't do it.'[22]

Peter Finch, the British actor, was said to have considered Rukmini as a foster mother. He had grown up in Madras as a child and lived with his grandmother, who was keen on the Theosophical Society and attended meetings with Annie Besant. Through circumstances, he ended up living with Buddhist monks, with a shaven head, and went begging for his food with them. Rukmini, who saw him every day, was horrified at the neglect of the child and took him into her home and nurtured him.[23]

She was first nominated to the Rajya Sabha in 1952 and then again in 1956, making her the first Indian woman to be nominated to the Rajya Sabha. An animal lover, she was associated with the cause of animal welfare. She was instrumental in getting the legislation for the Prevention of Cruelty to Animals Act passed in

1960, as well as in setting up the Animal Welfare Board of India in 1962, of which she was the chairperson until she passed away in 1986. She took the government of Pandit Jawaharlal Nehru head-on while she was a Member of Parliament (MP), against the exports of monkeys for experiments. While an MP, she studied the condition of animals destined for the slaughterhouse and formulated laws that might protect them. She first introduced the Prevention of Cruelty to Animals Bill in the house in 1953, and persevered until it was finally passed in 1960.[24]

To quote her on animal welfare:

> We always speak of rights of man and the freedom of the individual, but we forget that besides his rights, man has his responsibilities as well. These responsibilities do not merely extend to the poor and the suffering in the human kingdom, but also to the animal kingdom, which is even more helpless and in need of kindness and compassion.[25]

She spoke extensively about the living hells that animal slaughterhouses were, and devoted years of her life visiting and documenting the conditions in slaughterhouses, research laboratories, vaccine institutes and cattle markets, to name a few. Her love for animals led her to espouse the cause of vegetarianism. To quote her:

> We need to know not only 'why vegetarianism' but also what is right vegetarianism. Ancient systems of medicines taught the right diet, and grandmothers of earlier generations had a very good knowledge of food values. Today, we eat food that is not healthy...I know that while a vegetarian is not necessarily a better person, vegetarianism is a better way of life in every possible respect.[26]

Having grown up with Buddhist principles imbibed from her father, she admired and respected the Dalai Lama deeply, and was the head of the relief committee offering him and the other escapees from Tibet refuge as well as rehabilitation in 1959. She took in a hundred Tibetan refugee children at Kalakshetra along with a couple of *lamas* who would teach them their religion. The children grew up at Kalakshetra and she made sure they were well settled with jobs when they finished their education.[27]

She also founded the Indian Vegetarian Congress in 1959, serving as its president for many years, and the vice-president of the International Vegetarian Union for 31 years—another post she held until her death. She was the president of the Crafts Council of India from 1975 to 1986. This was a non-profit organization supporting the education of young people in traditional Indian crafts such as stone carving, pottery and textiles.

In fact, as mentioned earlier, in 1977, the then Prime Minister (PM) Morarji Desai wished to nominate her for the post of the president of India when Fakhruddin Ali Ahmed passed away, but she turned it down. She had more important work to do. If she had accepted she would have been the first woman president of India. Years later, in 2013, then President Pranab Mukherjee recounted the incident in his speech at the inaugural Rukmini Devi Memorial Lecture at Kalakshetra. To quote him:

> I was a Congress MP at the time and Morarji Desai proposed that Rukmini Devi fill the vacancy caused by the death of President Fakhruddin Ali Ahmed. The choice was very widely appreciated and if she agreed, she would have been elected unanimously. But her refusal spoke volumes of her character, wisdom and sagacity and exemplified the values of renunciation and sacrifice that India has traditionally inculcated.[28]

She set up the Kalamkari Centre at Kalakshetra in 1978 to revive the art of textile printing.

Her life's efforts have been acknowledged at the highest level. She was awarded the Padma Bhushan in 1956 and the Sangeet Natak Akademi award in 1957. Ten years later, she got the Sangeet Natak Akademi Fellowship in 1957, the Prani Mitra Award in 1968 and the Kalidas Samman in 1984, to name a few. Apart from these, she was awarded the Queen Victoria Silver Medal by the Royal Society for the Prevention of Cruelty to Animals, London, and was included in the roll of honour of the World Federation for the Protection of Animals, The Hague.

She spoke about her life's purpose in these words, 'To encourage the living of beautiful lives, of lives so refined and so artistic, so gracious and so compassionate, so true and so noble, so wise and so understanding, that everywhere the beautiful is extolled and ugliness fades away.'[29]

In December 1985, the Kalakshetra Academy began six weeks of celebration for its Golden Jubilee celebrations. Though besieged with ill health, Rukmini threw herself into organizing the event. Her body could not take the strain and she passed away on 24 February 1986. Her followers and admirers were shocked at her sudden demise. It was a simple funeral attended by students, disciples, admirers, friends and dignitaries at the highest level. There was a brief Christian memorial service which was attended by close family and friends at Arundale House and a 10th Day ritual, which was held according to the Hindu tradition.

The Indian government issued a postage stamp in her honour in 1987. In 1994, the Indian Parliament acknowledged the importance of the work she had begun by recognizing the Kalakshetra Foundation as an institute of national importance. The year 2004, her birth centenary year, saw celebrations through lectures, seminars and festivals, not just at Kalakshetra but around the world. On the Kalakshetra campus, 29 February saw a day-long celebration with ex-students from across the globe gathered to pay tribute to Rukmini. A photo exhibition on her life opened on this day at the Lalit Kala Akademi in Delhi, and President A.P.J. Abdul Kalam released a photo-biography on her life written by Dr Sunil Kothari. In 2016, Google celebrated Rukmini on her 112th birthday with a doodle. She was also featured in the 2017 Google Doodle for International Women's Day.

What we see and know of Bharatanatyam today, in its form and presentation, owes more to Rukmini Devi Arundale than we realize. In her gentle life, and her firm principles, she left behind a legacy that will endure each time the dance is performed on a stage somewhere in India or around the world.

NOTES

1 'Rukmini Devi Arundale: Indian Dancer and Theosophist,' *Britannica,* 20 February 2023, http://tinyurl.com/52nwpsu6. Accessed on 2 January 2024.

2 Ibid.

3 'Rukmini Devi Arundale,' *Kalakshetra Foundation,* http://tinyurl.com/2ed7cdtr. Accessed on 2 January 2024.

4 Ramani, Shakuntala (ed.), *Rukmini Devi Arundale: Birth Centenary Volume,* Kalakshetra Foundation, 2004.

5 Samson, Leela, 'From the Archives: Rukmini Arundale | Rhythm in Repose,' *India Today,* 5 January 2022, http://tinyurl.com/4dm8wkcp. Accessed on 2 January 2024.

6 Ibid.

7 'Two Dance Legends and an Untold Story,' *Deccan Herald,* 27 November 2010, http://tinyurl.com/y36ytd2n. Accessed on 2 January 2024.

8 Ramani, Shakuntala (ed.), *Rukmini Devi Arundale: Birth Centenary Volume,* Kalakshetra Foundation, 2004.

9 'Rukmini Devi Arundale,' *Kalakshetra Foundation,* http://tinyurl.com/2ed7cdtr. Accessed on 2 January 2024.

10 'Rukmini Devi Arundale: Indian Dancer and Theosophist,' *Britannica,* 20 February 2023, http://tinyurl.com/52nwpsu6. Accessed on 2 January 2024.

11 Ramani, Shakuntala (ed.), *Rukmini Devi Arundale: Birth Centenary Volume,* Kalakshetra Foundation, 2004.

12 V.R. Devika, 'Remembering Rukmini Devi Arundale, Whose Contested Reforms Shaped Modern-Day Bharatanatyam', *Firstpost.*, 26 February 2021, http://tinyurl.com/tv9d7jzf. Accessed on 2 January 2024.

13 Ibid.

14 Bandamede, Rishika, 'Rukmini Devi Arundale', *iFeminist*, 19 September 2020, http://tinyurl.com/bdhux6w3. Accessed on 2 January 2024.

15 V.R. Devika, 'Remembering Rukmini Devi Arundale, Whose Contested Reforms Shaped Modern-Day Bharatanatyam', *Firstpost.*, 26 February 2021, http://tinyurl.com/tv9d7jzf. Accessed on 2 January 2024.

16 'Rukmini Devi Arundale: Dancer, 1904-1986', *India Today*, http://tinyurl.com/yc3da3sk. Accessed on 2 January 2024.

17 V.R. Devika, 'Remembering Rukmini Devi Arundale, Whose Contested Reforms Shaped Modern-Day Bharatanatyam', *Firstpost.*, 26 February 2021, http://tinyurl.com/tv9d7jzf. Accessed on 2 January 2024.

18 'From Sadir Attam to Bharatanatyam', *Indian Culture.gov*, http://tinyurl.com/mrxzzad2. Accessed on 2 January 2024.

19 Samson, Leela, 'From the Archives: Rukmini Arundale | Rhythm in Repose', *India Today*, 5 January 2022, http://tinyurl.com/4dm8wkcp. Accessed on 2 January 2024.

20 V.R. Devika, 'Remembering Rukmini Devi Arundale, Whose Contested Reforms Shaped Modern-Day Bharatanatyam', *Firstpost.*, 26 February 2021, http://tinyurl.com/tv9d7jzf. Accessed on 2 January 2024.

21 Arundale, Rukmini Devi, *The Teacher and the Pupil*, European Committee of the Besant Cultural Centre.

22 Ibid.

23 Ibid.

24 Sanand, Swapna Raghu, 'Rukmini Devi Arundale: This Iconic Indian Dancer Was a Strong Crusader of Vegetarianism and Animal Rights', *FE Leisure*, 6 May 2019, http://tinyurl.com/mwysk93h. Accessed on 2 January 2024.

25 Ramani, Shakuntala (ed.), *Rukmini Devi Arundale: Birth Centenary Volume,* Kalakshetra Foundation, 2004.

26 Sanand, Swapna Raghu, 'Rukmini Devi Arundale: This Iconic Indian Dancer Was a Strong Crusader of Vegetarianism and Animal Rights,' *FE Leisure,* 6 May 2019, http://tinyurl.com/mwysk93h. Accessed on 2 January 2024.

27 Samson, Leela, 'From the Archives: Rukmini Arundale | Rhythm in Repose,' *India Today,* 5 January 2022, http://tinyurl.com/4dm8wkcp. Accessed on 2 January 2024.

28 Pal, Sanchari, 'Rukmini Devi Arundale, the Legend Who Chose Dance over Becoming the President of India,' *The Better India,* 8 March 2017, http://tinyurl.com/2pd7kwwa. Accessed on 2 January 2024.

29 Arundale, George S., 'Issue no.197 - Theosophy as Beauty', *Adyar Pamphlets,* Theosophical Publishing House, http://tinyurl.com/bdhu3d9k. Accessed on 9 January 2024.

6

CAPTAIN LAKSHMI SAHGAL

THE 'RANI' OF THE RANI OF JHANSI REGIMENT

To this generation of young girls and women she's perhaps just a name in their history textbooks that comes alongside Netaji Subhas Chandra Bose and the Indian National Army (INA). But long before women were officially inducted into the armed forces of free India, and long before diversity and inclusion became the catchword of corporate India, Captain Lakshmi Sahgal led a regiment of women in Netaji Subhas Chandra Bose's INA to fight against the British colonizers. The regiment was called 'Rani of Jhansi Regiment', most appropriately, and she not only fought on-ground in combat, but was also taken as prisoner of war in Burma (now Myanmar) during the Second World War. She is no less a hero of the Indian independence movement than those who marched in the streets, courted arrests and were incarcerated in prison by the British.

Hers is a legacy that is truly astounding, as it is the story of how a young woman back in pre-Independence India defied social mores. She studied and became a doctor; got married and then had the courage to leave an unhappy marriage back in 1940; travelled abroad to Singapore on her own; and then signed up to fight in armed combat, as part of a revolutionary army, putting her entire life at stake for the idea of Indian independence. Revolutionary fire was in her genes. Perhaps, it was inevitable that she would go on to lead the adventurous life she led.

She was born on 24 October 1914 to S. Swaminathan and A.V. Ammukutty (who eventually become better known as Ammu Swaminathan). Her father was a lawyer at the Madras High Court and her mother was a well-regarded social worker and Independence activist. Her mother, who was very young when she got married, went on to become a member of the Constituent Assembly of independent India.[1]

Her parents were truly revolutionary for their times. Her father was a Tamil Brahmin and her mother was a Nair from Kerala. Her mother's family was well-known, the aristocratic Vadakkath family from Anakkara in Malabar. Their marriage was quite scandalous at the time, given how strict societal rules were back then. Lakshmi was herself an early rebel. When she was a young girl spending her vacations at her grandmother's home in Kerala, she would hear people talking in the jungle around them. When she asked who these people were, her grandmother told her that they were tribals, and that they were the people 'whose very shadows are polluting.' Though she was young at that time, the injustice of this statement stayed with her. She went into the thick of the jungle, found a young tribal child and decided to play with her. Her grandmother was incandescent with rage, but Lakshmi was determined to have her way.[2]

These were tumultuous times before the formation of free India. Lakshmi and her family were irrevocably drawn into the freedom struggle. From being a lady from the upper strata of society, her mother was transformed into a staunch Congress supporter, who, one fine day, took away all of Lakshmi's foreign-made dresses and burnt them in a bonfire to protest against the British. The memory of that bonfire stayed with Lakshmi for years.

In South India, the freedom struggle ran parallel with the struggle for social reform. Political campaigns for independence also included campaigns for abolition of the caste system, dowry, child marriage and other ills of society. As a young girl, Lakshmi was deeply influenced by these campaigns and the messages they sent out. Another powerful influence on her was Suhasini Nambiar, Sarojini Naidu's sister and a radical activist who had spent many years in Germany. A book she read at this time that also influenced her thinking was Edgar Snow's *Red Star over China*, which was perhaps the first book she read on communism and its precepts and practice. This proved to be the start of a lifetime devoted to communist ideology.[3]

She completed her high-school education from Madras (now Chennai), went on to study at Queen Mary's College, got her MBBS degree from Madras Medical College and then got a diploma in gynaecology and obstetrics. She went on to work in Madras at the Kasturba Gandhi Hospital. She got married to P.K.N. Rao, who was a pilot, but that marriage didn't work out. They had no children and she ended the marriage without divorce, as it was not recognized by the colonial legal system. She went to Singapore after the break-up of her marriage in 1940. She was barely 26 at the time.[4] Her reason for moving to Singapore was to avoid being recruited into the British Indian Army to serve during the Second World War, as all doctors were being recruited.[5]

Singapore was where the course of her life changed irrevocably. It was here that she came in contact with members of the INA. When the British surrendered Singapore to the Japanese, there were a number of prisoners of war who needed urgent medical treatment and Lakshmi treated them. Many of them were keen to create a territorial army for the Indian independence movement. Based in Singapore at the time were K.P. Kesava Menon, S.C. Guha and N. Raghavan, who founded a Council of Action.[6]

To quote Lakshmi:

> The Japanese forces attacked Singapore on December 8, 1941. Rashbehari Bose, who was a veteran freedom fighter, had come with the Japanese. He started the India Independence League. [...] I joined the League but could only do welfare work and underground broadcasts. On February 15, 1942 the Indian National Army (INA) was formed by Captain Mohan Singh. [...]There were military officers in it from the INA. They all went to Tokyo to meet the Japanese government [...]. Unfortunately, the Japanese only verbally agreed to this but never officially ratified them. [...][7]

Things changed drastically with the arrival of Subhas Chandra Bose in Singapore on 2 July 1943. To quote her:

> In the meantime, news of Subhas Chandra Bose's arrival in Germany had come, and Rashbehari Bose pressurised the Japanese, through their ambassador in Berlin; to have Netaji sent from Berlin to Southeast Asia.[...]Netaji completely reorganised the whole movement and put it on a revolutionary basis. He first gave a call for total mobilisation of manpower and appealed to all able-bodied youth to volunteer for the INA.[...][8]

Lakshmi had already become an integral part of the INA and was determined to do her bit for the freedom struggle. At this point, Lakshmi got word that Netaji was contemplating drafting women into his organization. She requested a meeting with Netaji and her request was granted. The meeting went on for five long hours, and from this meeting emerged the proposal to set up a women's regiment in the INA.[9] As mentioned earlier, it was named the 'Rani of Jhansi Regiment,' in tribute to Rani Lakshmibai of Jhansi who rode into the battlefield against the British with her infant son strapped onto her back. To quote Lakshmi:

> At the second mass meeting, Netaji dropped a bombshell by saying that it was his intention to form a women's infantry regiment [...]. I already knew of this idea as he had told me earlier during an interview I had sought with him. I told him I was ready to join, [...] and I started recruiting women. The date was July 8, 1943.[10]

It was indeed a radical idea for the time, especially considering the recruitment of women into the Indian armed forces has started only recently. The fact that back in the 1940s a leader was keen to have a women's regiment was nothing less than revolutionary. But then, Netaji was a revolutionary leader—one who dared to take on the might of the British empire with arms and an army, in radical contrast to the non-violent movement spearheaded by Gandhi ji.

The INA put the call out to draft women who might be keen to take up arms against the British to liberate India, and applications started coming in. Lakshmi had initially been apprehensive about getting enough recruits, as most educated middle-class families had moved to India. Netaji had then advised her to not depend just on the middle class to bring about a revolution. The workers are the ones who bring the real revolution. They eventually had a regiment of 1,500 women soldiers, including 200 nursing staff.[11]

Lakshmi then took on a new role, one that changed the trajectory of her life irrevocably. She went from being a doctor in Singapore to a captain in an army. She went on to lead a regiment of women—something that was unheard of at the time, a first of sorts. From then on, she went down as Captain Lakshmi in the annals of history. Sahgal was a surname that would get appended to hers much later. Before that, she had history to create.

They began training the Rani of Jhansi Regiment in Singapore and Rangoon on 23 October 1943. A couple of days earlier, on 21 October, the provisional government of Azad Hind had been announced, and Netaji had appointed Captain Lakshmi as a minister in his government, giving her the portfolio of

Women's Problems in addition to her responsibilities in setting up and heading the Rani of Jhansi Regiment. Their training was only three months long and as rigorous as could be, given the circumstances and the very short duration they had to actually train. The women also had a uniform, a khaki bush shirt and trousers like the men, and they all had to cut their hair short. Cutting her hair short was a liberation of sorts for Lakshmi. Her mother had always insisted she keep her hair long, and she had kept it was down to her knees. Maintaining that length of hair was quite a burden, and was completely impractical for field combat.

They were trained by regulars from the Indian Army who were committed to making soldiers out of the new recruits. Weapons were limited, just rifles and hand grenades. The recruits also learnt essentials like military strategy and map reading. Hindi was taught to the new recruits in the Roman script. Netaji took their classes on politics. Lakshmi often said that Netaji helped them demolish many myths about themselves. He believed that a good soldier was as good as their training and often ridiculed the British categorization of Indians as martial and non-martial.[12]

The INA joined the Japanese Army in December of 1944 to march on towards Burma from Singapore. The Rani of Jhansi Regiment moved from Singapore to Burma after three months of training and then in May 1944, they moved from Rangoon to Imphal in small batches, focussing on guerrilla attacks. The male members of the INA would protect the female soldiers from the Japanese and local male populace. The Japanese soldiers were in fact strongly against the women's regiment, refusing to give them sites to camp at. Later, they saw how determined and efficient the women's regiment was and changed their mind.

By March 1945, the War had turned its course and Japan was on the back foot. The Regiment sadly could only go as far as the middle of Burma, with the British forces overpowering the INA. To their bad luck, the monsoon set in as well, making further advances impossible. The INA was forced to withdraw to Central Burma after suffering heavy losses, with the aim of re-grouping and attacking the British Army again.

The INA decided to retreat before they could reach Imphal. Lakshmi once recounted that all the members of the Rani of Jhansi Regiment sent Netaji a petition signed with their blood, stating that they did not want to retreat. That is how determined they were to give up their lives for the cause of Independence.[13]

At this point, she began volunteering in a hospital in the Shan jungles which had not seen any fighting. The hospital was for those who were severely wounded and incapacitated during the battle. The Allied forces bombed the hospital, and the medical personnel who survived tried to shift the severely wounded by bullock carts to Rangoon. They were intercepted and arrested by the British. Captain Lakshmi was arrested by the British in June 1945, and was kept in captivity for almost an entire year. She was separated from the rest of the INA prisoners.[14] The INA trials in Delhi caused great outrage and heightened opinion against the imperialist rule. Lakshmi was sent to India in March 1946. The INA trials became iconic with Pandit Jawaharlal Nehru himself defending the INA prisoners of war, and Bhulabhai Desai's speech at the trial becoming a much cited one in the annals of law history.

In 1947, Lakshmi married Col Prem Kumar Sahgal, also of the INA, in Lahore, a few months before India attained independence. The couple settled in Kanpur after their wedding. She continued her medical practice, and helped the refugees who arrived in India after Partition. They named their daughter Subhashini to pay tribute to Netaji. Post Independence, she returned to practising medicine and did not join any political party. When her daughter, Subhasini, returned from the United States in 1969, she joined the CPI (M). Lakshmi volunteered for relief work during the Bangladesh War after seeing Jyoti Basu's appeal, and worked for over six weeks in the border areas.[15]

Captain Lakshmi was at the Indo-Bangladesh border working with the refugees who needed supplies and medical assistance. On her return via Calcutta (now Kolkata), the politbureau of the Communist Party of India, Marxist (CPI [M]) was having a meeting. She decided to meet the leaders on an impulse, and then joined the party. She was part of the CPI (M) until she passed away.

She was always a communist at heart. On joining the CPI (M), she said it was 'like coming home. My way of thinking was already communist, and I never wanted to earn a lot of money, or acquire a lot of property or wealth.'[16]

She was among the founders of the All India Democratic Women's Association in 1981, working on-ground in Kanpur during the anti-Sikh riots of November 1984. They ensured that no Sikh in the area near her clinic in Kanpur was attacked by the mobs. She then went on to lead a medical team into Bhopal after the gas leak in December 1984, later writing a report on how exposure to the gas affected the women who were pregnant at the time and the children they gave birth to.

Active till the age of 92, she was seeing patients at her clinic in Kanpur. In a 2006 interview with Singeli Agnew, a filmmaker from the Graduate School of Journalism, Berkeley, who was making a documentary on her life, she said, 'The fight will go on. Freedom comes in three forms. The first is political emancipation from the conqueror, the second is economic [emancipation] and the third is social... India has only achieved the first.'[17]

Interestingly, although she is known as Captain Lakshmi, she was in fact a lieutenant colonel in the INA. She had been promoted—a fact she didn't really talk about or try to correct too vehemently.

She almost became the president of India in 2002 when four of the Leftist parties—the CPI, the CPI (M), the Revolutionary Socialist Party and the All India Forward Bloc—nominated her to be a presidential candidate. However, she lost to A.P.J. Abdul Kalam.[18] The result of the presidential elections was a foregone conclusion, but this didn't deter her from throwing herself wholeheartedly into a country-wide campaign, addressing issues of importance, while simultaneously frankly admitting that she had no chance of winning. She was awarded the Padma Vibhushan in 1998 by the then President K.R. Narayan. The University of Calicut conferred an honorary doctorate on her in 2010.

She passed away in Kanpur on 23 July 2012 from a cardiac arrest she had had a few days earlier on 19 July.[19] She was 97. She had been active at her clinic until a few years before her death, till she was 92. Her body was donated to medical research as per her wishes. With her passing ended a life that had been lived to the fullest in service to the nation—at first for the freedom from British rule, and then in service to the citizens of the nation, both through activism and through her training as a doctor.

NOTES

1 'Captain Lakshmi Sahgal,' *Azadi Ka Amrit Mahotsav*, http://tinyurl.com/3t8bk6m7. Accessed on 2 January 2024.

2 Banerji, Rishabh, 'Dr. Lakshmi Sahgal Set up the Women Regiment in Netaji's INA, but That's Not the Only Reason You Should Know Her,' *Indiatimes*, 18 December 2015, http://tinyurl.com/2vf8ftxk. Accessed on 2 January 2024.

3 Menon, Parvathi, 'Captain Lakshmi Sahgal (1914–2012)—A Life of Struggle,' *The Hindu*, 17 November 2021, http://tinyurl.com/ycxr7fcv. Accessed on 2 January 2024.

4 Ibid.

5 Sahgal, Lakshmi, 'My Days in the Indian National Army by Lakshmi Sehgal, *NDTV*, 23 July 2012, http://tinyurl.com/4dk5dn3k. Accessed on 2 January 2024.

6 Jayakumar, Vaibavi, 'Doctor, Captain, Politician: Remembering Lakshmi Sahgal,' *The Commune*, 10 August 2020, http://tinyurl.com/2fh4ut7a. Accessed on 2 January 2024.

7 Sahgal, Lakshmi, 'My Days in the Indian National Army

by Lakshmi Sahgal', *NDTV*, 23 July 2012, http://tinyurl.com/4dk5dn3k. Accessed on 2 January 2024.

8 Ibid.

9 Menon, Parvathi, 'Captain Lakshmi Sahgal (1914–2012)—A Life of Struggle', *The Hindu*, 17 November 2021, http://tinyurl.com/ycxr7fcv. Accessed on 2 January 2024.

10 Sahgal, Lakshmi, 'Memoirs of a Communist Freedom Fighter: My Days in INA', *People's Democracy*, Vol. XXXVI, No. 30, 2012, http://tinyurl.com/crkvpxkt. Accessed on 2 January 2024.

11 Sahgal, Lakshmi, 'My Days in the Indian National Army by Lakshmi Sahgal', *NDTV*, 23 July 2012, http://tinyurl.com/4dk5dn3k. Accessed on 2 January 2024.

12 Naim, Shahira, 'The Bose I Knew Is a Memory Now—Lakshmi Sahgal', *The Tribune Spectrum*, 12 June 2005, http://tinyurl.com/2t22wmdv. Accessed on 2 January 2024.

13 Gupta, Ateendriya, 'Women in Command: Remembering the Rani of Jhansi Regiment', *The Hindu*, 7 March 2020, http://tinyurl.com/4cmt526j. Accessed on 2 January 2024.

14 Sahgal, Lakshmi, 'My Days in the Indian National Army by Lakshmi Sahgal', *NDTV*, 23 July 2012, http://tinyurl.com/4dk5dn3k. Accessed on 2 January 2024.

15 Sahgal, Lakshmi, 'Memoirs of a Communist Freedom Fighter: My Days in INA', *People's Democracy*, Vol. XXXVI, No. 30, 2012, http://tinyurl.com/crkvpxkt. Accessed on 2 January 2024.

16 Menon, Parvathi, 'Captain Lakshmi Sahgal (1914–2012)—A Life of Struggle', *The Hindu*, 17 November 2021, http://tinyurl.com/ycxr7fcv. Accessed on 2 January 2024.

17 Ibid.

18 Jha, Avishek, 'Remembering Capt. Lakshmi, Freedom Fighter & Social Activist, on Her 6th Death Anniversary', *The Print*, 23 July 2018, http://tinyurl.com/kc4x74j6. Accessed on 2 January 2024.

19 PTI, 'Captain Lakshmi Sahgal Passes Away', *The Times of India*, 23 July 2012, http://tinyurl.com/yc3zwy87. Accessed on 2 January 2024.

7

JUSTICE ANNA CHANDY

LADY JUSTICE

In 1905, in Elaphi, in what was then the princely kingdom of Travancore in South India, a young girl was born. She was later raised in Trivandrum (now Thiruvanthapuram).[1] She was named Anna Chandy. Although an Anglican Syrian Christian by birth, she took to Catholicism much later in her life. Anna saw hardship early on in her life. She lost her father when she was very young, and her mother provided for Anna and her sister by working at a local store. She saw her mother's struggle to survive financially and to bring up her children in a world that was skewed towards men from an early age, even though Kerala was primarily a matrilineal society. At home, she learnt how women could take on the mantle of household responsibilities and earn an income. But as she grew, she saw that society around her still considered a woman's domain to be primarily the home. She saw that women were expected to be subservient to the men in their lives, and that they were not encouraged to be too educated. However, she grew up to defy the norm.

Her princely state was quite progressive for its time (compared to other states). The rulers set great store by women's education. The queen of Travancore, Maharani Sethu Lakshmi Bayi, a fierce advocate for women's empowerment herself, opened admissions for women in the Government Law College in 1927. Eager to make a mark for herself, the young Anna signed up for a postgraduate degree in law. She was the first woman in her state to do so. It wasn't easy; she faced unforeseen hostility from the men in the classroom itself, but she stayed the course, undeterred. She got her postgraduate degree in law in 1929, with distinction, and passed the Bar exam the very same year.[2] She immediately began practising as a barrister, with her focus on criminal law, getting much acclaim for the cases she fought.

She was also passionate about women's rights. In 1930, she founded a magazine on women's issues, *Shreemati*, that she also edited herself. It was the first women's magazine in Malayalam. Through *Shreemati*, she created a platform to talk about the misogyny that affected women's lives, and she espoused the causes of widow remarriage and gendered wage inequality, something we are still grappling with today. Back then, her area of concern was the wage inequality for farm workers.[3] She was a fervent advocate of women's right to work, and campaigned for support from other contemporary public figures and intellectuals like Sadasya Thilakan T.K. Velupillai, who authored *Travancore Manual* and was the first elected deputy speaker of Travancore, to put forth the demand for government offices to institute a quota for women.

To quote her from an argument she made when a fellow legislator opposed a quota for women in government jobs, 'From the elaborate petition, it is clear that the plaintiff's immediate demand is to ban all efforts by women to gain employment, on the grounds that they are a bunch of creatures created for the domestic pleasures of men, and that their lives outside the hallowed kitchen-temples will harm familial happiness.'[4]

Thanks to her relentless struggle, women could finally apply for government jobs, as the statute preventing women from working in government positions was abolished. She was one of the first women to fight for women's right to be in the workforce in India, that too in pre-Independence India. Her strong feminism could also be a product of the matriarchal culture she came from in Kerala as well as the circumstances of her childhood, when she saw how her mother navigated society alone. Her fight for equality was fair to both men and women. In 1935, she took on the law that exempted women from being given the death penalty and questioned its rationale. If women should have equal rights as men, she felt, they should also have equal punishment.[5]

At a time when the words 'agency' and 'consent' weren't even considered in the lexicon of women's rights, Anna Chandy was a fierce advocate of women's consent. While we are still struggling to get a definitive law on marital rape in twenty-first century India, she took a stand against the law in Travancore which permitted men to force their conjugal rights on their wives, without consideration for the latter's consent. She was always ahead of her time.[6]

Her stand on bodily autonomy for women stands out for how relatable it is even in contemporary times. To quote her from one of her speeches, 'Many of our sister-Malayalees have property rights, voting rights, employment and honours, financial independence. But how many have control over their own bodies? How many women have been condemned to depths of feelings of inferiority because of the foolish idea that women's body is an instrument for the pleasure of men?'[7]

She was an inspiration for the other 'first-generation feminists' from the region. According to J. Devika and Binitha V. Thampi in their book, *New Lamps for Old?: Gender Paradoxes of Political Decentralisation in Kerala*, the feminists of the time 'also explicitly connected women's political rights with other kinds of rights, for instance, legal and reproductive rights, an effort especially palpable in the writing of Anna Chandy'.[8] Justice Fathima Beevi has said that her father's insistence that she take up law instead of science, was thanks to him being inspired by the achievements of Anna Chandy, who at the time had already made a name for herself in Kerala as an icon for women.[9]

As mentioned earlier, though Travancore was a princely state, its rulers were much ahead of their times. They had been among the earliest rulers to set up their own democratically elected Legislative Assembly, as far back as 1888. A few decades later, in 1904, the Maharaja of Travancore set and inaugurated what was called the Shree Mulam Popular Assembly (*Praja Sabha*), which was essentially a non-legislative advisory body. While two-thirds of the members of this body were elected by votes, the rest of the members were nominated. Chandy campaigned to be elected to the Shree Mulam Popular Assembly in 1931—an audacious decision back in those times when positions of governmental importance were limited only to men. Her candidature was not met favourably; there was a lot of disparagement from the Opposition as well as the media which published unfavourable stories about her connections with the Dewan of the state. A Nair-run newspaper called *Malayala Rajyam* was reportedly at the forefront of the campaign to discredit her. However, *Nasrani Deepika*, another Malayalam newspaper, backed her wholeheartedly. She did not win then, but undeterred she contested again the next year; and this time round, she was elected and was part of the Assembly from 1932 to 1934.[10]

The dewan of Travancore, Sir C.P. Ramaswami Iyer appointed her as a *munsif* in Travancore in 1937, making her the first female judge in India and the first woman in a Commonwealth country to become a judge, along with Emily Murphy.[11] It is possible that she was the second woman in the world to be appointed to the post of High Court judge after Florence Allen in the United States, who was appointed as a judge back in 1922.[12]

All eyes were on her; her decriers were alert to the possibility of her putting a foot wrong so that they could put it down to a woman's inability to take 'logical unbiased decisions'. Anna was acutely aware of the precariousness of her position, thanks to the biases against her, and knew that on her shoulders rested the responsibility of shaping how the country would perceive the future generation of women in law. To quote her, 'I must admit that I was not free from trepidation when I first stepped up to the Bench. However, what was foremost in my mind was a fierce determination to make a success of this experiment. I knew I was a test case... If I faltered or failed, I would not just be damaging my own career, but would be doing a great disservice to the cause of women.'[13]

This was back when India was still under the British rule. By 1948, she was elevated to district judge. There were more firsts that came her way. She became the first female judge in India at an Indian High Court on 9 February 1959, when she was appointed as a judge at the Kerala High Court—a position she held until 5 April 1967. After she retired, she served on the Law Commission of India. She received staunch unstinted support from her husband, P.C. Chandy, who was an inspector general of police. In 1971, the popular Malayalam magazine, *Malayala Manorama*, serialized her autobiography, which was subsequently published in Thrissur by Carmel Books in 1973 under the title *Atmakatha*.[14]

She passed away at the age of 91 on 20 July 1996. With her passing, we lost a pioneering legal luminary—one who disregarded gender biases and fought not just for herself, but also mindfully worked towards helping other women get the rights they deserved, whether government jobs or wage equality.

NOTES

1 'Anna Chandy Death Anniversary: Remembering India's First Woman Judge in High Court', *CNBCTV18*, 20 July 2022, http://tinyurl.com/mwe3pfs4. Accessed on 2 January 2024.

2 Parmeshwar, K., and Medha Damojipurapu, 'Justice Anna Chandy: The Pioneer from Travancore and India's First Female Judge', *Bar and Bench*, 7 March 2022, http://tinyurl.com/ynb82rze. Accessed on 2 January 2024.

3 Wangchuk, Rinchen Norbu, 'How India's First Woman HC Judge Championed Gender Equality in Pre-independence India,' *The Better India*, 7 November 2019, http://tinyurl.com/4cszbe3x. Accessed on 2 January 2024.

4 Ibid.

5 Parmeshwar, K., and Medha Damojipurapu, 'Justice Anna Chandy: The Pioneer from Travancore and India's First Female Judge', *Bar and Bench*, 7 March 2022, http://tinyurl.com/ynb82rze. Accessed on 2 January 2024; Kumar, Adarsh, 'Justice Anna Chandy: The First Female High Court Judge', *DesiKaanoon*, 17 January 2021, http://tinyurl.com/4mwpe9ca. Accessed on 2 January 2024.

6 Wangchuk, Rinchen Norbu, 'How India's First Woman HC Judge Championed Gender Equality in Pre-independence India', *The Better India*, 7 November 2019, http://tinyurl.com/4cszbe3x. Accessed on 2 January 2024.

7 Shah, Aditi, 'Anna Chandy: India's First Woman Judge', *Peepul Tree Stories*, 26 September 2017, http://tinyurl.com/422e473m. Accessed on 2 January 2024.

8 J. Devika, and Binitha V. Thampi, *New Lamps for Old?: Gender Paradoxes of Political Decentralisation in Kerala*, Zubaan Books, 2012.

9 Agarwal, Khushi, 'Justice Fathima Beevi: The First Indian Woman to Become a Supreme Court Justice', *Feminism in India*, 13 September 2019, http://tinyurl.com/32eu4pr3. Accessed on 2 January 2024.

10 'Justice Anna Chandy', *Government College for Women, Thiruvananthapuram*, http://tinyurl.com/46dyk2y9. Accessed on 2 January 2024.

11 'Justice Anna Chandy', *Kerala Women*, http://tinyurl.com/mr3tavna. Accessed on 2 January 2024.

12 Nabil, Mohammed, 'Anna Chandy: India's First Female Judge in District and High Courts', *Heritage Times*, 7 March 2018, http://tinyurl.com/32248bzf. Accessed on 2 January

2024; 'Justice Anna Chandy', *Kerala Women,* http://tinyurl.com/mr3tavna. Accessed on 2 January 2024; Kumar, Adarsh, 'Justice Anna Chandy: The First Female High Court Judge', *DesiKaanoon,* 17 January 2021, http://tinyurl.com/4mwpe9ca. Accessed on 2 January 2024.

13 Kumar, Adarsh, 'Justice Anna Chandy: The First Female High Court Judge', *DesiKaanoon,* 17 January 2021, http://tinyurl.com/4mwpe9ca. Accessed on 2 January 2024.

14 'Justice Anna Chandy', *Government College for Women, Thiruvananthapuram,* http://tinyurl.com/46dyk2y9. Accessed on 2 January 2024.

8

TULASI GOWDA

TREE GODDESS

8 NOVEMBER 2021

The prestigious Padma Awards are being awarded in the magnificent Darbar Hall of the Rashtrapati Bhavan with all the pomp and splendour that the event mandates. Swishing silks and brocades, sparkling jewellery, fine suits, dapper *bandhgalas*, the attendees are all dressed in their best. And then, a name is announced. Tulasi Gowda. An old woman, dressed in a traditional fabric which is also tied around her neck. It is the fabric worn by the Halakki indigenous tribe from Karnataka. She wears a humble black and yellow bead necklace around her neck and walks barefoot towards the stage with a sprightly ease belying her age. She stops for a moment to greet Prime Minister Narendra Modi, before moving to where President Ram Nath Kovind is about to award her the Padma Shri for her work in the conservation of forests.[1]

The photographs went viral; her simplicity in the face of such pomp and grandeur was appreciated across the country, but 72-year-old Tulasi Gowda was not trying to make a statement. She was just dressed as she always was—she saw no reason to change the way she was just because she was going to the Rashtrapati Bhavan to receive the Padma Shri. Referred to as the 'encylopedia of the forest', the 'barefoot environmentalist' or *vruksha devata,* as the members of the Halakki Vokkalu community call her, Tulasi has devoted all her life to the protection of the forest.

Born in pre-Independence India, on 30 April 1943, in the Halakki tribe, she grew up in the Honnalli village, a humble settlement in the Uttara Kannada district in Mysore State (now Karnataka). As a state, Karnataka is blessed with an abundance of forests, with over 25 wildlife sanctuaries and five national parks. It was in this verdancy that she grew up, albeit in extremely impoverished circumstances. She lost her father when she was barely a toddler and, as a young girl, she was put perforce to work along with her mother, a labourer at a local government nursery. She got no education; day-to-day survival was all that mattered in such impoverished situations. She must not have been more than 10 or 12 when her mother got her married off to a much older man called Govinde Gowda.[2]

While working as a child at the nursery, Tulasi was part of the workers in charge of taking care of the seeds intended for planting and harvesting at the Karnataka Forestry Department. She worked at the nursery with her mother for 35 years as a daily worker. It was then, after 35 years of work, that she was offered a permanent job at the nursery thanks to her knowledge of botany—gained not through textbooks but through actual on-ground work with seeds and soil—and her efforts towards conservation.

For over five decades, she worked with the land. She worked with the forest department in their project to rejuvenate the land and repopulate it with indigenous trees and saplings at the Agasur Nursery. This was part of the ongoing afforestation efforts in the Mastikatta range of Honnalli village.

The people involved in the afforestation efforts turned to her for her traditional knowledge of growing things on the land. She not only worked on afforestation and planting saplings, but was also involved in efforts to prevent forest fires and to deal with poachers who were dangerous to wildlife.

She was awarded the Indira Priyadarshini Vriksha Mitra Award in 1986. The award is given to individuals or institutions involved in afforestation and wasteland development. She was awarded the Karnataka Rajyotsava Award in 1999, an award given every year to distinguished citizens of Karnataka over the age of 60. This is the second highest civilian honour in Karnataka. She came into the national spotlight when she got the Padma Shri in 2020. She received the award from then President Ram Nath Kovind. Of the award she is quoted as having said that while she is glad to have been awarded the Padma Shri, she 'values the forests and trees more'.[3]

While environmentalists call her the 'encyclopedia of the forest,' her tribe calls her the 'tree goddess'. She is respected for her ability to be uncannily accurate in identifying the mother tree of every species in the forest. The mother nodes are the most connected nodes in the forest; they are important because of their age and size. They grow underground and can connect the saplings and seedlings, with the mother tree exchanging nitrogen and nutrients.

She also has an incomparable skill in the extraction of seeds from the mother trees—an important process in the regeneration of a species of a plant. The seeds need to be collected at the very peak of the germination process from the mother tree so that the seedlings are able to survive the transfer. Her decades of experience working intimately with the earth and trees help her know intuitively when this collection should be done. Perhaps, 'intuitive' is the right word to describe Tulasi's knowledge of the forest. She is often hard-pressed when asked how she learnt about the forest, but says she can speak the language of the forest.[4]

It is perhaps something that has been passed on to her from her tribe, who have been caring for the land and the forests for centuries. With her Padma Shri, the Halakki Vokkalu tribe now has the honour of having two Padma Shri awardees from the community. In 2016, folk singer Sukri Bommagowda had also received the Padma Shri. A paper published in the *International Journal of Current Research* says that members of the Halakki Vokkalu community are known as the aboriginals of Uttara Kannada district in Karnataka, mainly distributed in four taluks of Ankola, Kumta, Karwar and Honnavar.[5]

Rough estimates state that Tulasi has planted over 1 lakh trees in Karnataka on her own. She is highly respected and is the pride of her community. To quote Nagaraja Gowda, a social worker working for the welfare of the Halakki tribe, 'She has invaluable knowledge of the forest and medicinal plants. Nobody has documented it and she is not a good communicator. So, it is difficult to understand her contribution unless you've seen her work.'[6]

She has now retired from the forest department but uses her time to teach children about the sourcing and care of seeds and seedlings. To quote environmentalist and former forest conservationist, Dr A.N. Yellappa Reddy, 'The plants she raises are like children for her. She knows each one down to its last roots. She can't explain how but she knows this because she speaks the language of the forest. Seeing her work is an incredible experience.'[7]

This intuitive knowledge she has of the language of the forests is what made Dr Reddy realize that she was no ordinary daily-wage worker. He realized her extraordinary capabilities in identifying the mother tree of any species in the forest, and he turned to her for help with his reforestation efforts. To quote him, 'I met Tulasi Gowda after putting in more than 28 years of service as an Indian forest service official trained at the Indian Forest Academy. [...] Gowda could identify a mother tree of any species anywhere in the forest. Regeneration is best done with the seeds from the mother tree.'[8]

When asked how she plants the trees, she answered in an interview, saying:

> We collect seeds, then dry it before planting. Some seeds of trees like mathi drop off by themselves which we would collect and plant them in select plots (in the nursery) and we would nurture them and plant them in the forest again. Mathi seeds are best planted in April or May. The seeds of honne, nandi, tamarind, gooseberry are all sown directly. It is only in April or May that we can find the seeds of bamboo. We would get the seeds, put it in a container with water and leave it in for four days. We would then scrub it until it turns white and then we would plant it for about 20-25 days. Then they would start sprouting.[9]

While she had joined the forest department as a daily wager, her dedication and knowledge got her a permanent job in the department, as mentioned earlier. She served as a permanent employee for 15 years before retiring.[10] She not only worked to help reforestation efforts by the forest department, but also helped stop forest fires and worked to prevent poachers from killing the wildlife of the forests she nurtured.[11]

Now retired, she does not go to the nursery every day, but spends her time with her grandchildren. To quote her, 'I'm retired, so, I don't go to the nursery unless I find a rare seed or a sapling. Then, I take it there.' In an interview, she said that when she worked in the department they would grow many different plants, including eucalyptus, saguwani (*Tectona grandis*), sheesham (*Dalbergia latifolia*), honne (*Pterocarpus marsupium*) and even mango and jackfruit. She has planted so many trees that she lost count of them.[12]

She is also an ardent advocate of women's rights. She came to the defence of another woman who had been threatened by guns after a fight in the village. Tulasi stated that she would 'protest fiercely if the perpetrator of this crime isn't punished'.[13]

Her message is simple. One that we need to spread as much as we can: 'I always explain to children that the forest must be protected and nurtured. We all have to pitch in. Let children plant seeds and look after the plants as they grow.'[14] One can only hope that the message she has spent her entire life espousing is heard by the people, and the value of the forests, beyond economic considerations, is heeded. Hers is a life that has been spent in selfless service to the environment, without her even being aware of the concept of 'environmentalism.' It is this unassuming, yet dedicated, service to the forests that makes her an icon for all environmentalists and forest conservationists to look up to.

NOTES

1 Sarkar, Snehadri, 'Meet Tulsi Gowda, the "Encyclopedia of Forest" Who Collected Her Padma Shri Barefooted', *The Logical Indian*, 9 November 2021, http://tinyurl.com/4y84txzk. Accessed on 4 January 2024.

2 'Padma Shri: Smt. Tulsi Gowda', *Padma Awards*, http://tinyurl.com/bdd4sddj. Accessed on 4 January 2024.

3 Menon, Arathi, and Abhishek N. Chinnappa, 'Tulasi Gowda: How She Brings Forests to Life', *roundglass sustain*, 25 September 2023, http://tinyurl.com/3x9nbcna. Accessed on 4 January 2024.

4 Ibid.

5 Hoogar, Praveen, Ashwini Pujar and Dr Basavanagouda, 'Life Cycle Rituals among Halakki Vokkalu Community of Uttar Kannada District, Karnataka', *International Journal of Current Research*, Vol. 9, No. 10, 2017.

6 Menon, Arathi, and Abhishek N. Chinnappa, 'Tulsi Gowda: Barefoot Ecologist Brings Forests to Life', *The Beacon*, 10 June

2021, http://tinyurl.com/2w8jktk2. Accessed on 4 January 2024.

7 D., Aditi, 'Tulasi Gowda, 77-Year-Old "Encyclopedia of the Forest" Came Bare-Foot to Receive Her Padma Shri!', *women's web*, 10 November 2021, http://tinyurl.com/438dd6zc. Accessed on 4 January 2024.

8 Menon, Arathi, and Abhishek N. Chinnappa, 'Tulasi Gowda: How She Brings Forests to Life', *roundglass sustain*, 25 September 2023, http://tinyurl.com/3x9nbcna. Accessed on 4 January 2024.

9 Menon, Arathi, and Abhishek N. Chinnappa, '[Video] the Barefoot Ecologist Who Brought Forests to Life', *Mongabay*, 24 February 2020, http://tinyurl.com/5ypyy4ut. Accessed on 4 January 2024.

10 'Meet Environmentalist Tulsi Gowda, Who Collected Her Padma Shri Award Barefooted. Watch Video', *mint*, 10 November 2021, http://tinyurl.com/5pcdkcn4. Accessed on 4 January 2024.

11 Hamsadhwani Alagarsamy, 'Tulasi Gowda: The Encyclopedia of the Forest', *Feminism in India*, 22 June 2020, http://tinyurl.com/4nwte94a. Accessed on 4 January 2024.

12 Menon, Arathi, and Abhishek N. Chinnappa, 'Tulsi Gowda: Barefoot Ecologist Brings Forests to Life', *The Beacon*, 10 June 2021, http://tinyurl.com/2w8jktk2. Accessed on 4 January 2024.

13 Beltramelli, Estella, 'Tree Goddess Tulasi Gowda, the Barefoot Indian Activist Protecting the Forest', *Lifegate Daily*, 1 September 2020, http://tinyurl.com/45pamfju. Accessed on 4 January 2024.

14 Ibid.

9

IROM CHANU SHARMILA

THE IRON LADY OF MANIPUR

In the end, it was a scoop of honey. After 16 long years of voluntarily not eating a single bite, she tasted a scoop of honey. She said that the honey felt bitter[1]—perhaps, the bitterness came from her experience of denying herself food, a mirror, a comb or any comfort for 16 years. This was a promise she had made to herself, a promise that took her story across the world. She had last eaten on 4 November 2000. On that day in 2000, she ate two packets of pastries, filling her stomach to her heart's content, before she went on her fast.

There's a particular image that remains entrenched in everyone's mind: a pale, wan face, with a nasal pipe attached to her nostril, her hair falling unruly on her forehead, almost obscuring her face, draped in a shawl, wearing a simple cotton saree. The nasal pipe was to force-feed her and it stayed in place for 16 years, when she was on a hunger strike to abolish the Armed Forces (Special Powers) Act, 1958 (AFSPA). It was a fast that caught the attention of the world, a fast that changed the trajectory of her life in ways she could never have imagined.

Through her fast, Irom Chanu Sharmila became a saint for her people, a martyr; someone they adored and worshipped, someone they elevated to a pedestal. However, later, they tore her down from the same pedestal when she decided she didn't want to be a saint and martyr anymore. She was just a young woman who wanted to live a normal life. But first, the journey to sainthood.

Born on 14 March 1972 in Manipur, one of nine children born to Irom Nanda and Irom Sakhi, Irom Sharmila grew up in the environment of insurgency and unrest in Manipur—one of the seven sister-states in the Northeast of India. She was 28, working as an intern in a human rights group, when on 2 November 2000, a bomb exploded while an army convoy was crossing a bus stop at Malom, a village near Imphal Airport. The soldiers stated that gunfire followed and they retaliated with fire themselves.[2] The gunfire from the soldiers led to 10 civilians losing their lives. Among those who died were Leisan Leisangbam Ibetombi, a 62-year-old woman, and 18-year-old Sinam Chandramani (a 1998 National Bravery Award winner).

By this time, Irom Sharmila was already in the thick of trying to get justice for those who were victims of human rights abuses: slain civilians; survivors of gang rape; and parents and relatives of those who had been killed in conflicts with the armed forces. The AFSPA that then applied to the seven Northeastern states and Jammu & Kashmir, gave the Indian armed forces blanket permission to search properties without a warrant, and to arrest people if they felt so. They also had permission to use force if they had reasonable suspicion that a person was acting against the state, without any repercussions for their actions.[3] The draconian law, originally put into place to tackle the insurgency and conflict in the state, had made civilian life extremely difficult, to put it mildly.

Sharmila didn't come from a wealthy family; she could barely afford to complete high school. The news of the Malom massacre came to her a day later, when the photographs of the bullet-riddled bodies were on the front pages of the local newspapers. She was enraged by the needless deaths, and realized that it was now or never. She needed to take a stand, and do whatever she could to stand up against the injustice of what was unfolding around her. Protests and rallies seemed futile to her. She decided to follow the path set by Mahatma Gandhi, that of non-violent protest through fasting. After all, it was his non-violent protests and fasts throughout the freedom struggle that had helped India achieve freedom from the yoke of colonization.

Three days later, on 5 November 2000, she went to the site of the Malom massacre and sat under a shelter there with a placard that simply said she would be fasting there until AFSPA was repealed.[4] With this act, she morphed irrevocably from the young girl working in the field of human rights into the very embodiment of the Manipuri people's aspirations for the repeal of AFSPA. However, people didn't really take her too seriously in the beginning.

On the first day, a crowd gathered; they sat with her through the day, but, come dusk, they dissipated. The head of the human rights organization she was interning with thought it was too big a challenge for her. He dissuaded her from doing it. She was undeterred; she had received her mother's blessings, and went ahead with what she had decided. At times, though, she wondered if she was doing the right thing. The crowd, back then, felt like the fast was a circus. They were yet to understand the seriousness of her mission. That moment of realization arrived when she was arrested three days later for the crime of attempted suicide and then force-fed on 10 November 2000.

Her fast ended on 9 August 2016, after 16 years. She refused food and water for over 500 weeks.[5] She was force-fed nasally while she was in jail. She became the 'world's longest hunger striker' with this fast. To quote her from an interview with *The Guardian*, she tried to resist the feeding tube, 'but I convinced myself it was futile. My position was like a bird who had shattered her wings.'[6] What she did do was request the prison authorities to feed her through a nasal tube rather than through the mouth, as that would help her keep the promise to not eat anything until AFSPA was repealed by the Indian government.

The authorities inserted a 3-ft-long tube that went from her nose to her stomach, through which a mixture of nutrients and water was fed directly into her stomach. This continued for 16 years. She would be released from jail every year, as one can only be kept in custody for the crime of attempted suicide for a year, and then re-arrested when she began fasting again. Then she would go back again to the isolation ward of the Jawaharlal Nehru Institute of Medical Sciences in Imphal after her re-arrest. From that isolation ward, far in the remote Northeast of India, her story reached out to the world and the world took notice.

Her hunger strike made her an 'icon of public resistance' in 2004 when there was another flashpoint in Manipur: the death of a young girl called Manorama. On 10 July 2004, soldiers came for a 32-year-old woman, Thangjam Manorama, and dragged her from her home, stating that she was a member of the People's Liberation Army and was responsible for many bomb blasts. Her body was found near her home with 16 bullet wounds, and also wounds suggesting torture. The autopsy confirmed the presence of semen, indicating rape. No one was held responsible, and AFSPA was invoked. The people were outraged. This killing led to the historic 'Mothers of Manipur' protest.

On 15 July 2004, 12 *imas* (mothers) flung their clothes off outside the Kangla Fort. Anubha Bhonsle wrote about the protest: 'No one is sure who was the first to disrobe. But they had come prepared, leaving behind their petticoats, blouses and fear. They hardly exchanged a glance, they didn't wince or hide. No one spoke. But in a few moments the air was ringing with slogans, like a chant. [Indian Army] Rape us, kill us! Rape us, kill us!'[7]

With her continued fast, Sharmila became the hero they had all been searching for and they rallied around her. She became the face of the Manipur resistance. It was an elevation she had not asked for—all she had been doing was protesting in her own way. It was a crippling weight, the burden of the expectations of all the people on her fragile shoulders.

It had been a long, lonely struggle for years. She met her mother only once during her years of fasting; she was afraid that her mother's tears would have broken her resolve. She said at the time, 'The day AFSPA is repealed I will eat rice from my mother's hand.' Her mother, Irom Sakhi Devi, was heartbroken that her daughter hadn't had a drop of water for years. She had said to a journalist, 'Even if the Act can be repealed for five days, I think she can be saved. Just five days.'[8]

To quote Sharmila, 'I really loved life. Just because of that love, those long years of endurance were possible. This kind of living with nasal feeding, just observing day and night and getting all that blind fame—I just knew this was not life.'[9]

She realized people were treating her like an icon, a symbol, rather than as a human being in anguish. She was alone, lonely and in agony. She was being written about in media all around the world, Nobel laureates were seeking to meet her, she was being lauded as the 'Iron Lady of Manipur', but underneath it all she was a woman who was acutely lonely and longing for love. It came her way in the form of a British-Indian man named Desmond Coutinho. It wasn't easy, being alone, away from family and friends, in an isolation ward. Time passed slowly; she walked the corridors for hours, read the Bhagavad Gita, did yoga to keep herself fit, wrote poetry and read books. It was books that brought Desmond into her life in 2009.

Desmond had come to India after the demise of his mother, searching for his roots and a purpose to life. He chanced upon Sharmila's story when he read a newspaper article about her, and its ending stayed with him. She had said she liked to read books but didn't get any. He sent her books and a letter, and they began a correspondence. He sent her P.G. Wodehouse's writings, books on postmodernist economics and biographies. He even sent her a Valentine's card. They made a commitment to each other, despite the fact that she was not free.

Desmond's arrival in Manipur in 2011 led to strong objections from those surrounding her. Her desire to have a life partner shocked them. They had placed her on a pedestal, made her a goddess.[10] But she was very much human, and she yearned to live an ordinary life—a life that had passed her by all these years when she was deified. She decided she would end this relentless cycle of fasting, arrest and release that had been her life for the past 16 years.

On 26 July 2016, she announced that she would end her fast on 9 August 2017. She said that she would marry Desmond and continue her struggle by running for Manipur's Parliament. She had a public fallout with the anti-AFSPA struggle in Manipur. A group that was instituted in support of her, called the Sharmila Kanba Lup (SAKAL), a Meira Paibi group, dismantled itself and severed ties with her, announcing that they would neither support nor oppose her in her decision to enter politics. The Meira Paibis took strong objection to Sharmila's relationship with a 'non-Meitei' man. A student activist, Anirban Bhattacharya, described the conclusion of Sharmila's fast in these terms: 'a fast that ended in hunger' because 'AFSPA has stayed, [and] the atrocities under it has [sic] also stayed'.[11] But she had decided that she would break her fast. She had begun it without caring about what the world would say, and she would end it on her own terms as well. And so, she did.

On an overcast August morning in Imphal in 2017, with the gaze of the world on her, she put a finger dipped in honey into her mouth. Tears streamed down her eyes. With that taste of honey, Irom Sharmila ended her 16-year-long fast. She now wanted to live as happy a life as she could: finding love, getting married, having children; things she had denied herself all these years. To quote her, 'That first drop of honey was bitter, so caustic. The taste spread throughout my whole body.'[12]

Eating again after 16 years was not easy; she would throw up anything she ate. Her body couldn't even take coconut water initially. It took months before her stomach stopped rejecting everything she ate, throwing it up violently. Ending her fast also ended the support and worship that she had enjoyed all these years, when those around her had made her larger than life—a symbol of the Manipuri resistance.

She found herself out in the cold with nowhere to go. She spent a few weeks in the same isolation ward of the hospital where she had been held prisoner, now a free woman but with no roof over her head. The very people to whom she'd given 16 years of her life turned their back on her when she decided she had had enough of being an icon. They were irate that she no longer wanted their worship, that she dared to dream of being ordinary again.

She was undeterred; she decided she would contest the elections. However, this was not an overnight decision. Her political ambitions had first been stirred up way back in 2011, when she contacted the anti-corruption activist Anna Hazare, who sent across two representatives to Manipur to meet her. Back in 2011, the Communist Party of India (Marxist) had stated their support for her and the cause of repealing AFSPA, and in October, the Manipur Pradesh All India Trinamool Congress had done the same. She had called on the then Prime Minister Dr Manmohan Singh in November to reiterate her call to end AFSPA. Ordinary citizens, too, had come out in support of her. One hundred women in Ambari had formed a human chain to support her in November; civil society groups had gone on 24-hour fasts in solidarity with her. The Save Sharmila Solidarity Campaign had been launched in 2011 to bring public attention to her long struggle, and Pune University had announced a scholarship for 39 female Manipuri students in her name.

To quote her from 2016, 'I have to change my strategy. Some people are seeing me as a strange woman because I want to join politics. They say politics is a dirty, but so is society. I want to stand in the elections against the government. [I have to] try a different [form of] agitation because I have been fasting for 16 years and I have not got anything from it yet.'[13] To this end, she announced the launch of a political party called Peoples' Resurgence and Justice Alliance in order to contest from two Assembly constituencies in Manipur, namely Khurai and Khangabok.[14] Incidentally, Khangabok was the home constituency of the then Chief Minister Okram Ibobi Singh.

Interestingly, despite her international stature as a political activist, it failed to translate into on-ground votes at the hustings. The Manipur Legislative Assembly election held in March 2017 saw her get only 90 votes, the least of all the five candidates in the fray. That was the end of her attempt to enter electoral politics and she left Manipur two days after the results.[15] She went to South India, and celebrated her forty-fifth birthday at the Santhigramam rehabilitation centre, seeking peace and tranquillity to clear her mind.[16] She then went to Kodaikanal with Desmond, and married him on 17 August 2017 under the Special Marriages Act.[17]

Two years later, on 12 May 2019, she delivered twin daughters in Bengaluru. The babies were born one minute apart at 35 weeks, after Sharmila was rushed to the hospital with labour pains. Incidentally, it was Mother's Day as well. She was 47, and she was finally reclaiming her life. They named their daughters Nix Shakhi and Autumn Tara. She hasn't returned to Manipur since, and has left that part of her life behind. She lives in Bengaluru with her husband and children, living the ordinary, everyday life that she had always wanted.

About her hunger strike, she later spoke to the *Hindustan Times* after the removal of AFSPA from several parts of the Northeast, saying, 'Just three days after I started my protest, police arrested me and I went through a lot of torture. I did not want to drink even a drop of water, but the people force-fed me nasally in hospital and jail. My hunger strike later became the world's longest hunger strike... I stood for a cause and after decades, the mainland leaders in Parliament have understood.'[18]

When asked about going back to Manipur, she says that she isn't sure if she would be welcome. She is finally living her own life. She said in an interview, 'No more bondage, controlling by others all the time. That sense of freedom, my own view, reaching out to the farthest point.'[19] In 2022, she told the students of St Joseph's College in an address, 'I was not educated. I was physically, academically and financially weak. The society laughed at me and mocked me. But neither did I stop what I was doing nor did I wait for someone to come and support me. I was and have always been a one-woman army.'[20]

She's received multiple awards. In 2007, she was awarded the Gwangju Prize for Human Rights, sharing it with Lenin Raghuvanshi of People's Vigilance Committee on Human Rights, a Northeastern Indian human rights organization. In 2009, she was awarded the inaugural Mayilamma Award of the Mayilamma Foundation for her non-violent struggle in Manipur. The year 2010 saw her being awarded a lifetime achievement award from the Asian Human Rights Commission. She also got the Rabindranath Tagore Peace Prize from the Indian Institute of Planning and Management, and the Sarva Gunah Sampannah 'Award for Peace and Harmony' from the Signature Training Centre. In 2013, Amnesty International declared her a prisoner of conscience, stating that she was being held solely for a peaceful expression of her beliefs.[21]

She's firmly out of the limelight now and that's the way she prefers it, living a quiet life in Bengaluru with her husband and daughters. Life in the spotlight might be glorious for those of us who look on, but for the one who is in the spotlight, perhaps, stepping out of it might be their moment of true freedom.

NOTES

1 Safi, Michael, 'How Love and a Taste of Honey Brought One Indian Woman's 16-Year Hunger Strike to an End', *The Guardian*, 11 November 2018, http://tinyurl.com/2snpcpba. Accessed on 4 January 2024.

2 Prabhakara, M.S., 'Ordinary Woman, Extraordinary Will', *The Hindu*, 23 September 2009, http://tinyurl.com/muut5uah. Accessed on 4 January 2024.

3 *The Armed Forces (Special Powers) Act, 1958*, Ministry of Home Affairs, http://tinyurl.com/2543sv3j. Accessed on 4 January 2024.

4 '2000: Irom Sharmila Begins Fast for Repeal of AFSPA', *The Hindu Frontline*, 15 August 2022, http://tinyurl.com/3xxcj2km. Accessed on 4 January 2024.

5 'Manipur's Iron Lady Irom Sharmila Ends 16-Year-Long Hunger Strike', *The Times of India*, 9 August 2016, http://tinyurl.com/2c2s3vts. Accessed on 4 January 2024.

6 Safi, Michael, 'How Love and a Taste of Honey Brought One Indian Woman's 16-Year Hunger Strike to an End', *The Guardian*, 11 November 2018, http://tinyurl.com/2snpcpba. Accessed on 4 January 2024.

7 Dasarathi, Amala, 'Remembering Thangjam Manorama | #Indianwomeninhistory', *Feminism in India*, 9 March 2017, http://tinyurl.com/2p96486v. Accessed on 4 January 2024.

8 Shah, Binjal, 'Manipur's "Iron Lady" Irom Sharmila to End Her 15-Year-Long Hunger Strike', *YOURSTORY*, 27 July 2016, http://tinyurl.com/2878k7wp. Accessed on 11 January 2024; Bhattacharjee, Kishalay, 'How Irom Sharmila Changed the Narrative of AFSPA in Manipur', *the quint*, 14 March 2019, http://tinyurl.com/mtht9bar. Accessed on 4 January 2024.

9 Safi, Michael, 'How Love and a Taste of Honey Brought One Indian Woman's 16-Year Hunger Strike to an End', *The Guardian*, 11 November 2018, http://tinyurl.com/2snpcpba. Accessed on 4 January 2024.

10 Buncombe, Andrew, 'Hunger Striker's Declaration of Love Angers Her Supporters', *Independent*, 17 September 2011, http://tinyurl.com/36ahassz. Accessed on 4 January 2024.

11 Thoudam, Natasa, 'Irom Sharmila: The Curious Case of Manipur's Human Rights Activist and the Politics of Representation', *Women Community Leaders and Their Impact as Global Changemakers*, Patricia Goodman Hayward, Sahar Rehman and Zirui Yan (eds), IGI Global, 2022.

12 Safi, Michael, 'How Love and a Taste of Honey Brought One Indian Woman's 16-Year Hunger Strike to an End', *The Guardian*, 11 November 2018, http://tinyurl.com/2snpcpba. Accessed on 4 January 2024.

13 Buncombe, Andrew, 'Irom Sharmila: Indian Activist Ends World's Longest Hunger Strike—But Continues Fight for Justice,' *Independent*, 9 August 2016, http://tinyurl.com/4nbr2hbr. Accessed on 4 January 2024.

14 Verma, Vidhushi, 'AFSPA Revoked in Parts of N-E: "It Is Horrible That It Still Exists," Says Irom Sharmila', *The Citizen*, 25 April 2018, http://tinyurl.com/dczzd36r. Accessed on 4 January 2024.

15 Agarwala, Tora, 'Far and Away from Manipur, Irom Sharmila Says: '"I Get the Political System Now... It's Corrupt"', *The Indian Express*, 18 March 2022, http://tinyurl.com/27t4hfen. Accessed on 4 January 2024.

16 'Lost the Election, Manipur's Iron Lady Seeks Peace of Mind in Kerala's Tribal Village', *Outlook*, 15 March 2017, http://tinyurl.com/mrxr9htj. Accessed on 4 January 2024.

17 PTI, 'Rights Activist Irom Sharmila Marries Long-Time Partner Desmond Coutinho', *NDTV*, 17 August 2017, http://tinyurl.com/sh2tzy8p. Accessed on 4 January 2024.

18 Purkayastha, Biswa Kalyan, '"This Is Real Sign of Democracy": Irom Sharmila on Centre's AFSPA Changes', *Hindustan Times*, 1 April 2022, http://tinyurl.com/5n7ft6nj. Accessed on 4 January 2024.

19 Safi, Michael, 'How Love and a Taste of Honey Brought One Indian Woman's 16-Year Hunger Strike to an End', *The Guardian*, 11 November 2018, http://tinyurl.com/2snpcpba. Accessed on 4 January 2024.

20 'Enough Is Enough: Irom Sharmila on Political Plunge', *Deccan Herald*, 5 May 2022, http://tinyurl.com/39kcafh6. Accessed on 4 January 2024.

21 Karmakar, Rahul, '10 Things You Need to Know About "Iron Lady" Irom Sharmila', *Hindustan Times*, 9 August 2016, http://tinyurl.com/58nfaxu9. Accessed on 4 January 2024.

10

SEEMA RAO

COMMANDO TRAINER

Dr Seema Rao's profession is most unlikely. She is the first civilian female special forces commando trainer in India, and probably the only one in the world so far. She is a marathoner, and a sharpshooter who can shoot an apple off a target's head at a distance of 75 yards. She can use a Glock pistol, defuse explosive devices within minutes and neutralize armed opponents within seconds. That's a lot to pack into her lean, lithe frame.

For the past two decades, she has trained over 20,000 soldiers of the Indian armed forces, paramilitary and the police. This was not the career that she had envisaged for herself. It came about on its own. It probably all began with her father, Professor Ramakant Sinari. He was a freedom fighter, one who fought against the Portuguese colonizers in Goa. To quote her, 'My dad was an underground rebel. I was certainly inspired by his stories of rebellion and strength.'[1]

She grew up on the stories of how he was imprisoned by the Portuguese in Goa, and then managed to escape with the help of a fellow inmate. The story still gives Dr Rao goosebumps. In fact, her most prized possession is a sword that her father had inherited from his father.

Her first stint with martial arts came when she was around 16 and decided to learn Taekwondo. Interestingly, she was studying to be a doctor and never imagined that she would become a commando trainer. She began learning various skills and martial arts because of her fascination with the life of commandos. To quote her:

> I was thrilled when I thought about the life of commandos. I started learning martial arts and got trained in military martial arts, Israeli krav maga and MMA. I did a professional course in sailing and yachting as well as in scuba diving to understand the problems faced in deep waters, a course in mountain climbing to understand the challenges posed in high altitude and extreme cold, and a jungle survival course to survive on land. To understand altitude, I also did a skydiving course.[2]

She found out that she was surprisingly good at martial arts, but by then had already been studying to become a doctor. She went on to complete her studies and then got married, putting all plans of learning martial arts on the back-burner. A turning point came about in the early 1990s after a scuffle with anti-social elements at Girgaum Chowpatty in South Bombay (now Mumbai), while she and her husband were out on their morning walk. The assaulters attacked her husband and her with knives, and the couple only had their training in martial arts as their defence. Her husband told her at the time that she was ready and trained for it. He told her, 'This is your fight, deal with it.' And so, she did. She had the swift reflexes and moves from years of training, and in that fight, she found her true calling. None of their attackers' knives managed to draw blood, only her t-shirt got slashed. To quote her, 'I still get goosebumps. But after that, I felt like a different person was born. I knew I had finally moved from weakness to strength—from being controlled to being in control.'[3]

Her tryst with training elite forces began serendipitously. On a morning walk, the couple bumped into a senior official of the Pune police force. The husband-and-wife duo demonstrated their skills to him; he was impressed and invited them to conduct a workshop in unarmed combat for the Pune Police. They did so, and then he was even more impressed and recommended them to the Mumbai Police. That's how it all started. Over the years, she got 8th degree black belt in Military Martial Arts. By 35, she had trained the NSG Black cats and was also training different Special Forces. This was where she found her calling.

To have a civilian, and that too a woman, train the police and then the armed forces was a huge testament to the excellence of what she offered. From martial arts, she began training to be a sharpshooter. She, along with her husband, jointly created the Rao System of Reflex Fire, which has now been adopted by some of the Forces. This method allows you to shoot swiftly and accurately without aim. It focusses on shooting by reflex without taking aim. Seema can also shoot five rounds of a 9mm pistol at a target in under two minutes. The Reflex shooting method trains soldiers to fire at and injure their opponents before being hit by enemy fire. Seema and her husband went on to train different forces.

In 1997, the then Mumbai Police Commissioner R.D. Tyagi was made the director general of the National Security Guard (NSG) and asked them to train the NSG troops. Also, around that time, Retired Brigadier Balbir Singh introduced them to the then Army Chief General Roy Shankar Chowdhury, and he commissioned them to conduct a six-week training course for the Parachute Regiment Training Centre in Bangalore (now Bengaluru). To quote Singh on them, 'There are a lot of sharpshooters outside the Army. Once you get into the art of warfare, you don't have to be in uniform to make a difference.'[4]

Amongst the things she faced, one was scepticism. But she learnt to deal with it. To quote her, 'Although I was a professional combat shooting instructor, the first question to be thrown at me was, "How can you train male commandos as a woman?" So before commanding my trainees to perform any task, I'd make sure I'd mastered it. When they saw me perform, they were convinced I knew what I was doing.'[5]

When questioned by a trainee at a camp about her skills, she shot an apple off her husband's head with an AK-47 at 75 yards. It effectively silenced all the doubts the trainees might have had about her ability and competence to train military and paramilitary troops. This is something they then incorporated into their training. For commando training, she put herself through extreme situations in difficult terrains to understand the specific challenges of each team. She's qualified in mountaineering, rock climbing and scuba diving—all to know how to deal with different terrains.

To up her skills, she also studied immunology from Harvard Medical School and leadership from Westminster Business School. She is among the few instructors qualified to teach *Jeet Kune D*o (JKD). She learnt skydiving from the Indian Air Force course. On top of being a combat shooting instructor, she is also an army mountaineering Himalayan Mountaineering Institute medalist. Dr Seema Rao has an MBA in crisis management and is an expert in close quarter battle (CQB), which is the art of fighting in close quarters that forces people to engage in special ops. She and her husband began training the forces in CQB after the Ministry of Home Affairs had them conduct a pilot course to check the effectiveness of their training in 2010. To quote her, 'Terrorist encounters take place at 30 to 40 yards, rather than 500 yards of conventional battle, and may include civilian hostages and concrete walls. So, you need CQB techniques.'[6]

Her 8th Degree black belt in unarmed combat helps her teach soldiers how to tackle targets without using ammunition at close quarters. This is essential because ammunition can run out and soldiers need to know hand-to-hand combat or hand-to-weapon combat. She brought to the table Bruce Lee's philosophy of martial arts—JKD, which she has trained in, as previously mentioned. She is one of the five senior female Instructors of JKD in the entire world. The JKD is based on intercepting an attack before it takes place, retaliating with economy of motion. To quote her, 'It teaches us the vital areas in a human body. The science is where I strike with my hand or weapon, to handicap, maim or cripple the enemy. This helps in close encounters.'[7]

She's done the training for decades, pro bono, for the cause of the nation. To quote her, 'I am the first and only woman to train some of the most elite special forces in India. It's a great honour, but I've had my share of struggles. My work was a service to the nation, and I'd never charged a penny for it!'[8] She's seen dire days when they were so financially strapped that she had to sell her gold and cash in her savings. The forces provided lodging and boarding and travel expenses. That was it. They were, according to her, two enthusiastic youngsters trying to make a difference. To quote her, 'Former Army Commander General Deepak Kapoor directing us to train battle schools in the Kashmir Valley, and later, former Army Commander General VK Singh asking us to train counter terror training schools in Assam.'[9] Seema and her husband steadfastly refused all offers of sponsorship to retain their independence. Circumstances improved financially when they set up the Academy of Combat Training in Mumbai in 2003, branching out into training corporates.

An unexpected feather in her cap is the title of 'Mrs India World Finalist', a contest she had entered in as a lark. Truly, she embodies beauty with brawn, an unusual combination indeed. She has sacrificed a lot for her calling, not just financially, but also by choosing not to have a child due to the physical demands of her profession. It required her to be in top physical form at all times, and she did not have time to devote to motherhood. The couple chose to adopt a daughter much later in their career. Her work is intensely physically demanding, and comes at immense physical risk to her. She's had a head injury that led to amnesia for a week; a spinal fracture from a monkey rope exercise up at 50 ft; been shot at and fractured almost every bone in her body, not to mention other minor injuries that come with the territory.[10]

In her 20 years as a commando trainer, she has trained commandos from every elite force in the country, like the Army special forces, National Security Guards (Black Cats), Garud Commando Force, Indian Navy Marine Commandos, Border Security Force Commando Wing, Indo-Tibetan Border Police commando school, Army paratroopers and Ghatak Platoons. For her service, she has been awarded three Army Chief Citations, a rare honour for a civilian. Her husband was made an honorary major with a commission into the Parachute Regiment TA by the President of India, in acknowledgement of the stellar work done by the couple.

Apart from the armed forces of India, she's also trained the police forces of over 12 states. The home secretary at the time, G.K. Pillai, made her an approved resource to train State Police Anti-Terror Squad (ATS) and Quick Response Teams (QRT) in anti-terror ops. After 26/11 in Mumbai, the couple were called upon to train key state police ATS -QRT commando teams across India. They also did urban counter-terror training at the National Police Academy. Ever since 1994, they have been training both Mumbai and Maharashtra Police, including 500 police sub-inspectors, 200 assistant police inspectors, State Reserve Police Force, Unconventional Ops Training Centre and the very first batches of special units such as the Anti-Naxal units of Gadchiroli, Gondia, Special Protection Unit, Riot Control Unit, ATR and QRT.[11]

She's received many prestigious awards too. The former President of India Ram Nath Kovind awarded her the Nari Shakti Puraskar on International Women's Day, 2019. She was in the 2019 *Forbes India* W-Power Trailblazer list. She was voted 'Woman We Love' by *Femina*; named among the most influential women alongside Theresa May and Melinda Gates as rated by *BBC* host Ruth Davidson; was named as *The Indian Express*'s 'Dynamic Woman of the Year'; selected by *Reebok* as the 'Fit to Fight Woman of the Year' and as *Harper Bazaar*'s 'Most Inspiring Woman'. The laurels rest easy on her lithe frame. She has also authored the book, *World's First Encyclopedia of Close Combat Op*, which is now in the FBI, Interpol and the Buckingham Palace libraries.[12]

She no longer trains on the field, but spends her time working on issues regarding women's empowerment. Her joy now comes from encouraging young women to realize that they too can be physically empowered. In her journey was the reward, and a lesson we could all pay heed to. Find your passion, even if it means going against what you trained and studied for.

Excerpts from a conversation with her:

Your father fought against the Portuguese and was even imprisoned. Tell us about him and how his life has probably been the one that put you onto the path you have chosen.

My father, Prof. Ramakant Sinari, was a freedom fighter during the freedom struggle against the Portuguese rule. My dad often told me stories about his participation in the freedom struggle. He used to pen inflammatory anti-Portuguese propaganda, owned a sword which was used by my grandfather in defence against a Portuguese soldier. One day my father gifted it to me. He said, 'If you can, carry on the legacy of allegiance to our country.' I inherited the sword from my father. And maybe, inherited the patriotism too. Those words stayed in my mind. Forever.

As a woman, did you have to recondition your mindset to be able to be fearless when you took on this path of martial arts and skilling yourself in this sphere? How did you conquer fear and train yourself to become fearless?

Fear is a part of everybody. Either it conquers you or you

conquer it. One needs to deal with it and confront it. That's the only way to be rid of it. In martial arts, I was put to test with various opponents, bigger and more aggressive than me. I would shudder with fear but eventually I started harnessing my fear and began overcoming the opponents with superior skill.

In your journey, there might have been many moments where you grappled between life and death, and where your very survival was at risk. Can you tell us about them?

Apart from many minor injuries and few fractures during the 25-year tenure, falling on my head and getting amnesia was the biggest and scariest event during my training. It brought me closer to the reality of life and death. But it only made me work with greater passion and ferocity. When the obstacle gets large, you have to get larger!

Over the years, I honed my skills doing courses on survival, scuba diving, sailing and yachtsmanship, mountaineering, firefighting, sport shooting and earned an 8th degree black belt in Military Martial Arts. Every field that I achieved in had an influence on me understanding my subject of CQB better. Medicine helped because I was able to understand vital areas in the human body which when attacked, would maim or fatally injure the enemy soldier. I did leadership and management from Westminster Business School. The MBA taught me about managing tasks and men under me. I earned my Para Wings under the Indian Air Force and did an adventure sky-diving course. All I learnt helped me understand the subject of commando training and CQB better.

To learn a martial art is one thing, but to train elite forces as a woman civilian is quite another. What were the biases and sexism you had to deal with and what were the moments that gave you pride and joy at the task you were doing?

When you are serious, skilled and passionate in your pursuit, the world senses and respects it. For me, every day has been a new challenge. It's never been easy. I instil confidence in my trainees by my attitude of 'it may be tough but impossible is a just a word'. I lead by personal example. And when they see my prowess in the skills I impart to them, I have earned their respect forever. My work entails selecting participants, training them in physical unarmed combat, reflex shooting, team tactics and commando battle simulation exercises. At the end of the day, I am soaked with grit and grime, my face [is] burnt with gunpowder from continuous firing from assault rifles. If any task was to be done, I would do it first, before asking them to do it and I would win their respect. In teaching them unarmed combat, I would spar with them, wrestle with them. On the firing range, I would prove my skills and prowess at shooting. I can shoot an apple off a man's head without protracted aiming. That's how they knew I was the boss.

My trainees are always male. But I've learnt over a period of time that respect is to be earned. So, before I commanded my trainees to perform any tactic, I would see to it that I personally do it. When they would see my capabilities, they were convinced. There's nothing that a man can do which a woman cannot do. At the end of every course, I remember with fondness the goodbyes exchanged with my trainees on the last day of training. What I saw in their eyes was true admiration and respect. As a woman, to have gained this respect from tough commandos and soldiers, is a compliment and my greatest wealth.

You were also a finalist at the Mrs India pageant. What was your experience like of something so completely different from your professional space, and what were the lessons, if any, that you learnt from it?

I believe life is lived but once, and in a lifetime if you can experience different colours of life then it's a life well-lived. When the Mrs India pageant was announced, my friends coaxed me to go in for it. I joked with them, 'It's a beauty pageant and I'm an action woman. It is not my cup of tea.' After all the coaxing, I went for the elimination round and was pleasantly surprised when I was selected. I met women from different states and cities who were competing. It was a different experience. I walked the ramp confidently and even flexed my biceps. I was runner-up for Mrs India World pageant without even dyeing my grey stands of hair. However, my core fidelity has always been to my work for the country as a commando trainer. One must always stay centred and rooted to what is good for you.

Your husband was made an honorary major of the territorial army, while you missed out on that because of gender provisions. Do you wish this was redressed now that the forces are opening up to women across all functions?

I always feel at home when I'm in any force location. It's like I was meant to be there, among our brave soldiers, battling odds to keep our country safe and secure. For this, I have survived the extremes of cold in the mountains and scorching heat in deserts. Serving the Indian forces for almost two decades as guest trainers; travelling every month to training centres in hostile locations like freezing valleys, the high altitude of Siachen, the jungles of Madhya Pradesh, the para units in deserts; getting three Army Chief Citations as well as getting multiple injuries; getting bedridden for as long as six months at times; losing out on having a family or children; escaping getting shot by random terrorist fire and going bankrupt many a times but never charging a rupee from our forces—there was never any doubt in our minds of continuing the selfless work.

And yes, after all these hardships, my hubby Dr Deepak Rao received the President's rank honour to become Major Deepak Rao. He is one of six Indians since independence, to receive the President Rank Award along with cricketer M.S. Dhoni and

Abhinav Bindra. He was neither a top sportsman nor a high-level actor, but was an ordinary person who spent his entire life sweating it out training the forces with his wife instead of making money as a doctor or raising a family. When he got recognized, it was the biggest moment in my life. I consider that to be my achievement too. I never had any regrets that my contribution was not recognized. And now, receiving the Nari Shakti Award from the President, I feel honoured too. Our government is doing a lot to empower women. We need to believe in them and with time there will be many positive changes for empowering women.

You decided to adopt a child rather than have one. What made you take this decision, and would you say motherhood and physically carrying a baby and giving birth affects a woman's body to the extent that she might not regain her previous level of fitness?

I don't deny that motherhood is a beautiful experience for a woman, and due to my training commitments I had to let go of this wonderful experience. Getting back my fitness was not really the issue. A lot of women in athletic fields do get back their fitness after motherhood. I also believed that as a mother I would need to give at least the first few years of undivided attention in the upbringing of the child. For this, I would have to stay off my training assignments for years. Considering both these aspects, I decided to postpone it. I am fortunate to have an understanding hubby (I like to refer to him as a life partner) who understood my decision. Eventually, I decided to adopt a girl child and complete the family.

What have been the most challenging training assignments you have undertaken across the decades that you've trained elite forces, and are there any moments that stand out for you when you look back upon them?

Every force I trained has been elite in its own way. I have never underestimated any of the forces. They were highly trained and it was always a challenge to keep up with them. Every experience was deeply satisfying, though challenging. And the mementoes gifted to me by all those organizations are my greatest wealth.

You have now set up a training academy. How do you see the awareness towards learning martial arts and related skills increasing among regular citizens today, as well as girls and women?

At the age of 50, I decided to retire from active field training. In the meanwhile, I had opened an academy catering to the fitness of the busy corporate man and woman. We teach holistic fitness programmes including martial arts and a DARE (Defence Against Rape and Eve teasing) programme designed by me to make women confident and capable of handling unexpected situations.

You have received countless awards for the work you've done. Which are most precious to you, and could you share your emotions and memories from the award function, specifically the Nari Shakti award?

I have never worked for awards, accolades, recognition. Even my selfless work for 25 years for the forces was done with the feeling of patriotism and duty. I always thought it was satisfying and honourable work. I'd go to different force locations, do my work and come back home, only to be travelling again to another academy. Life was perfect and I never looked for anything. When one day I received a call saying that I was to be receiving the Nari Shakti Award, I was pleasantly surprised. Going to Delhi, and receiving the award from our [former] Honourable President Shri Kovind ji at the Rashtrapati Bhavan. Every moment is memorable. Those moments are etched forever in my mind. I felt honoured that my work was appreciated and acknowledged by the highest office in the country.

Through your life and your achievements, what message would you like young girls and women to take away?

Be the best you can be. Compete with yourself not with anyone else. Be better today than you were yesterday. And I think the qualities required for a woman to achieve and excel in her chosen field are:

- Dedication (not getting deterred from the chosen path);
- Focus (balancing marriage and parenthood with your forward movement towards your personal goals);
- Endurance (to keep at it even when the going gets tough); and
- Conscience (to do what you do with utmost sincerity, without expectation of gains, like the Mahabharata philosophy of doing your karma and not waiting for material gain).
- Win over people by self-expression and honesty.

NOTES

1 Arivalan, Kayalvizhi, 'Wonder Woman: Dr Seema Rao, India's First and Only Woman Commando Trainer', *Femina*, 30 September 2021, http://tinyurl.com/msesjcyp. Accessed on 4 January 2024.

2 'Singh, Aishwarya, '"Young Girls Keen on Joining Forces": Meet Seema Rao India's Only Woman Commando Trainer', *TimesNow*, 8 December 2023, http://tinyurl.com/2va3asur. Accessed on 4 January 2024.

3 Rashid, Sumaira, 'Women Who Conquered Men Like No One Else-Seema Rao', *The Indianness*, 14 January 2020, http://tinyurl.com/yr92fsxn. Accessed on 4 January 2024.

4 Shah, Ruchika, 'Dr Seema Rao: India's First Female Combat Trainer, Fighting Stereotypes', *Forbes India*, 5 March 2019,

http://tinyurl.com/4breym3t. Accessed on 4 January 2024.

5 Prakash, Priya, 'Meet Dr Seema Rao, India's First Female Commando Trainer', *shethepeople,* 29 January 2022, http://tinyurl.com/4ss78hkt. Accessed on 4 January 2024.

6 Shah, Ruchika, 'Dr Seema Rao: India's First Female Combat Trainer, Fighting Stereotypes', *Forbes India,* 5 March 2019, http://tinyurl.com/4breym3t. Accessed on 4 January 2024.

7 Ibid.

8 Prakash, Priya, 'Meet Dr Seema Rao, India's First Female Commando Trainer', *shethepeople,* 29 January 2022, http://tinyurl.com/4ss78hkt. Accessed on 4 January 2024.

9 Shah, Ruchika, 'Dr Seema Rao: India's First Female Combat Trainer, Fighting Stereotypes', *Forbes India,* 5 March 2019, http://tinyurl.com/4breym3t. Accessed on 4 January 2024.

10 Kapoor, Aekta, 'Meet India's Only Woman Commando Trainer Dr Seema Rao', *CNBCTV18,* 15 June 2019, http://tinyurl.com/374w8wek. Accessed on 4 January 2024.

11 Jain, Reshma, 'Fusion of Brain, Beauty and Brawn, Dr Seema Rao's Journey from Weakness to Strength Has Been Incredible', *sociostory,* 9 April 2022, http://tinyurl.com/28xvc2v2. Accessed on 4 January 2024.

12 Kapoor, Aekta, 'Meet India's Only Woman Commando Trainer Dr Seema Rao', *CNBCTV18,* 15 June 2019, http://tinyurl.com/374w8wek. Accessed on 4 January 2024.

11

KALPANA CHAWLA

TOUCH THE STARS

There are two iconic images of Kalpana Chawla in her space suits, her dark long hair falling down her back, a soft smile on her face, that we remember her by: one in an orange NASA (National Aeronautics and Space Administration) launch and re-entry pressurized suit; and the other in a blue NASA flight suit, the United States (US) flag prominent in the corner of the frame, along with a model of a space shuttle in the other corner.

It was a long journey for the young girl—from Karnal in Haryana, one of the most rigidly patriarchal states in India, to the US, as an astronaut with NASA. It took a dream, immense gumption and the ability to defy all traditional expectations that bound her to the pre-defined notions of what a woman's life should be in India. It took a Kalpana Chawla to become an icon for young girls in India, for them to know that the sky wasn't their limit, and that if they so chose, they could touch the stars.

∞

On 17 March 1962, a young girl was born into an ordinary family in Karnal. Her parents had migrated from Multan (now in Pakistan).[1] Little did her parents, Banarasi Lal and Sanjyothi Chawla, know then that Kalpana (the youngest of their four children) would go on to become a global icon for young girls.

In fact, she was not even called 'Kalpana' until she started going to school. At home, her parents called her 'Montu'. When she had to enrol in school, her parents gave her options of names to choose from and she picked 'Kalpana', meaning imagination. An apt choice for someone who dared to dream of going to space. When she became an astronaut, she was popularly known by her initials, 'KC'.

The flying bug bit her young, when she was barely three. It all started with her seeing planes flying over her home in Karnal. They fascinated her. Her father indulged his darling Montu's fascination. He would take her to local flying clubs to watch planes take off and land, and also managed to wrangle her a joyride on one. To quote her father:

> Kalpana was about three or four years old when she first saw a plane. She had been playing on the rooftop when she saw a plane flying above our house. She seemed so excited. I took her to the flying club near our house where a pilot agreed to take us for a ride. Kalpana's joys knew no bounds. She had always wanted to fly.[2]

She studied at the Tagore Baal Niketan Senior Secondary School and was a precocious and gifted child. Her father altered her date of birth by one year on her documents, to allow her to be eligible for the matriculation exams. Her school teachers would say that she spent her time making paper planes and flying them in class. In an interview before the Columbia Mission, she recalls how she and her brother used to cycle to see the aeroplanes. The seeds of her fascination with space were perhaps sown back then. To quote her, 'We gazed dreamily at the Milky Way and once in a while caught some shooting stars. Times like those gave me the opportunity to wonder and ask all those very basic questions. That sense of awe for the heavens started there.'[3]

She grew up in the state of Haryana which was, and still is, to a large extent, rigidly patriarchal. To quote her, 'Forget about space, I didn't even know if my folks were going to let me go to engineering college.' It was her mother who pushed her to pursue her dreams and supported her all the way. Her father says in a documentary, *Dreams that Touched the Sky*, that while Kalpana wasn't a naughty child, she wasn't a very studious child or a class topper either. Nonetheless, she was a sincere student.[4]

To quote Rakesh Sharma, the first man from India to go into space, about her, 'Here was this small-town girl in Karnal who dreamt of going into space. She chased her dream. It wasn't available in the country. She went halfway around the world and went after her dream and grabbed it.'[5]

She went on to get a Bachelor of Engineering in aeronautical engineering from Punjab Engineering College. Her choice of major had her professors dissuade her from choosing it initially, as according to them, it didn't make sense for her to become an aeronautical engineer. What opportunities did she have in India to pursue this field as a girl? She refused to pay heed to them, completed her aeronautical engineering and then moved to the US in 1982 for a Master of Science degree in aerospace engineering from the University of Texas at Arlington in 1984.[6]

She also found love during this time. On 2 December 1983, she got married to Jean-Pierre Harrison, a flying instructor and a writer on aviation. She was barely 21 at the time, and they had known each other for barely a year.[7]

The couple moved to Boulder, Colorado. In 1986, she got a second masters, and in 1988, she was awarded a PhD in aerospace engineering from the University of Colorado, Boulder. She did her research on computational fluid dynamics on vertical and short take-off and landing concepts. Her research is still cited in many technical journals and academic papers. In 1988, Kalpana joined NASA's Ames Research Center in the field of powered-lift computational fluid dynamics. Her research focussed on simulation of complex air flows encountered around aircraft such as the Harrier in 'ground-effect'. Post this project, she worked on research in mapping of flow solvers to parallel computers, and did the testing of these solvers by carrying out powered lift computations. She became a naturalized citizen of the US in 1991. In 1993, she joined Overset Methods Inc., Los Altos, California as vice president and research scientist, and formed a team to specialize in simulation of moving multiple-body problems.[8] She also was a certified flight instructor for airplanes and gliders, and held commercial pilot licences for single- and multi-engine airplanes, seaplanes and gliders.

She was selected by NASA in December 1994. In March 1995, she reported to the Johnson Space Center as an astronaut candidate in the fifteenth group of astronauts. She went through a year of training and evaluation before she was assigned as crew representative to work on technical issues for the Astronaut Office EVA/Robotics and Computer Branches. Among her assignments were the development of robotic situational awareness displays and testing space shuttle control software in the Shuttle Avionics Integration Laboratory.

A year later, in November 1996, she was assigned as mission specialist and prime robotic arm operator on the STS-87. Two years later, in January 1998, she was assigned as crew representative for shuttle and station flight crew equipment, and subsequently served as lead for Astronaut Office's Crew Systems and Habitability Section. She flew on STS-87 (1997) and STS-107 (2003) and logged 30 days, 14 hours and 54 minutes in space.[9]

She was part of the six-astronaut crew that flew the Space Shuttle *Columbia* STS-87, making her the very first Indian woman to go into space. As mentioned earlier, Kalpana was a mission specialist and prime robotic arm operator for the flight; the other astronauts on-board were Kevin Kregel, Steven Linsey, Winston Scott, Takao Doi and Leonid Kadenyuk.[10]

The Mission saw her travel 10.4/6.5 million miles in 252 orbits of the earth, logging more than 376 hours (15 days and 16 hours) in space. The Mission on this shuttle included conducting a number of experiments which included studying plant reproduction in microgravity as well as how materials behave in space.

On this Mission, she was responsible for the deployment of the Spartan Satellite which was to study the outer layer of the Sun (or its corona). The Satellite malfunctioned and could not control its position on deployment. This resulted in the astronauts Winston Scott and Takao Doi needing to do a space walk in order to capture the satellite, which was not deployed again on the Mission. After the mishap of the Spartan release from the shuttle and its going out of control, Kalpana went incommunicado for two months. She was exonerated after a five-month internal investigation by a committee at NASA, which called her a 'terrific astronaut'.[11]

Later, in an interview with Raj Chengappa, published in *India Today*, she spoke about her experience of her first flight into space. To quote from the interview:

> But as soon as the engines cut off and you get to zero gravity, you felt as if you were being pushed off your seat. You feel disoriented. [...] In fact, you are in a free fall—that's what zero gravity is all about. But the first few hours, the workload was so much that it was hard to realise the magic of the experience. But afterwards the feeling was literally out of this world.[12]

She was then assigned to technical positions in the astronaut office. Of being in space, she said that it changed her perspective about being human. She said that she realized that she was only aware of her thoughts. She philosophized saying that in a sense, we all just become our consciousness and intelligence when in space.[13]

Interestingly, according to author Harish Bhat, in an interview with *moneycontrol.com*, Kalpana was inspired by J.R.D.

Tata piloting an aircraft. According to him, as a young woman, Kalpana had first heard of J.R.D. Tata piloting an aircraft in 1982. At the time, he was commemorating the fiftieth anniversary of the inaugural air mail flight. The fact that J.R.D. Tata did this when he was 78 was very inspiring to the young Kalpana. In 2003, after she had passed away, her family wrote to Ratan Tata enclosing 'special memorabilia'. To quote Bhat:

> There was a crew autographed group picture of the Space Shuttle Mission STS-87, (her first Space Shuttle Mission), a pair of medallions commemorating her two space journeys, and an old black and white photograph. This was the photograph of JRD Tata's inaugural mail flight, which Kalpana Chawla had carried along with her, on her first mission into space.[14]

These medallions and photographs are now on display at the Tata Archives in Pune, outside the re-created office of J.R.D. Tata, as a tribute.

Her second flight was the STS-107, which was the final flight of the Space Shuttle *Columbia,* in 2003. She was one of the seven crew members. The crew included Mission Commander Rick Husband; Pilot Willie McCool; Mission Specialists Kalpana Chawla, Laurel Clark and David Brown; Payload Commander Michael Anderson; and Payload Specialist Ilan Ramon. Kalpana was selected for the flight in 2001, and the Mission kept getting repeatedly delayed due to various issues, including scheduling conflicts as well as technical problems. The technical issues included cracks in the shuttle engine flow liners, found in July 2002.

Despite all these issues, the Space Shuttle *Columbia* was launched into orbit on the STS-107 Mission. While on the Mission, the crew performed nearly 80 experiments studying the Earth, space science, advanced technology development and astronaut health and safety. It was a 16-day flight, and the crew worked in shifts to ensure that they carried out research continuously through the flight. The STS-107 crew tested technology to recycle water for the then new International Space Station. They conducted experiments developed by elementary school students, analysing how insects and fish responded to space and space flight. Some experiments studied the Sun. A large pressurized chamber, called the SPACEHAB Research Double Module, within the shuttle's payload bay was dedicated towards biological and health research.[15] While on the flight she had said, 'You simply do not have time to dwell on yesterdays because you have to finish the whole mission properly. I think once we get back to Earth we will have a lot of time to talk about this and that's when I plan to do that.'[16]

The flight though, was a doomed one; doomed from take-off itself, although the crew didn't realize it then. During the launch of this Mission, *Columbia*'s twenty-eighth Mission, a piece of the foam insulation broke off from the space shuttle's external tank and hit the port wing of its orbiter. While there had been foam shedding in previous missions as well, the damage had been minimal. This time, though, the damage was more substantial. More importantly, the investigation conducted in the aftermath of the disaster confirmed that the crew could not have rectified the problem, even if they had known about it.[17]

That bit of foam insulation proved to be the undoing of the Mission. On 1 February 2003, when the *Columbia* Space Shuttle re-entered the atmosphere after the 16-day mission, the damage caused by the loose piece of foam insulation allowed the heated atmospheric gases to enter and destroy the internal wing structure, damaging the thermal protection system—a shield that protected the shuttle from intense heat during re-entry into the atmosphere. The shuttle became unstable, and within a minute, it de-pressurized, killing the crew instantly and disintegrating over Texas and Louisiana upon re-entry, barely 16 minutes before its landing.

Kalpana was barely 40 at the time of her death. She loved the mountains and had written in a letter that if she didn't come back from the Mission, her remains should be cremated and scattered across the Himalayas or the Zion National Park in Utah. In keeping with her wishes, her remains, when identified, were cremated and scattered across the Zion National Park in Utah. In fact, when her parents went there, they found a young girl sitting there and crying. She told them that Kalpana had helped her complete her education by sending her money.[18] To quote her father:

> She earned well while working at NASA. But she never cared for materialistic things. She would spend all her money on helping underprivileged kids with education. She would reach out to students who were unable to complete their education due to financial constraints and help them out as far as she could.[19]

She was always keen to encourage young girls to harbour ambitions of a career in space and to pursue scientific education. Often, NASA would invite young girls from her secondary school back in India to be part of their Summer Space Experience Program, and the school would send two girls each year from 1998 onwards to the Foundation for International Space Education's United Space School in Houston. Kalpana would interact with these girls, and invite them to her home for a home-cooked Indian dinner.[20]

The disaster led to a suspension of all space shuttle flights for over two years; even the construction of the International Space Station was put on hold in this time. This accident was the second disaster for the US Space Shuttle Program, the first of which was the 1986 explosion of the Shuttle *Challenger*. It was the last fatal mission of the US Space Program. The *Columbia* accident ultimately led then President George W. Bush to announce plans to retire NASA's space shuttle fleet (which was more than 20 years old at the time), once the construction of the International Space Station was complete. A capsule-based spacecraft was planned to replace the shuttles.

As mentioned earlier, with her two missions, Kalpana logged a total of 30 days, 14 hours and 54 minutes in space. She was awarded the Congressional Space Medal of Honor posthumously, as well as the NASA Space Flight Medal and the Distinguished Service Medal. She's had streets, universities and institutions named in her honour. In India, she is considered an icon for young girls looking to reach the skies and beyond. She had a spacecraft mission named after her—the 14th Northrop Grumman Cygnus Spacecraft Mission—which delivered supplies to the ISS. The *Columbia* crew members had asteroids named after them. The Asteroid 51826 was named after Kalpana Chawla. She has a crater on the moon named after her.[21] In India, then Prime Minister Atal Bihari Vajpayee announced that the meteorological series of satellites, MetSat, were to be renamed Kalpana-1. The first satellite had already been launched on 12 September 2002 but was renamed in 2003 as Kalpana-1.[22]

Speaking of her in a documentary, her father said:

> I think she came into this world with some blessing from the almighty. She was different and special from her childhood. As a father all that I did was not to clip her wings. She wanted to fly, I just let her fly. She came, conquered and flew after inspiring many lives. She was one of the girls who excelled in everything she did, every job she tried.[23]

He is proud to be known as Kalpana's father. To quote him from an interview with *IANS*, 'I feel proud that my daughter's life and her achievements have inspired so many people. People know me because of my daughter. They don't say ki, "*arey ye Banarasi Lal hai...*" they greet me by calling me "Kalpana's father".'[24]

Her husband, Jean-Pierre Harrison, wrote a biography called

The Edge of Time, which he published in 2011. Perhaps, that is where she always belonged—the edge of time, a resident of the Milky Way, as she had confessed to *India Today*. Perhaps, it would be appropriate to end this chapter with her own words, where she speaks about her place in the universe:

> On one of the night passes, I dimmed the lights in the flight deck and saw the stars. When you look at the stars and the galaxy, you feel that you are not just from any particular piece of land but from the solar system. I could extend the whole thing—maybe one day people will go to other galaxies and then what would we say? Where did we come from? I am a resident of the Milky Way?[25]

NOTES

1 Targhotra, Prerna, 'Kalpana Chawla Birth Anniversary 2023: 10 Interesting Facts about the First Indian Woman to Go to Space That You Must Know', *EnglishJagran,* 17 March 2023, http://tinyurl.com/2c3rhtpr. Accessed on 4 January 2024.

2 Banerjee, Disha, 'Born to Fly: Kalpana Chawla's Father Talks about Her Moving Journey 17 Yrs after Her Death', *STORYPICK.*, 12 October 2020, http://tinyurl.com/4by7raxk. Accessed on 4 January 2024.

3 'Padmanabhan, Anil, 'The Journey Matters as Much as the Goal: Kalpana Chawla', *India Today,* 4 July 2012, http://tinyurl.com/mrzcmmrw. Accessed on 4 January 2024.

4 Lamba, Aditi, 'Recalling Kalpana Chawla, Groundbreaking Astronaut on Space Shuttle Columbia Flight', *SpectrumNews1,* 8 March 2023, http://tinyurl.com/3exnk5ux. Accessed on 17 January 2024; IANS, '"She Wanted to Fly, I Let Her Fly"', *the pioneer,* 29 October 2019, http://tinyurl.com/5bhanbrp. Accessed on 4 January 2024.

5 'Kalpana Chawla: Tracing the Incredible Journey

of a Karnal Girl', *Factual News,* 17 March 2022, http://tinyurl.com/3pzxs7jx. Accessed on 4 January 2024.

6 'Biographical Data: Kalpana Chawla (Ph.d.)', *National Aeronautics and Space Administration,* http://tinyurl.com/3achhjv7. Accessed on 4 January 2024.

7 Varsha, 'Kalpana Chawla Love Story with Jean Pierre Harrison Has a Tragic Ending', *Jodistory,* 7 December 2023, http://tinyurl.com/26drxdem. Accessed on 4 January 2024.

8 'Biographical Data: Kalpana Chawla (Phd.)', *National Aeronautics and Space Administration,* http://tinyurl.com/3achhjv7. Accessed on 4 January 2024.

9 Ibid.

10 Harvey, Ailsa, and Nola Taylor Tillman, 'Kalpana Chawla: Biography & Columbia Disaster', *SPACE.com,* 11 February 2022, http://tinyurl.com/y4ur8bhh. Accessed on 4 January 2024.

11 'On Kalpana Chawla's Death Anniversary, a Tribute to the First Woman Astronaut from India', *The NEWS Minute,* 1 February 2017, http://tinyurl.com/tbnn73xd. Accessed on 4 January 2024.

12 Chengappa, Raj, 'From the Archives: I Really Felt Responsible for the Earth | Kalpana Chawla,' *India Today,* 16 March 2022, http://tinyurl.com/2kxw2zms. Accessed on 12 January 2024.

13 Ibid.

14 Sengupta, Ankita, 'Kalpana Chawla Death Anniversary: How JRD Tata Inspired Her to Become an Astronaut', *moneycontrol,* 1 February 2022, http://tinyurl.com/mw828uyf. Accessed on 4 January 2024.

15 'STS-107 Columbia', *CBS News Space,* http://tinyurl.com/2nhsnpxp. Accessed on 4 January 2024.

16 'Kalpana Chawla: Tracing the Incredible Journey of a Karnal Girl', *Zee5,* 17 March 2022, http://tinyurl.com/ay7mtmud. Accessed on 4 January 2024.

17 Tate, Karl, 'Columbia Space Shuttle Disaster Explained

(Infographic)', *SPACE.com*, 1 February 2013, http://tinyurl.com/79a63e6. Accessed on 4 January 2024.

18 IANS, 'She Wanted to Fly, I Let Her Fly: Kalpana Chawla's Dad', *On Manorama*, 1 November 2019, http://tinyurl.com/bdz554dz. Accessed on 4 January 2024.

19 Banerjee, Disha, 'Born to Fly: Kalpana Chawla's Father Talks about Her Moving Journey 17 Yrs after Her Death', *Storypick.*, 12 October 2020, http://tinyurl.com/4by7raxk. Accessed on 4 January 2024.

20 Harvey, Ailsa, and Nola Taylor Tillman, 'Kalpana Chawla: Biography & Columbia Disaster', *SPACE.com*, 11 February 2022, http://tinyurl.com/y4ur8bhh. Accessed on 4 January 2024.

21 'Kalpana Chawla 59th Birth Anniversary: From Asteroid 51826 Being Named after Her to "Kalpana Chawla Award", Everything You Want to Know about the First Indian-Origin Woman to Go to Space', *LatestLY*, 17 March 2021, http://tinyurl.com/mpt85rhk. Accessed on 4 January 2024.

22 'Kalpana-1 Introduction', *MOSDAC*, http://tinyurl.com/32mmrrrm. Accessed on 4 January 2024.

23 IANS, 'She Wanted to Fly, I Let Her Fly: Kalpana Chawla's Dad', *On Manorama*, 1 November 2019, http://tinyurl.com/bdz554dz. Accessed on 4 January 2024.

24 IANS, 'Kalpana Chawla's Father on Her Biopic: Would Be Happy to See a Film on My Daughter's Life', *India Today*, 24 March 2022, http://tinyurl.com/ymmymu5f. Accessed on 4 January 2024.

25 Chengappa, Raj, 'From the Archives: I Really Felt Responsible for the Earth | Kalpana Chawla', *India Today*, 16 March 2022, http://tinyurl.com/2kxw2zms. Accessed on 12 January 2024.

12

BEGUM AKHTAR

QUEEN OF THE GHAZAL

They called her the queen of the *ghazal*: *Mallika-e-Ghazal.* It was a title she bore with the insouciant elegance with which she also led her life. Akhtari Bai Faizabadi or Begum Akhtar, the queen of the ghazal, the *dadra* and the *thumri* continues to reign in the hearts of her devoted listeners even today, decades after her passing.

Hers was an unconventional childhood. She was born in Bada Darwaza, Bhadarsa Bharatkund, Faizabad, in present day Uttar Pradesh on 7 October 1914. She was the child of Asghar Hussain, a young lawyer, and Mushtari Bai, a former courtesan or *tawaif.* Begum Akhtar saw tragedy unfold when still very young. Her father disowned her mother, and his twin daughters, Zohra and Bibbi (Begum Akhtar).[1] He did not acknowledge his wife or his daughters for years. It was a harsh rejection that Begum Akhtar could never understand. All her life, she pined for her absent father without being able to understand what it was that she had done wrong to cause him to withdraw from their lives.

It is believed that she was a very mischievous child. Anecdotally, she is believed to have chopped off her school teacher's plait, and then refused to go back to school after the incident, terrified about the repercussions of her actions. Luckily for her, she was not doomed to suffer from a lack of formal education. She showed both interest and promise in music and singing, and her mother decided that she would get her trained in the art form.[2]

However, another tragedy was yet to come, one that scarred her childhood. Unknowingly, she and her twin sister Zohra both ate sweets that were poisoned. Zohra didn't survive. Begum Akhtar was devastated, as she was very close to her sister. At the time, young Bibbi didn't even understand the concept of death. She asked her mother what had happened to Zohra. Her mother replied that Zohra had gone to live with Allah in his home. In fact, that was Begum Akhtar's first introduction to the concept of religion.

Bibbi, the mischievous girl, who had experienced being abandoned by a parent and the death of a sibling whilst still young, grew up to become Begum Akhtar, the doyenne of the ghazal, who sang with a voice that was steeped in sorrow and an inexplicable melancholy. It was a long and arduous journey from Bibbi to Begum Akhtar. It saw her go through various phases, taking her from 'Bibbi Sayyed' to 'Akhtari Sayyed' to 'Akhtari Bai Faizabadi' to 'Begum Ishtiaq Ahmed Abassi' and, finally, to a name by which she is now immortalized in the minds of all music lovers: Begum Akhtar.[3]

Music came into young Bibbi's life early. When she was barely seven years old, she became fascinated by the singing of Chandra Bai, an artist with a touring theatre group. It was then that the family recognized that she had perhaps both the inclination and, more importantly, the talent towards music and singing. Her mother was keen for her to learn conventional Hindustani classical music, but she eventually found her métier in the forms of the ghazal and the thumri. She was barely seven or eight when she began training formally under the sarangi maestro Ustad Imdad Khan of Patna, who was then the accompanist of Mallika Jaan of Agra and the fabled Gauhar Jaan of Calcutta (now Kolkata). She trained under him for six months, then moved to Gaya with her mother and continued her music training under Ustad Ghulam Mohammed Khan. In 1923, she moved to Calcutta with her mother and Ustad Ata Mohammed Khan. They lived in a small room on Ripon Street.[4] Her training would go on for hours, beginning early in the morning. Months would go perfecting a single note. Though the popular anecdote goes that her first concert was when she was 15, her disciple Rita Ganguly says, 'She was 11 when she had her first performance in Calcutta. She stole the hearts of the audience by singing "Deewana Banana Hai to Deewana Bana De".' In fact, it was at this same event that the *shehnai* maestro, Bismillah Khan, made his debut, too, according to Ganguly.[5] This was a music concert at Alfred Theatre, Calcutta. The concert was organized to raise funds for the victims of the Nepal–Bihar earthquake in 1934.

The young Akhtari gave a solo concert, singing four ghazals and five dadras to an enthralled crowd, captivating even Sarojini Naidu, who was in the audience. She would later talk about the experience, saying, 'I had never before faced an audience. My knees turned to water and I began to tremble all over with sheer stage fright. I thought I would collapse on the stage. I started with a favourite ghazal of mine. Suddenly I felt my nerves relax and my voice sore in full-throated ease.'[6]

Anecdotally, it is popularly believed that the legendary Gauhar Jaan told the young Akhtari that she would be famous. Encouraged by the response to her early performances, Akhtari began singing ghazals regularly in public. It was at this time that she cut her first disc for the Megaphone Record Company in 1933, which later released the gramophone records of her popular ghazals, thumris and dadras.

By June 1944, the number of recordings rose to 154. She shot to popularity with her seventh single 'Deewana Banana Hai to Deewana Bana De', written by Behzaad Lakhnavi. Interestingly, in many of her early recordings, Ustad Bade Ghulam Ali accompanied her on the harmonium.

She saw her fortunes turn as an artiste with the Megaphone Record Company. She got a monthly salary of ₹500, which was a princely amount at the time. While continuing to live at Ripon Street, she now had a car for her use. But alas, just as things seemed to be turning around, further tragedy unfolded in her life. While she learnt from the great names in music, she also faced what we understand and acknowledge now as abuse. Her first music teacher reportedly slipped his hand on her thigh in the course of a lesson. Later, she was reportedly molested by the Maharaja of one of the states of then Bihar Presidency, who was a musical patron, and is said to have given birth to a girl she would say was her sister. Young as she was, she had already experienced so much trauma. Is it any wonder, then, that this sorrow percolated into her singing, and enhanced her voice with a rare timbre and melancholy that no amount of training could infuse?[7]

The combination of her beauty and mellifluous voice soon got her the title of Mallika-e-Ghazal, and offers from the film world began pouring in. She acted in a few movies in the 1930s. Her very first movie was *Ek Din Ki Badshahat*, followed by *Nal Damayanti, Nach Rang, Mumtaz Begum, Ameena, Jawani Ka Nasha, Naseeb Ka Chakkar* and *Roti*. Many years later, she did a small performance as a guest appearance in the classic movie, *Jalsaghar*, but this time, she portrayed the fabled singer she had become. She also acted in stage productions of famed theatre companies like Corinthian, where she acted in mythological plays like *Sita* and *Nal Damayanti* with stars like Master Fida Husain. Her first theatrical performance was *Nai Dulhan*.[8]

While unfortunately none of these films survive today, she got her big break by being cast by Mehboob Khan in his landmark film *Roti* with Chandramohan, Sheikh Mukhtar and Sitara Devi. Unfortunately, six songs sung by her were removed from the final film because of contractual issues with the Megaphone Record Company, but are now available as audio online. In *Panna Dai* she sang two songs which became quite famous.[9]

While the lure of the world of glamour was firmly wrapping itself around her at this time, her guru, Ustad Ata Mohammad Khan, is believed to have given her an ultimatum: 'Either you concentrate on your music or go to become an actress.' Around this time, at a music conference held in Bombay (now Mumbai), she heard legends like Gauhar Jaan and Zohra Bai Ambalewali. This made her acutely aware of the lack of preparation in her voice when compared to their voices, and she went back to training again. She was now firmly on the route to becoming a singer, laying aside the charms of the film world. Soon, she was invited to the courts of Ayodhya, Hyderabad, Rampur, Darbhanga and Kashmir. She became a court singer and never went back to the world of films again.

She left Bombay and returned to Lucknow in 1934, after finishing her stint in the movies. She now moved to Cheena Bazaar, Lucknow, and began training under Ustad Abdul Wahid Khan, from the Kirana *gharana*. He was the one who honed Akhtari's *purab-ang gayaki*, which was a style that was considered characteristic of the Lucknow and Benares regions. Then, she trained to be a classical *khayal* singer, and was known as Akhtaribai Faizabadi.[10] She was given the name by one of her gurus, Ustad Zamiruddin.

Begum Akhtar's charm is still spoken about by everyone, and is evident in the recordings of her live performances. The wit and charm were part of the tawaif culture and performance. Begum Akhtar could sing for a live audience, and hold their attention without even a microphone at times, and she understood the deep and complex nuances of the poetry she sang.

She had a lavish home in Lucknow where she invited most of her patrons, and by the late 1930s she was perhaps the wealthiest and most sought-after woman in Lucknow. By the early 1940s, she was the court singer for royalty, invited by the son of the Nizam of Hyderabad, Moazzam Jah, and later by the Nawab of Rampur, Raza Ali Khan. She was also under the patronage of the Maharaja of Kashmir and the Maharaja of Darbhanga for brief periods.[11] Of the Rajwaadas of pre-independent India who were her patrons, Raza Ali Shah Khan of Rampur was her most steadfast patron, gifting her expensive gifts, including a Packard car. To quote her friend Sheila Dhar on the Nawab of Rampur's fascination for Begum Akhtar, 'There was this seven-stringed necklace of Basra pearls in the Rampur collection. And from the seventh string of this necklace, hung a big diamond pendant. The Nawab used to say that if there is anything more lustrous than the diamond, it's the smile of Akhtari.'[12]

The nobility sent their cars for her to come perform in their palaces, according to Yatindra Mishra, the author of *Akhtari: The Life and Music of Begum Akhtar.* He said, 'I got the story of the Mercedes Benz being sent to ferry her to the palace from there. Dadi's father, Raja Narayan Pratap Singh, used to send his Merc to fetch Begum in 1938-1945 for mehfils at the durbar.'[13] In another interview, Mishra elaborates:

> The period from 1935 to 1945 was when Akhtar was making appearances in darbar and holding Khadi Mehfils. She performed in Ayodhya Darbar especially on Dussehra and Holi. [...] Her visits and performances made up for interesting anecdotes that have been passed down to us from generations. Talking to my elders, I came to know that there was a fight amongst drivers as to who would go to receive her. [...] My grandma mentioned her rendition of thumri Chala ho pardesiya naina lagaye, and Holi ki thumri Daff kahe ko bajaye main toh aawat rahi were something magical. She was fortunate enough to learn these from the great doyen.[14]

At this point in her life, she sought stability and respectability. To this end, she approached her friend, Sayeeda Raza, who worked at All India Radio (AIR), Lucknow with an unusual request. She wanted to get married to a recently widowed lawyer from an 'established' Lucknow family, Ishtiaq Ahmad Abbasi, a landowning *taluqdar* and a barrister from the aristocratic family of Kakori. Sayeeda was Akhtari's best friend and confidante back in the early 1940s. She facilitated this marriage. Akhtari's transition from a performing artist to the daughter-in-law of a respectable household was not easy. To quote her, 'I was the daughter-in-law of that house, I would shrink every time I heard my records play anywhere. My voice was my biggest treasure and now that was scaring me.'[15] It was after her marriage that she came to be known as Begum Akhtar.

Regula Qureshi in her essay, 'In Search of Begum Akhtar: Patriarchy, Poetry, and Twentieth-Century Indian Music,' talks about how Begum Akhtar transformed herself from a hereditary singer to a 'respectable married lady'. She talks about how Begum Akhtar tried to give up her singing career but later emerged larger than ever. Qureshi adds, 'Recording provided an opportunity for courtesans to continue as singers and entertainers even as their opportunities for live performance diminished. Many courtesans became singers for films. Interestingly, it was also through sound recordings that Begum Akhtar's re-entry into public as a singer after she had married and her persona had changed from courtesan to respectable married woman was facilitated.'[16]

According to historian Saleem Kidwai, who studied the lives of courtesan performers, the stigma of her origins as the daughter of a courtesan was erased by her becoming Abbasi's wife, and being introduced into 'respectable' society by him. She was always conscious of her background. To quote her, 'I am proud of my family singing background. I accept that. How can you blame someone for her background? What can you do about your birth? You must accept what God gave you and make your own life.'[17]

It was almost a year before Abbasi told his family about

his marriage to Begum Akhtar. There are conflicting reports on why she gave up singing when she got married. Some say her husband preferred that she didn't sing in public, others say that she chose to give up singing so as to not bring any disrepute to her husband's family, which was among the elite of the city. She wanted to have children and raise them, but she suffered multiple miscarriages in her quest for a child. Her beloved mother, Mushtari, passed away at this time as well. She fell into a deep depression. Of those days, she would say,

> I gave up everything for him but he could not give up even a little for me; I was not allowed to perform in any program or gathering-I was almost not allowed to sing at all. For a year and a half even, the radio was a distant thought, even humming a tune was impossible for that girl, for whom singing was life. I gave up everything. I looked sick. Even then I didn't realize just how thoroughly song had penetrated my heart. How could I uproot what had spread its tendrils throughout my inner being?[18]

Other conflicting accounts from her disciples say that her husband was rather proud of his talented and renowned wife. Her disciple, Rita Ganguly, says that Begum Akhtar wanted a home, so she didn't sing for a long period. After her miscarriages, she went back to singing. To quote Ganguly, 'Contrary to popular media perception, her marriage with Nawab of Kakori, Ishtiaq Ahmed Abbasi, wasn't an unhappy one. It wasn't friendship that they shared. He was more like her guardian. A great scholar himself, he would explain poetry to her. Ammi had innate intelligence. She wasn't academically very qualified but was intellectually very bright.' Her student Shanti Hiranand was quoted as saying, 'She wanted respectability but never forgot her courtesan roots. She always saw upper class women as being better than she was.'[19]

She was keen to be accepted into the closed inner circles

of upper-class society. Her marriage to a nobleman from a land-owning family helped her do just that. To quote Kidwai from an article, 'And when she met them, she charmed everybody.' It was a marriage that also helped Akhtar escape from the control of her mother. To quote Mehru Jaffer from an article in the *Women's Feature Service,* 'Akhtari Bai managed to escape the matriarchal hold by arranging a marriage for herself into high society. She did this knowing that the price of respectability was a life in purdah, giving up the arts and individual freedom.'[20]

She made her first AIR recording in 1948, as Akhtar Ishtiaq and not as Akhtaribai. In her singing comeback, she sang three ghazals and a dadra at the AIR station in Lucknow, and was so overwhelmed with emotion that she broke down and cried when she finished recording. She then returned to singing in public concerts, and sang right until the time she passed away.

Often, she would come home and break down after a major performance and sob uncontrollably. She would never perform in Lucknow in deference to her status as the wife of a barrister, but in 1962, she sang at a women's only concert in Lucknow in order to raise funds for the war against China. It was now, in this phase of her career, that she began singing verses from renowned poets. She moved from the private *mehfils* where she would sing earlier to public performances. She also sang on AIR, which helped carry her voice to millions across the country, and made her a phenomenon.

According to Regula Qureshi, Begum Akhtar 'epitomized (Lucknow's) feudal high culture both in her music and poetry, but also in her speech and manners, as well as her personal style. Her entire persona evoked a nostalgic, feudal Lucknow.'[21]

With time and maturity, the timbre of her voice changed—it became deeper, richer. She came to be known for her own inimitable style. A regular performer on AIR, she has over 400 songs to her name. She composed her own ghazals, which were based on classical *ragas*. Her voice brought to life the exquisite words of great poets like Mirza Ghalib, Kaifi Azmi, Shakil Badayuni, Mir Taqi Mir and Jigar Moradabadi. To quote Saleem Kidwai, 'There came a time when every poet, expert or novice, yearned for Begum Akhtar to sing his creation. With complete command over her musical idiom, she inflected nuances into the love poems that might have surprised and delighted the poets themselves.'[22]

This is a sentiment that is echoed by Yatindra Mishra as well. To quote him from his book *Akhtari: The Life and Times of Begum Akhtar*:

> Begum Akhtar attained unparalleled success with her lilting voice, and the unique way of singing in a fast tempo. Her voice was so imbued with pathos and rhythm that at one time the pain in her voice echoed the pain of every listener. Anyone who had suffered heartbreak and betrayal in life found refuge in Begum's voice. [...] It remains an example as well as a milestone in the history of music. Be it the ghazals of Shakeel Badayuni and Jigar Moradabadi or those of novice poets like Sudarshan Faakir, Begum Akhtar added value to their words with her voice.[23]

It was the magic of her voice that made Pandit Jasraj become a singer when he was barely six, and her singing that made Agha Shahid Ali turn to poetry. He had met her when he was a teenager and would attend her concerts and record her with a tape recorder. It was his intense study of the nuances in her singing that Ali used in his poems and ghazals.[24]

In the documentary *Hai Akhtari!* made by the critic S. Kalidas, Sheila Dhar states that Begum Akhtar had a remarkable ability to create complex musicality from what had hitherto been perceived as a limited space of the thumri and the ghazal, infusing her music with the panache of her own captivating personality.

In fact, she was the only singer or musician who was given

the permission to smoke in the AIR recording studios. Rita Ganguly writes in her book, *Ae Mohabbat...Reminiscing Begum Akhtar*, that her *taseer* (soulful sound) came from a lifetime of 'loneliness, pain, suppression and silence'. According to vocalist Shruti Sadolikar, Begum Akhtar had said, 'It is important to have that pain inside you. When that pain is a part of you, you can convey whatever you want, and it will be effective. It is with pain that music is enriched.'[25]

To quote Ganguly, 'Her forte was not necessarily the audibility of her music, for she had a defective area where her voice cracked at a high-pitch, with a limited one-octave range, but she turned it into her virtue for she knew how to mould her voice.'[26] Of her voice, the shehnai maestro Bismillah Khan said, 'Her voice was flawed. But that was the beauty of it. I would wait patiently for her voice to crack as she approached the higher notes and when it came, I would exclaim, "Wah! This is what I wanted to hear!"'[27]

In the preface to her book, Rita Ganguly says, quoting a psychiatrist, that the unresolved abandonment and early trauma that Akhtar experienced manifested in a lifetime of melancholy. She was always worrying about what was the worst that could happen at any given moment, thinking, '*Ya Allah, ab kya hoga* (Oh god, what next)?' Ganguly states that Begum Akhtar smoked cigarettes and drank whiskey, unconcerned about the effect on her voice. She had given up drinking for two years after coming back from Hajj, but had started again later. She was a devotee of Lord Krishna, and loved a simple meal with *arhar dal*. She was also lonely, and she hated coming back to an empty hotel room after a performance.

She broke barriers that female singers had been up against for centuries. She formalized the *guru-shishya* relationship with her students. She did so by tying the *ganda* (sacred thread) in a *ganda-bandh* ceremony on two of her students, Shanti Hiranand and Anjali Banerjee. This was yet another bastion broken by a female musician in the Hindustani classical music tradition. As the classical music world was conservative and male-dominated, this ceremony had hitherto been considered the prerogative of male musicians.[28] She followed the guru–shishya *parampara* under which she herself had been trained.

She did not take any fee from her students, and also taught at the Bhatkhande College of Music in Lucknow.[29] She was an unpredictable teacher, according to her disciple, Shanti Hiranand. According to Shanti, 'Her methods were unorthodox. There were no fixed hours. She sang as and when the muse beckoned. She would sing for hours together and told me to learn by listening. Sometimes if I got a note wrong she would threaten to throw the harmonium at me! And yet she was the most loving, generous ustad one could have.'[30]

She also defied norms in other ways. She had the generosity of spirit that one normally associates with those born into immense wealth. In an unprecedented gesture, when Raza Ali Khan, the Nawab of Rampur, who was besotted with her and wanted to marry her, visited her at her home, she gifted all her furniture to his courtiers and her expensive new car to his son. It was a reversal of the norm where rich patrons showered gifts on a courtesan. The courtesan here was showering gifts on the entourage of a rich patron. When she left Faizabad in the 1930s, she returned the 50-odd acres that the ruler of Faizabad had gifted her. When the ruler of Bauri admired a mirror in her house, she is said to have promptly gifted it to him.

She lived like a queen. To quote her foremost disciple, Shanti Hiranand, 'Begum Akhtar was different from her peers, her thinking, her style set her apart. She wasn't even educated. Yet she had what you call the "sharifana" blood... she would fit into any society. She would just live like a queen.'[31] She had an innate refinement in the little things that belied her humble origins. She wore Lucknowi chikan sarees at home, but draped herself in the most elegant silks for her performances, with her diamond nose pin sparkling and her lips painted red. She noted little lapses of grace. According to Sheila Dhar, she was terribly insulted when once a concert organizer gracelessly handed over notes as her fee without even the courtesy of putting them in an envelope.

She was a performer who could mesmerize the audience. Poet Kaifi Azmi said of her, 'When in an audience with Begum Akhtar, you not only get to hear ghazals but also to see one.'[32]

She became a pioneer by taking the thumri and dadra to the common man through public concerts, breaking out of the *kotha*. She brought respectability and public acceptance to these forms of singing. She sang for Vilayat Khan in Satyajit Ray's *Jalshagar*; she was cutting LPs of Ghalib as well as of contemporary poets, bridging the gap between Urdu poetry and music. She soon towered over the ghazal, the thumri, the dadra and overtook the legacy set by greats like Gauhar Jaan, Jaddan Bai and Benazir Bai.

To quote the noted critic Raghava Menon on what made her an icon:

> Akhtar was constantly caught up in a male-dominated world. She could never escape, even in the middle class, for there were inescapable social stigmas. But, it seems to me, she had an understanding of the predicament of the human being, and she used her life as a source of understanding of the masses who have looked for things, searched for things, gone on a journey to discover things and, in some cases, come back empty handed, finally realising that the important thing is the journey. She seemed like that to me. She was a remarkable, highly evolved woman.[33]

To quote Sheila Dhar on Akhtari, 'Akhtari Bai sang the ghazal with such insight and sensitivity she created a new area where poetry and music were simultaneously enhanced. She flowered into almost a cult figure, an ideal figure invested with such charm and charisma, an entire generation of women passionately wished to emulate her.'[34]

Her fan following spanned the gamut of society—from poets and writers to cricketers, business tycoons, politicians and the ordinary citizens of India. Not everyone would be familiar with the nuances of the verses she sang, but her enthralling voice, with the curious break in it, her style of performing and the way she was infused with verse and poetry made her a legend.

As she neared 60, her heart began troubling her, and she suffered from heart attacks. In a concert in 1974, she felt her singing had not been up to the mark and tried to raise the pitch of her voice. This effort resulted in undue stress on her already fragile system. She suffered her third heart attack on 26 October 1974 during a concert in Ahmedabad; and on 30 October 1974 she died in Ahmedabad itself.[35] Barely eight days before she passed away, she had recorded a ghazal by Kaifi Azmi which has now become iconic, and is forever associated with her soulful voice, '*Sunaa karo merii jaan un se un ke afsaane, sab ajanabi hain yahaan kaun kis ko pehchaane...*'

The day she died, Agha Shahid Ali was in New Delhi along with Saleem Kidwai. He recalled, 'From the airport we decided to come to Lucknow. I think the ticket was 300-400 rupees. We had to borrow the money so that we could join the funeral.' They stayed up all night, and Ali wrote an elegy to her that very night, later published as 'In Memory of Begum Akhtar'.[36]

She was interred in a mango orchard in her home, Pasand Bagh, in the Thakurganj locality in Lucknow, next to her beloved mother. She was mourned by all who loved her—from the rickshaw pullers in her city to the nobility who gave her patronage. Composer Madan Mohan is said to have sobbed at her grave. Anecdotally, it is believed that a devout listener went about inscribing the walls of old Lucknow with the words '*Hai Akhtari*' the night she died.

Over the years, her grave had been long neglected, the

garden had been taken over by the encroaching city and the tomb had fallen into disrepair. In 2014, it was restored by Shanti Hirandand and Saleem Kidwai, among others, along with the Sanatkada Trust, a non-profit run by Madhavi Kukreja. The architect Ashish Thapar restored the original pietra dura work on both graves. The graves are now enclosed in a red-brick enclosure. There are efforts to turn her home in China Bazaar, Lucknow into a museum. On her birth anniversary every year, there is a performance of her most well-known songs there.[37]

On her 103rd birthday, 7 October 2017, Google dedicated a doodle to commemorate her life and works. One of her foremost disciples, Shanti Hiranand, who was later awarded the Padma Shri, wrote a biography on her, titled, *Begum Akhtar: The Story of My Ammi*. She was awarded the Sangeet Natak Akademi Award in 1972 and the Padma Shri in 1968. The Government of India awarded her the Padma Bhushan posthumously.

But at the end of it all, after all the books and documentaries, can one really know who Akhtari was? Robert Charles Ollikkala, academician and researcher, wrote, 'Who Akhtari Bai really was, an individual separated from any specific role or combination of roles, will always remain something of a mystery.'[38] While there were thousands of singers in the times she lived in, the one thing everyone—whether a connoisseur, an academician or just a music lover—agrees upon is that Akhtari was unique, one of a kind, imbued with a magic that mesmerized her listeners.

And when she passed away, something precious and irretrievable was lost to us forever. In the elegy Agha Shahid Ali wrote to her, we get a sense of the unfathomable bereavement that assails all those who knew her, as well as those who just know her by her voice:

Ghazal, that death-sustaining widow,
sobs in dingy archives, hooked to you.
She wears her grief, a moon-soaked white,
corners the sky into disbelief.[39]

NOTES

1 'Remembering Begum Akhtar', *DailyExcelsior.com*, 2 November 2014, http://tinyurl.com/2kz92952. Accessed on 4 January 2024.

2 Singh, Anisha, 'Begum Akhtar as a Student and a Teacher', *NDTV*, 7 October 2017, http://tinyurl.com/2v2b866k. Accessed on 4 January 2024.

3 '"Loneliness Was Begum Akhtar's Constant Companion"', *The Telegraph Online*, 5 October 2013, http://tinyurl.com/5n785ed7. Accessed on 4 January 2024.

4 'Akhtaribai Faizabadi', *Begum Akhtar Centenary*, http://tinyurl.com/fhfdpy5z. Accessed on 4 January 2024.

5 '"Loneliness Was Begum Akhtar's Constant Companion"', *The Telegraph Online*, 5 October 2013, http://tinyurl.com/5n785ed7. Accessed on 4 January 2024.

6 Bhardwaj, Aditi, 'Begum Akhtar: A Glance into the Music and Life of the "Mallika-E-Ghazal"', *Feminism in India*, 28 October 2022, http://tinyurl.com/4ydvkw2z. Accessed on 4 January 2024.

7 '"Loneliness Was Begum Akhtar's Constant Companion"', *The Telegraph Online*, 5 October 2013, http://tinyurl.com/5n785ed7. Accessed on 4 January 2024.

8 'Akhtaribai Faizabadi', *Begum Akhtar Centenary*, http://tinyurl.com/fhfdpy5z. Accessed on 4 January 2024; Ramani, Priya, 'What a Life,' *mint*, 7 November 2008, http://tinyurl.com/43dncm7v. Accessed on 15 January 2024.

9 'The Lonely Ghazal Queen: Begum Akhtar', *Songs of Yore*, 7 October 2014, http://tinyurl.com/5n7d4dh5. Accessed on 4 January 2024.

10 'Akhtaribai Faizabadi', *Begum Akhtar Centenary*, http://tinyurl.com/fhfdpy5z. Accessed on 4 January 2024.

11 Ibid.

12 Bhardwaj, Aditi, 'Begum Akhtar: A Glance into the Music and

Life of the "Mallika-E-Ghazal"', *Feminism in India*, 28 October 2022, http://tinyurl.com/4ydvkw2z. Accessed on 4 January 2024.

13 Sathya Saran, 'Music Recall. Begum Akhtar: The Legend and the Woman', *The Hindu businessline*, 25 May 2021, http://tinyurl.com/sb387vdb. Accessed on 9 January 2024.

14 Khanna, Anshu, 'It Was Ayodhya's Honour That It Hosted Begum Akhtar's Art: Yatindra Mishra', *The Daily Guardian*, 23 July 2021, http://tinyurl.com/2yp87kat. Accessed on 4 January 2024.

15 Khanna, Shailaja, 'Enduring Legacy of Begum Akhtar', *The Tribune*, 2 May 2021, http://tinyurl.com/u8jmt4pm. Accessed on 4 January 2024.

16 Burckhardt Qureshi, Regula, 'In Search of Begum Akhtar: Patriarchy, Poetry, and Twentieth-Century Indian Music', *The World of Music*, Vol. 52, No. 1/3, 2010, pp. 347–86, http://tinyurl.com/2p9kmy8u. Accessed on 4 January 2024.

17 Bhardwaj, Aditi, 'Begum Akhtar: A Glance into the Music and Life of the "Mallika-E-Ghazal"', *Feminism in India*, 28 October 2022, http://tinyurl.com/4ydvkw2z. Accessed on 4 January 2024.

18 'Akhtaribai Faizabadi', *Begum Akhtar Centenary*, http://tinyurl.com/fhfdpy5z. Accessed on 4 January 2024.

19 Bhardwaj, Aditi, 'Begum Akhtar: A Glance into the Music and Life of the "Mallika-E-Ghazal"', *Feminism in India*, 28 October 2022, http://tinyurl.com/4ydvkw2z. Accessed on 4 January 2024; '"Loneliness Was Begum Akhtar's Constant Companion"', *The Telegraph Online*, 5 October 2013, http://tinyurl.com/5n785ed7. Accessed on 4 January 2024.

20 Wangchuk, Rinchen Norbu, 'Begum Akhtar, the Queen of Ghazals Who Turned Her Pain into Soul-Stirring Music', *thebetterindia*, 7 October 2019, http://tinyurl.com/2nwwvwj3. Accessed on 4 January 2024.

21 Burckhardt Qureshi, Regula, 'In Search of Begum Akhtar: Patriarchy, Poetry, and Twentieth-Century Indian Music',

The World of Music, Vol. 52, No. 1/3, 2010, pp. 347–86, http://tinyurl.com/2p9kmy8u. Accessed on 4 January 2024.

22 'Enduring Legacy of Begum Akhtar', *The Tribune*, 2 May 2021, http://tinyurl.com/u8jmt4pm. Accessed on 4 January 2024.

23 Mishra, Yatindra (ed.), *Akhtari: The Life and Music of Begum Akhtar*, Maneesha Taneja (trans.), HarperCollins Publishers India, 2021.

24 Kapoor, Manan, 'How the Legendary Begum Akhtar Influenced the Life and Poetry of Agha Shahid Ali', *DAWN*, 19 June 2019, http://tinyurl.com/mwh2ua49. Accessed on 4 January 2024.

25 Ganguly, Rita, and Jyoti Sabarwal, *Ae Mohabbat...Reminiscing Begum Akhtar*, Stellar Publishers, 2008; 'Enduring Legacy of Begum Akhtar', *The Tribune*, 2 May 2021, http://tinyurl.com/u8jmt4pm. Accessed on 4 January 2024.

26 Chakraborty, Debdutta, 'Her Lips Painted Red, Ghazal Queen Begum Akhtar Sang with a "Pain in Her Voice"', *ThePrint*, 7 October 2022, http://tinyurl.com/ep6k82fj. Accessed on 4 January 2024.

27 'Remembering Mallika-E-Ghazal Begum Akhtar Ahead of Her 102nd Birth Anniversary', *The Economic Times, Panache*, 1 October 2016, http://tinyurl.com/35shc44f. Accessed on 4 January 2024.

28 Chakraborty, Debdutta, 'Her Lips Painted Red, Ghazal Queen Begum Akhtar Sang with a "Pain in Her Voice"', *ThePrint*, 7 October 2022, http://tinyurl.com/ep6k82fj. Accessed on 4 January 2024.

29 Singh, Anisha, 'Begum Akhtar as a Student and a Teacher', *NDTV*, 7 October 2017, http://tinyurl.com/2v2b866k. Accessed on 4 January 2024.

30 'Remembering Mallika-E-Ghazal Begum Akhtar Ahead of Her 102nd Birth Anniversary', *The Economic Times, Panache*, 1 October 2016, http://tinyurl.com/35shc44f. Accessed on 4 January 2024.

31 Bhatia, Bhavita, 'In Memory of Begum Akhtar', *The Times of India,* 16 January 2011, http://tinyurl.com/435y32dh. Accessed on 4 January 2024.

32 Kapoor, Manan, 'How the Legendary Begum Akhtar Influenced the Life and Poetry of Agha Shahid Ali', *DAWN,* 19 June 2019, http://tinyurl.com/mwh2ua49. Accessed on 4 January 2024.

33 Wangchuk, Rinchen Norbu, 'Begum Akhtar, the Queen of Ghazals Who Turned Her Pain into Soul-Stirring Music', *thebetterindia,* 7 October 2019, http://tinyurl.com/2nwwvwj3. Accessed on 4 January 2024.

34 'Enduring Legacy of Begum Akhtar', *The Tribune,* 2 May 2021, http://tinyurl.com/u8jmt4pm. Accessed on 4 January 2024.

35 'The Lonely Ghazal Queen: Begum Akhtar', *Songs of Yore,* 7 October 2014, http://tinyurl.com/5n7d4dh5. Accessed on 4 January 2024.

36 Kapoor, Manan, 'How the Legendary Begum Akhtar Influenced the Life and Poetry of Agha Shahid Ali', *DAWN,* 19 June 2019, http://tinyurl.com/mwh2ua49. Accessed on 4 January 2024.

37 Chakraborty, Tapas, 'Tomb Tribute to Begum Akhtar - No Hitch in Grave Renovation despite Faizabad Clashes', *The Telegraph online,* 30 October 2012, http://tinyurl.com/wsj5jnnn. Accessed on 17 January 2024.

38 Bhardwaj, Aditi, 'Begum Akhtar: A Glance into the Music and Life of the "Mallika-E-Ghazal"', *Feminism in India,* 28 October 2022, http://tinyurl.com/4ydvkw2z. Accessed on 4 January 2024.

39 Gupta, Anukriti, 'Agha Shahid Ali's "In Memory of Begum Akhtar"', *Zikr-e-Dilli,* 6 March 2021, http://tinyurl.com/2s3bck4t. Accessed on 17 January 2024.

13

CORNELIA SORABJI

LADY LAWYER

There is a bust of Cornelia Sorabji at the Great Hall in Lincoln's Inn, London. Her expression is firm, even formidable as she no doubt was, and her head is draped. Unveiled in May 2012 by Baroness Brenda Hale, the bust of Cornelia Sorabji is a tribute to her spirit that helped her overcome the many blocks that came her way, merely because of her gender.[1] The bust was an honour she had earned. It was made by S. Unavane, and was presented to the Inn by Dr Kusoom Vadgama.[2] Indian lawyer, social reformer and writer—Cornelia Sorabji had many firsts to her name. She was the first female graduate from Bombay University, and the first woman to study law at University of Oxford. This also made her the first Indian woman to study law abroad. And this bust, installed at the Great Hall in Lincoln's Inn, commemorates all that.

Born on 15 November 1866 in Nashik, in what was then called the Bombay Presidency in British India, she was named in honour of Lady Cornelia Maria Darling Ford, her adoptive grandmother. She was the fifth daughter out of nine children. Her father was Reverend Sorabji Karsedji, a Christian missionary who had converted to Christianity from Zoroastrianism. Her mother, Francina Ford, was formerly Hindu, from the Toda tribe in Tamil Nadu, and had been adopted at the age of 12 by an aristocratic English couple living in India. Francina, who sowed the seeds of social work early in young Cornelia's mind, had established many girls' schools in Poona (now Pune), and worked towards the upliftment of the underprivileged. In her later years, Cornelia stated that her mother had been a major influence in her social activism.[3] Religion was not a major part of Cornelia's life; she barely wrote about it in her books, apart from describing Parsi rituals. Her autobiographic writing did not talk about religious conversion either.

Among her siblings were the educator and missionary Susie Sorabji and the doctor Alice Maude Sorabji Pennell. Two of her brothers passed away while still infants. While the family dressed according to and followed Parsi cultural practices and spoke Gujarati, they followed the Christian faith and the children were raised with British customs. Cornelia's early childhood was spent in Belgaum, and they then moved to Poona. She was at first homeschooled and then went to missionary schools. Her parents were visionaries, and they encouraged all their daughters to apply to Bombay University. However, their applications were consistently rejected as women were not allowed admission. This led to her father eloquently persuading the college authorities to consider accepting female students. It was with Cornelia that he was finally successful.[4] She was admitted into Deccan College, where she pursued literature, and, astoundingly, graduated at the top of her batch. It was a phenomenal achievement by any standard.[5] She had become the first woman to graduate from Bombay University, with a first-class degree in literature.

However, as she was a female student, she was denied the Oxford scholarship that was usually given to the top student of the year. There was no provision for a woman to avail of the scholarship, as it was traditionally only given to men. Cornelia was outraged at this denial of what she had earned through her hard work and innate ability, and refused to give up. She took up a teaching position at a men's college in Gujarat, where she worked for two years. Simultaneously, she kept trying to get the scholarship due to her, by writing to all those she thought would be able to help. In 1888, she wrote to the National Indian Association requesting them to help her get her further qualifications. Mary Hobhouse was instrumental in helping her raise funds. Adelaide Manning, Florence Nightingale, Sir William Wedderburn and Madeleine Shaw Lefevre, among others, contributed to help fund Cornelia's education in England.

To quote from a letter Mary Hobhouse wrote pleading Cornelia's case:

> Miss Sorabji is very desirous to come to England and to pass the examination requisite to gain an Oxford or a Cambridge degree (the degree itself being as yet not granted to womenkind) since this would be a great advantage to her in her destined career in India. Difficulties, chiefly of a pecuniary character, prevent her at present from following this course, and unless an opening or a friend should arise she means to prepare to take the MA degree at the Bombay University, with a view to continuing the useful work of teaching and of helping her countrywomen directly and indirectly by the stimulus of her example. The thought that perhaps others, like myself, may feel interested in watching Miss Sorabji's courageous course must be my excuse for troubling you with this letter.[6]

The issue of her being denied a scholarship became a raging debate in the House of Commons. Sir John Kennaway raised a question asking if a woman in the British Raj was being denied a scholarship to an English university merely because of her gender, and the Secretary of State for India confirmed it.[7]

In 1889, she arrived in England and the Hobhouses' saw Cornelia regularly, encouraging her to take up the legal line rather than medicine, as she had originally envisaged. When she arrived in England, she was hosted by Elizabeth Adelaide Manning, secretary of the National Indian Association, whom

Cornelia had met on the former's visit to India in January of that year.[8] In 1892, she received special permission by Congregational Decree (influenced by the petitions submitted by her supporters in England) to take the postgraduate Bachelor of Civil Law (BCL) exam at Somerville College, Oxford, and thus became the first ever woman to take this exam.[9] Interestingly, she wasn't encouraged to take law. She was told she needed to choose English literature as her subject but she remained adamant. She had come to England to study law and so she would. The academic and philosopher Benjamin Jowett intervened and made a special law course for her to read.[10]

Lord Hobhouse, whose wife was one of those who had funded her scholarship, got her permission to read in the library at Lincoln's Inn; something that was hitherto not permitted to women. She was then admitted as a reader to the Codrington Library of All Souls College, Oxford, owing to Sir William Anson's invitation in 1890. With this, she became the first woman reader at Oxford.[11]

Back then, female students needed to be chaperoned to their lectures. Cornelia was asked to sit alone at her college for her exams, supervised by the warden, and not with the other male students taking their exam. The examiner refused to assess a female student, and Cornelia argued against this because she felt that in later years, her degree might not count. Her appeal was taken into consideration and the university made special arrangements, permitting her to take the exams with the male students.[12]

While she was at Oxford, she became acquainted with renowned Indologists and Sanskrit scholars like Max Müller and Sir Monier-Williams. Interestingly, she also became great friends with Florence Nightingale, who had earlier contributed to the effort to bring her to Oxford. She began working at a solicitor's firm called Lee & Pemberton in London.[13] She cleared her BCL exam while practising at the solicitor's office. She was very fond of her college and her stay at Oxford. She wrote to her mother, saying, 'Next to home there is no place like Somerville.'[14]

There's an anecdote about this exam. On the eve of her BCL exams in 1892, she dreamt that an elderly man had stopped her as she entered a graveyard, and told her, 'Go elsewhere. You cannot be buried here.' Benjamin Jowett, the then Master of Balliol and vice chancellor, was her mentor. He introduced a resolution in Congregation which allowed her to sit for the BCL exams with the other students in the examination schools. She passed the BCL exams. To quote Benjamin Jowett, 'My big responsibilities, as you call them, didn't blind me to the fact that a young woman, seeking to train as a lawyer to fit herself to help her fellow country-women in difficulties was something very important indeed. It was a sign of something big. An omen perhaps too.'[15]

She became the first woman to pass the BCL examination in 1892 from Somerville, Oxford. However, she was not granted the degree, as no woman was allowed to register as an advocate. This was a postgraduate degree, normally taken by barristers and undergraduates in London who had a minimum five years of training, and Cornelia had cracked it in two years. Despite passing the exam, she could not collect her degree for the next 30 years, as such were the rules for women.[16] At Oxford, she held the record for being the first woman student from India to study at any British university. So, even though Cornelia was technically the first woman to study law in England, she was not allowed to enrol at the Bar until 1923.[17]

She returned to India in 1894, hoping to find a legal post. However, this proved to be a long and fruitless search. With the Chief Justice of Bombay passing an order instructing legal practitioners to not employ women, her hopes of working as a solicitor were dashed.[18] Nonetheless, she found a cause to occupy herself with—a cause that she felt passionately about, namely that of helping the women known as *purdah nashins*.

This referred to veiled women of a particular elite segment of society who were not permitted to step out into the world and interact with men outside their family. These women had no way to fight their legal battles and get the rights due to them.

Many of these women, while very wealthy, were not educated. They were not allowed to speak to any male, so they had no access to lawyers who could fight their cases for them. Cornelia worked on these cases as a solicitor, preparing cases for the purdah nashin women from many princely states. She asked for and received special permission to enter pleas on behalf of these women before the British agents of the princely states of Kathiawar and Indore, but her law degree held no standing in Indian courts and she could not fight their cases.

She decided to rectify that and presented herself for the LLB examination of the Bombay University in 1897, and the pleader's examination of the Allahabad High Court in 1899, making her the first female advocate in India. Nonetheless, despite qualifying, she could still not practice in court. However, she fought for the purdah nashins to be allowed to learn teaching and nursing, which helped them get out of the confines of the home and earn an independent living.

For a short while, she worked with her younger brother in his law firm, based in Allahabad. She could not get the designation of a barrister until 1923, when the law was changed to include women. Earlier in 1902, she had decided to make a position for herself, and requested the India Office to appoint her as the female legal advisor for women and minors in the provincial courts. In 1904, she was appointed lady assistant to the Court of Wards in Bengal—a responsibility that was later extended to Bihar, Orissa (now Odisha) and Assam as well. Over the next 20 years, she helped an estimated 600 women and orphans in their legal battles, often pro bono.[19] In her book, *Between the Twilights*, and the two autobiographies she wrote, she talked about some of these cases. She began practicing in Calcutta (now Kolkata) but still could not plead her cases in court. She was restricted to preparing her opinions on cases.

Oxford began awarding degrees to women in 1920, and the London Bar allowed women with law degrees to practice. After all these years, Cornelia travelled to England to collect her degree, and was called to the Bar in 1922. She returned to Calcutta in 1924 and was enrolled as a barrister in the High Court there. With this, she became the first woman to practice law in India.[20]

She had a strong social conscience and was part of many social service campaigning groups like the National Council for Women in India, the Federation of University Women and the Bengal League of Social Service for Women. She was a cautious social reformer for Indian women and did not believe that the Western model could be directly transposed to the Indian situation.

She was awarded the Kaisar-i-Hind Gold Medal in 1909 for her service to the nation.[21] An Anglophile to the core, she was against the self-governance movement that had gathered momentum, although she had initially supported the campaign for Indian independence. A supporter of Indian traditional values, she nonetheless was against the practice of child marriage and Sati, and pushed for a change in the laws allowing these. Her focus was completely on educating women, because she believed that without education, women would not be informed supporters and advocates of social change and the Suffragette Movement. She worked extensively with Pandita Ramabai, the renowned social activist of Maharashtra.

By 1927, she began promoting the support for British rule. She supported the American author, Katherine Mayo, who defended British rule in India in her book *Mother India*.[22] Cornelia was fiercely against the Civil Disobedience Movement, travelling across India and the United States to promote her views. This cost her public support for her cause of educating and empowering women. Her initiatives in the space of social welfare bore the fallout from this loss of support. One of the projects that was impacted was the League for Infant Welfare, Maternity and District Nursing. She gave up her practice in 1929 and devoted her time entirely to social work. In 1931, she moved to England and permanently settled there, visiting India only during winters.

In 1932, she had a widely reported public spat with Gandhi ji while he was attending the Round Table Conference in London. She had met him to interview him for a British journal but the interview had to be truncated when they got into an altercation. This was widely reported in the media in India and Britain.

According to Pallavi Rastogi, in her review of Cornelia's autobiography, *India Calling,* Cornelia's life was 'fraught with contradictions'. The historian Geraldine Forbes said that Cornelia's stand on nationalism and feminism 'caused historians to neglect the role she played in giving credibility to the British critique of those educated women who were now part of the political landscape'. Interestingly, Sorabji was a close friend of the poet laureate Alfred Lord Tennyson and read his elegiac poem 'Crossing the Bar' at the poet's funeral in Westminster Abbey.[23]

She was a prolific writer, authoring many works, two of them autobiographical: *India Calling: The Memories of Cornelia Sorabji* and *India Recalled.* She also served as the editor of *Queen Mary's Book for India* and contributed to a number of periodicals, including *The Asiatic Review, The Times Literary Supplement, Atlantic Monthly, Macmillan's Magazine, The Statesman* and *The Times.*

She retired from the High Court in 1929. She died when she was 87, on 6 July 1954, in her Northumberland house in London.[24] Along with the bust unveiled at Lincoln's Inn, London in 2012, there is also a large portrait of Cornelia in the prestigious National Portrait Gallery in London. In 2017, Google Doodle celebrated her 151st birthday on 15 November by making a doodle for her. In 2016, Somerville and University of Oxford launched the Cornelia Sorabji Graduate Scholarship Programme for students from India who were passionate about leading societal change upon returning to India.[25]

She wore her clothes distinctively, perhaps calling upon the hybrid culture and ancestry she came from. In her 1934 autobiography, *India Calling,* she begins with the clothing clause of the seventh-century treaty that came into place when the Parsis came to India. Dressing differently signified 'visible apartness', she wrote. The Parsis were not allowed to dress in the Persian manner, and so the women wore sarees to integrate into the Indian culture they'd settled in. They draped it differently, over the right ear and tucked behind the left, to signify their difference. She wore her sarees similarly, over a thousand years later, in a self-imposed dress code.[26]

To quote Dr Antoinette Burton, specialist in colonial India and professor at the University of Illinois (Chicago), Cornelia's 'letters and diaries are filled with struggles over what to wear'. A saree or a dress; whether to dress to fit in or stand out. Sartorial choices were important to her and her photographs show a woman who took great pride in her appearance. She distanced herself from the feminists of the day because she was uncomfortable with how they dressed in a masculine fashion. She wrote in a letter, 'What comes of trying to appropriate a sex not one's own?'[27]

Another anecdote is about her travels to Italy in the early 1980s, where the custom officials thought her sarees were silks for sale. She wrote in her book that they refused to let her clear the customs unless she 'undress and dress before them'. She says, 'We went into the Customs shed—one pull and my draperies were at my feet ... how we laughed at their faces! ... everything was free, and they were most apologetic.'[28]

There was this constant sense of being the 'other', not completely accepted anywhere she went. She expressed her otherness in her sartorial choices that integrated all facets of who she was.[29] Historian Cynthia Green writes of her, saying:

> Sorabji knew that wherever she went she was the 'other'. In England, she was Indian. In India, she was a minority. She was a mixture that floated across colonial boundaries without belonging to either side. Considering this, it's not surprising that Sorabji became known for her work representing Hindu and Muslim segregated women (*zenani* and *purdahnashins* or women restricted to the inner chambers of their homes), or that she returned so frequently to England, or that she chose to dress in sarees and long, dangling necklaces.[30]

Perhaps, it would be appropriate to end this chapter with her own words, using the metaphor of life as woven cloth, to speak about her life: 'Scraps of silk and wool and cotton—bits of colour, glowing or dull, snipped off too soon, or never taken into use...But there is no re-weaving it now.'[31]

NOTES

1 'Cornelia Sorabji', *Somerville, University of Oxford*, http://tinyurl.com/yf69euy5. Accessed on 4 January 2024.

2 'July 2018 – Cornelia Sorabji', *The Honourable Society of Lincoln's Inn*, 27 July 2018, http://tinyurl.com/bdhdmcnp. Accessed on 4 January 2024.

3 Prasad, Akshita, 'Cornelia Sorabji: India and Britain's First Female Attorney | #Indianwomeninhistory', *Feminism in India*, 8 March 2018, http://tinyurl.com/2kc98svp. Accessed on 4 January 2024.

4 Ibid.

5 Bagchi, Dishha, 'Helped by Florence Nightingale, Cornelia Sorabji Became India's 1st Woman Lawyer at Oxford', *ThePrint*, 15 November 2022, http://tinyurl.com/39spap6k. Accessed on 4 January 2024.

6 'Sorabji', *The Open University*, http://tinyurl.com/55ayzss8. Accessed on 4 January 2024.

7 Aranha, Jovita, 'Here's How India's First Woman Lawyer, Cornelia Sorabji Opened Law for Women in 1924!', *thebetterindia*, 16 September 2017, http://tinyurl.com/dputdfrz. Accessed on 12 January 2024.

8 'Cornelia Sorabji', *The Open University*, http://tinyurl.com/8m2mez4a. Accessed on 4 January 2024.

9 Prasad, Akshita, 'Cornelia Sorabji: India and Britain's First Female Attorney | #Indianwomeninhistory', *Feminism in India*, 8 March 2018, http://tinyurl.com/2kc98svp. Accessed on 4 January 2024.

10 Sharma Pant, Nidhi, 'Cornelia Sorabji – Meet India's First Female Lawyer', *POSToast*, 7 August 2019, http://tinyurl.com/5xnhsmnv. Accessed on 4 January 2024.

11 'About: All Souls College Library', *DBPedia*, http://tinyurl.com/ut9dkbtm. Accessed on 4 January 2024.

12 Singh, Anisha, 'Cornelia Sorabji Honored in Google Doodle: Lesser Known Facts and Her Oxford Legacy', *NDTV*, 15 November 2017, http://tinyurl.com/3h62hd34. Accessed on 4 January 2024.

13 Sharma Pant, Nidhi, 'Cornelia Sorabji – Meet India's First Female Lawyer', *POSToast*, 7 August 2019, http://tinyurl.com/5xnhsmnv. Accessed on 4 January 2024.

14 'Alumna: Cornelia Sorabji', *University of Oxford*, http://tinyurl.com/mpdyvbs9. Accessed on 9 January 2024.

15 Ibid.

16 Sharma Pant, Nidhi, 'Cornelia Sorabji – Meet India's First Female Lawyer', *POSToast*, 7 August 2019, http://tinyurl.com/5xnhsmnv. Accessed on 4 January 2024.

17 Ganesan Ram, Sharmila, 'The Veiled History of India's First Woman Lawyer', *The Times of India*, 9 July 2019, http://tinyurl.com/mr46u4kj. Accessed on 4 January 2024.

18 Sharma Pant, Nidhi, 'Cornelia Sorabji – Meet India's First

Female Lawyer', *POSToast*, 7 August 2019, http://tinyurl.com/5xnhsmnv. Accessed on 4 January 2024.

19 Ibid.

20 'Cornelia Sorabji: India's First Woman Lawyer', *National Portrait Gallery*, http://tinyurl.com/4sydretk. Accessed on 17 January 2024.

21 Sharma Pant, Nidhi, 'Cornelia Sorabji – Meet India's First Female Lawyer', *POSToast*, 7 August 2019, http://tinyurl.com/5xnhsmnv. Accessed on 4 January 2024.

22 Ganesan Ram, Sharmila, 'The Veiled History of India's First Woman Lawyer', *The Times of India*, 9 July 2019, http://tinyurl.com/mr46u4kj. Accessed on 4 January 2024.

23 Forbes, Geraldine, *Women in modern India*, Cambridge University Press, 1996; 'Cornelia Sorabji', *Somerville, University of Oxford*, http://tinyurl.com/yf69euy5. Accessed on 4 January 2024.

24 Bagchi, Dishha, 'Helped by Florence Nightingale, Cornelia Sorabji Became India's 1st Woman Lawyer at Oxford', *ThePrint*, 15 November 2022, http://tinyurl.com/39spap6k. Accessed on 4 January 2024.

25 'Cornelia Sorabji', *Somerville, University of Oxford*, http://tinyurl.com/yf69euy5. Accessed on 4 January 2024.

26 Green, Cynthia, 'The Sari Closet of India's First Female Lawyer', *The Voice of Fashion*, 10 June 2019, http://tinyurl.com/2ce4zjx9. Accessed on 4 January 2024.

27 Ibid.

28 Ibid.

29 Ganesan Ram, Sharmila, 'The Veiled History of India's First Woman Lawyer', *The Times of India*, 9 July 2017, http://tinyurl.com/ycy93c3k. Accessed on 4 January 2024.

30 Green, Cynthia, 'The Sari Closet of India's First Female Lawyer', *The Voice of Fashion*, 10 June 2019, http://tinyurl.com/2ce4zjx9. Accessed on 4 January 2024.

31 Ibid.

14

ISMAT CHUGHTAI

WALKING A CROOKED LINE

Short cropped hair; a pair of spectacles over sharp, twinkling eyes; a hearty and quick laugh; and piercing wit—Ismat Chughtai was a legend in the space of the Urdu short story. Novelist, short-story writer, humanist and filmmaker: Ismat Chughtai wore many hats and wore each disarmingly. She began writing in the 1930s, a time of political and creative ferment, and wrote on themes considered daring at the time. She wrote about female sexuality, feminism, middle-class gentility and class conflict viewed through a Marxist lens, written in the style of literary realism.

She came from noble antecedents; the Chughtai clan traced its ancestry back to the Mongol warlord Taimurlane. She was born on 21 August 1915 in Badayun, Uttar Pradesh. Her parents were Nusrat Khanam and Mirza Qaseem Baig Chughtai, and she was the ninth and the youngest child.[1] Her father was a civil servant, and this resulted in her always being on the move in her childhood, thanks to his job transfers. She lived in Jodhpur, Agra and Aligarh as a child. Her sisters were much older than her and were married off when she was still a child. As a result, she grew up in the midst of brothers, which perhaps accounted for her tomboyish nature. To quote her on tomboyishness from one of her fictional stories, 'At my age my other sisters were busy drawing admirers while I fought with any boy or girl I ran into! [...] Amma always disliked my playing with boys. Now tell me, are they man-eaters that they would eat up her darling?'[2]

Competing with her brothers, she would play street football, ride horses, climb trees and defy all set norms at the time for 'good girls' to follow. To quote her, 'I do not think men and women are two different kinds of beings. Even as a child, I always insisted on doing everything that my brothers did.'[3] The family was quite unconventional, in that no topic of discussion was considered taboo. She once said:

> I never had the feeling that, being a woman, I should be shy and nervous. Because of that upbringing, I am this way. And we discussed sex freely; even in those days sex was not a taboo subject for conversation in my house. We freely discussed it. [...]That was a peculiar thing and we were all considered quite mad. Peculiar, mad people![4]

She studied up to the fourth grade in Agra, and then till the eighth grade in Aligarh, when her parents felt she did not need to study further. They instead wanted her to learn to be a good housewife. Ismat had absolutely no intention of being a good housewife. Instead, she threatened her parents that she would run away from the house and join the missionary school. Her father decided to convince her of the need to learn cooking and household chores. As quoted in one of her works:

> 'Women cook food Ismat. When you go to your in-laws what will you feed them?' he asked gently after the crisis was explained to him.
>
> 'If my husband is poor, then we will make khichdi and eat it and if he is rich, we will hire a cook,' I answered.[5]

Her father relented, and she had her way and went on to complete her education. Her brothers had a great influence on her. In her later years, her second-eldest brother, Mirza Azim Beg Chughtai, who was also a novelist, was her mentor. When her father retired from the civil services, the family settled in Agra.

She received her education from the Women's College at the Aligarh Muslim University (AMU), and graduated from the Isabella Thoburn College with a bachelor of arts degree in 1940. She went against her family's wishes and decided to get her bachelor of education (BEd) from AMU.[6] It was at this time, while studying for her BEd, that she became acquainted with the Progressive Writers' Association (PWA). She attended her first meeting in 1936, where she became acquainted with Rashid Jahan, who was, at the time, one of the leading feminist writers in the movement.

Rashid Jahan had a powerful influence on Ismat. It was possibly her influence, along with that of her older brother, that led Ismat to begin writing. Jahan was a formidable woman, with multiple accomplishments. Along with being a qualified doctor, she was also a journalist, a short-story writer and a playwright, who wrote and directed her own theatre and radio plays, as well as adapted the stories of Chekhov, Gorky, James Joyce and Premchand for the radio. Rashid Jahan was one of first women to join the Communist Party of India (CPI) back in the 1930s.[7] She introduced Ismat to the basics of communism. About Jahan's influence on her, Ismat later said, 'Fidelity and beauty, which are considered a woman's virtues; I condemn them. Love is a burden on the heart and nothing else. I learned this from Rashid Aapa.'[8] Rashid Jahan's influence on Ismat's thinking, and, eventually, her writing, was immense. Ismat speaks of it, saying:

> She actually spoiled me. That was what my family used to say. [...] She influenced me a lot; her open-mindedness and free-thinking. She said that whatever you feel, you should not be ashamed of it, nor should you be ashamed of expressing it, for the heart is more sacred than the lips. She said that if you feel a thing in your mind and heart and

> cannot express it, then thinking it is worse and speaking it better, because you can get it out into the open with words.[9]

To quote Ismat on her early writings from a 1972 interview with *Mahfil*, 'When I started writing, there was a trend—writing romantic things or writing like a Progressive. When I started to write, people were very shocked because I wrote very frankly. [...] I didn't write what you'd call "literarily". I wrote and do write as I speak, in a very simple language, not the literary language.'[10]

She first wrote a drama titled *Fasadi* which was published in the Urdu magazine *Saqi* in 1939. It was her first published work.[11] She had been writing since she was 11 or 12 but had never tried to get her work published. Interestingly, when her first work was published, most readers thought it was written by her brother who was already an acclaimed humourist. To quote her, 'In the beginning, people thought these pieces were by my brother, Azim Beg Chughtai, but under a different name. He was also shocked and said "Who's writing in my name and in my style?" Our styles were similar because we were brother and sister.'[12]

Her brother was a mentor to her, and encouraged her to read widely and across Western literature. The Progressive Writers' Movement (PWM) had a profound bearing on her writing. She was fascinated by *Angarey* (an anthology of short stories in Urdu written by members of the PWA). Among her other influences were William Sydney Porter, George Bernard Shaw and Anton Chekhov.

Emboldened by the success of her first work, she began sending her work out for publication to newspapers and magazines. Her early writing included *Bachpan*, an autobiographical work; *Kafir*, which is considered her first short story; and *Dheet*, a soliloquy. In *Lifting the Veil: Selected Writings of Ismat Chughtai*, selected and translated by M. Asaduddin, she says 'Purdah had already been imposed on me, but my tongue was an unsheathed sword. No one could restrain it.'[13]

Reminiscing on her early years, she later wrote: 'I had

studied so much that whenever there was a debate, I would beat to pulp all the young men who were scared of the sight of books. They considered themselves superior to women merely because they were men.'[14] She published *Kalyan* (*Buds*) and *Coten* (*Wounds*), two collections of short stories, in 1941, and 1942 respectively. Her first novella, *Ziddi,* published in 1941, spoke of a romance between a domestic help and her employer's son. The novella was commended for its compelling prose. Her work was compared with that of the American writer Toni Morrison, and was later translated into English and made into a feature film in 1948 with the same title. Her short stories (*Gainda, Khidmatgaar*) and the play *Intikhab* written at this time were very well received.

With her BEd degree under her belt, she joined an Aligarh Girls' School as the principal. She continued to write during her stint at Aligarh. It was while she was there that she met Shaheed Latif, who was then pursuing a master's degree at AMU. Theirs was a stormy romance, but Shaheed moved to Bombay (now Mumbai) and Ismat followed. She moved to Bombay to become an inspector of schools and married Shaheed in a private ceremony in 1942. When Shaheed proposed to her, she replied, 'I am not an ordinary girl. All my life I've cut the chains that fettered me, I won't be able to take up another shackle. Obedience, chastity, and other virtues expected of a woman do not suit me. Lest you repent in the end.' However, Shaheed was persistent, so Ismat relented and accepted his proposal. About her relationship with Shaheed, Ismat later said, 'A man can offer love, respect, and even prostrations to a woman, but he can't give her an equal status; Shahid gave me an equal status.'[15]

Shaheed was already working as a dialogue writer for Hindi cinema at the time. One of the witnesses for the wedding ceremony was Khwaja Ahmed Abbas, the noted director, screenwriter and novelist.

To quote Ismat on love and relationships, 'I consider love to be a very important thing; it's the very strength of heart and mind, but a person should not become stingy in it, one should not become suicidal for its sake. There is an innate bond between love and sex, gone are the days when loved used to be a pious thing.'[16]

It was with her short story, 'Lihaaf' ('The Quilt') that she shot into the limelight. Published in *Adab-i-Latif*, a Lahore-based literary journal in 1942, it was reportedly inspired by the rumoured relationship of a begum with her female masseuse. It chronicled the sexual awakening of the protagonist Begum Jan through a same-sex relationship, given her unfulfilling marriage with a Nawab. The Begum later preys upon a young girl, the narrator, for her sexual needs.

To quote her from an interview:

> When I wrote on this subject, I thought—how stupid of me!—that this was something only women did. I thought that men always went to prostitutes, but because girls can't go to prostitutes, they do this. [...] People started calling me bad names. Nobody knew my address, so they could only write me through my editors.[17]

People critiqued her a lot and ridiculed her family as well. She has talked about how before she got married her editors would refrain from sending the letters to her. However, after her marriage they sent everything across, as they wanted her to act like a responsible person. She said that the things mentioned in the letters scared her, and she never wrote that way again.[18]

The story led to a trial because it depicted female homosexuality, and Ismat was called to the Lahore High Court to defend herself against charges of obscenity. She was accompanied by Saadat Hasan Manto, who was similarly charged with obscenity for his story, 'Bu' ('Odour').

She wrote about her experience at the Lahore Court,

defending herself and Manto in her autobiography, *Kaghazi Hai Pairahan*:

> The Judge called me to his chambers and greeted me very warmly.
>
> 'I've read nearly all your stories and they're not obscene, nor is *Lihaaf* obscene. But there's a lot of dirt in Manto's writing.'
>
> 'The world too is filled with a lot of dirt,' I said meekly.
>
> 'But is it necessary to fling it about?'
>
> 'Flinging it about makes it visible and one's attention can be drawn to the need of cleansing it.'
>
> The Judge Sahib laughed.[19]

Both were exonerated of the charges brought against them. The trial, though, remained her nemesis for the rest of her life. The trial in 1945 made both Ismat and Manto famous. Ismat got a lot of public support, and support from other members of the PWM like Majnun Gorakhpuri and Krishan Chander. She detested the attention the case got her. She would say, '[Lihaaf] brought me so much notoriety that I got sick of life. It became the proverbial stick to beat me with and whatever I wrote afterwards got crushed under its weight.'[20]

She later wrote about her meeting with the woman who inspired *Lihaaf*, saying:

> We stood face to face during a dinner. I felt the ground under my feet receding. She cruised through the crowd, leaped at me and took me in her arms [...] I felt like throwing myself into someone's arms and crying my heart out. She invited me to a fabulous dinner. I felt fully rewarded when I saw her flower-like boy. I felt he was mine as well. A part of my mind, a living product of my brain. An offspring of my pen.[21]

The woman had divorced her husband, remarried and had a child with her second husband. According to Ismat's biographers Sukrita Paul Kumar and Sadique, the meeting between the two women was a kind of closure for Ismat. In the biography, *Ismat: Her Life, Her Times,* they wrote, '[Chughtai] felt greatly rewarded when the begum told [her that Lihaaf] had changed her life and it is because of her story now she was blessed with a child.' In her memoir, Chughtai wrote about the meeting and the emotions she felt about it, saying, '...flowers can be made to bloom among rocks. The only condition is that one has to water the plant with one's heart's blood.'[22]

Chughtai's semi-autobiographical novel, *Tedhi Lakeer* (*The Crooked Line*) was published in 1943. She was pregnant at the time. In a 1972 interview, she speaks about the circumstances she wrote the novel under, saying, '[It was] during the war that I wrote my novel *Tedhi Lakeer,* a big, thick novel. I was sick then, pregnant with my daughter. But I was always writing that novel.'[23]

The book is a chronicle of the lives of Muslims, specifically the women, in the years of the decline of the British Raj. She drew from her lived experiences with the women in her family and those around them, in the neighbourhood. To quote her about her creative process, 'I write about people I know or have known. What should a writer write about anyway?'[24]

In the course of their marriage, Ismat also got a ringside seat to the Hindi film industry, thanks to Shaheed, and began writing scripts. Her debut was *Ziddi,* starring Kamini Kaushal, Pran and Dev Anand. It was Dev Anand's first major role and set him on the road to becoming a star. The film, as mentioned earlier, was based on a similarly-titled short story Ismat had written in 1941. It became a success at the box office.

After *Ziddi,* she wrote dialogue and screenplay for the 1950 movie *Arzoo,* with Kamini Kaushal and Dilip Kumar in the leading roles. She also attempted directing with the 1953 movie, *Fareb,* with a cast comprising Amar, Maya Daas, Kishore Kumar, Lalita Pawar and Zohra Sehgal. This screenplay was also written by her, and was again based on her short stories. She co-directed this film with her husband. Both movies did well at the box office.

Emboldened by their success, Ismat and Shaheed co-founded a production company called Filmina. In 1958, they made the movie *Sone Ki Chidiya,* which Ismat wrote and co-produced. The film had Nutan and Talat Mahmood in the leading roles, and was a poignant telling of the story of a child actor and the traumatic journey she faced. The movie was called significant for showcasing the grime behind the glamour of the film industry.

In 1958, again, Ismat produced her second movie titled *Lala Rukh* with Mahmood and Shyama. Making films did not deter her from writing her short stories. She published a short story collection, *Chui Mui,* in 1952. The collection received largely positive reviews, with critics commenting on its pertinent dissection of our society, and challenging the pedestal motherhood is put on by society. The famous movie *Garam Hawa,* based on the Indo-Pak partition, was written by Ismat. She also wrote Shyam Benegal's *Junoon* and played a small role in it. Other films she has written include *Chhed-Chaad, Buzdil, Shikayat, Shisha* and *Fareb.*

From the short story form, Ismat made a leap to novels in the 1960s, writing a total of eight. The first was *Masooma* (*The Innocent Girl*) which was published in 1962. She followed it with a novella titled *Saudai,* published in 1966, based on the screenplay of the 1951 film *Buzdil,* which she had co-written with her husband. Her fifth novel, *Dil Ki Duniya,* received rave reviews. Critics placed it second to *Tedhi Lakeer* in her body of work. The novel focusses on the lives of Muslim women living in Uttar Pradesh, with Ismat yet again drawing heavily on her lived experiences. In the 1970s, she wrote *Ajeeb Aadmi* and *Jangli Kabootar* which were based on her experiences in the film industry. *Ajeeb Aadmi* is said to have been inspired by Guru Dutt, and *Jangli Kabootar* on the real-life story of an actress of the times.

Sadly, in the late 1980s, she was diagnosed with Alzheimer's disease. This, naturally, impacted her work, and the slow progression of the disease meant that the world saw no notable writing from her pen post her diagnosis.[25] She died at home in Bombay, on 24 October 1991. She was 80 at the time. She was cremated in keeping with her wishes. She had mentioned her terror at the thought of being buried in conversations with the noted writer Qurratulain Hyder. To quote her, 'I am very scared of the grave. They bury you beneath a pile of mud. One would suffocate [...] I'd rather be cremated.' She was cremated at Chandanwadi crematorium in Bombay.[26]

It was the re-readings of 'Lihaaf', once it was widely anthologized, that renewed popular interest in Ismat's writings. It was noted that Ismat consistently kept exploring new themes and expanding the repertoire of her writing. In recent years, *Tedhi Lakeer* has come to be known as her magnum opus and one of the most significant works in Urdu literature. The novel has been termed a bildungsroman, one that explored themes of feminism, nationalism and female identity in the period it was set in. She is widely acknowledged as one of the four pillars of the modern Urdu short story as we know it, with Saadat Hasan Manto, Rajinder Singh Bedi and Krishan Chander being the three others. To quote Rakhshanda Jalil, 'When it comes to Ismat Chughtai, nobody has gone beyond the adjectives. She is appropriated by radicals, progressives, feminists and liberals.'[27]

While her writing was in the space of the Muslim identity, she remained a liberal, with her daughter, nephew and niece married to Hindus. She often said that she came from a family of 'Hindus, Muslims and Christians who all live peacefully'. She claimed to have read the Quran, the Gita and the Bible.[28]

She was awarded the Padma Shri by the Government of India in 1976 for her contribution to literature. In 1990, the Madhya Pradesh government awarded her the *Iqbal Samman*; she has also received the Ghalib Award. She is sometimes called 'the female Manto'. Those who call her so do both her and Manto a disservice. She is also sometimes called 'Lady Changez Khan' because she could trace her family tree back to the Mongol warlord Taimurlane. What she leaves behind is a legacy that is stronger than any award could commemorate—the legacy of an independent woman, who knew her mind and was not afraid to speak of things considered taboo.

NOTES

1 'Profile of Ismat Chughtai', *Rekhta.org,* http://tinyurl.com/yeymfhvw. Accessed on 4 January 2024.

2 '"Lihaaf" [The Quilt]. Short Fiction by Ismat Chugtai', *The Beacon,* 20 March 2021, http://tinyurl.com/4zu9ewu9. Accessed on 4 January 2024.

3 'Celebrating Ismat Chughtai, the Urdu Writer Who Dared to Talk about Feminine Sexuality', *India Today,* 21 August 2018, http://tinyurl.com/ystsfpv9. Accessed on 4 January 2024.

4 'Ismat Chughtai: A Talk with One of Urdu's Most Outspoken Woman Writers', *Mahfil,* Vol. 8, No. 2–3, 1972, pp. 169–88, http://tinyurl.com/54mr3fwt. Accessed on 4 January 2024.

5 'Celebrating the Fearless Ismat Chughtai's 107th Birth Anniversary', *The Times of India,* 21 August 2018, http://tinyurl.com/3428yvmc. Accessed on 4 January 2024.

6 Krishnatray, Shreya, 'Ismat Chughtai: An Inspiration for Many. Everything You Need to Know', *TN,* 23 January 2020, http://tinyurl.com/2xsathd2. Accessed on 4 January 2024.

7 Khanna, Neetu, 'Marxist Feminisms in India: The Visceral Materialism of Rashid Jahan and Ismat Chughtai', *S&F Online,* 2021, http://tinyurl.com/2p8an54x. Accessed on 4 January 2024.

8 'Profile of Ismat Chughtai', *Rekhta.org,* http://tinyurl.com/yeymfhvw. Accessed on 4 January 2024.

9 'Ismat Chughtai: A Talk with One of Urdu's Most Outspoken

Woman Writers', *Mahfil*, Vol. 8, No. 2–3, 1972, pp. 169–88, http://tinyurl.com/54mr3fwt. Accessed on 4 January 2024.

10 Ibid.

11 Krishnatray, Shreya, 'Ismat Chughtai: An Inspiration for Many. Everything You Need to Know', *TN*, 23 January 2020, http://tinyurl.com/2xsathd2. Accessed on 4 January 2024.

12 'Ismat Chughtai: A Talk with One of Urdu's Most Outspoken Woman Writers', *Mahfil*, Vol. 8, No. 2–3, 1972, pp. 169–88, http://tinyurl.com/54mr3fwt. Accessed on 4 January 2024.

13 Mohammad Asaduddin (trans.), *Lifting the Veil: Selected Writings of Ismat Chughtai*, Penguin, 2009.

14 Singh, Saumya, 'Why Ismat Chughtai Remains Relevant as a Feminist Icon', *the punch magazine*, 21 August 2021, http://tinyurl.com/mn3wcuuk. Accessed on 4 January 2024.

15 'Profile of Ismat Chughtai', *Rekhta.org*, http://tinyurl.com/yeymfhvw. Accessed on 4 January 2024.

16 Ibid.

17 'Ismat Chughtai: A Talk with One of Urdu's Most Outspoken Woman Writers', *Mahfil*, Vol. 8, No. 2–3, 1972, pp. 169–88, http://tinyurl.com/54mr3fwt. Accessed on 4 January 2024.

18 Ibid.

19 Jain, Ritika, 'Ismat Chughtai Felt Crushed under the Weight of Her Greatest Creation, Lihaaf', *The Print*, 24 October 2018, http://tinyurl.com/4xh6x7ce. Accessed on 4 January 2024.

20 'Naatak Radio', *buzzsprout.com*, 22 August 2020, http://tinyurl.com/yc7643fr. Accessed on 4 January 2024.

21 'About: Ismat Chughtai', *DBPedia*, http://tinyurl.com/43a6vt4j. Accessed on 4 January 2024.

22 Kumar, Sukrita Paul, and Sadique, *Ismat: Her Life, Her Times*, A Katha Book, 2000; Bahuguna, Urvashi, 'Born on India's Future Independence Day, Ismat Chughtai Wrote of the World She Saw, Not Aspired To', *Scroll.in*, 15 August 2017, http://tinyurl.com/yhh59www. Accessed on 4 January 2024.

23 Bhardwaj, Aditi, 'On Ismat Chughtai', *Zindaginama*, 1

November 2020, http://tinyurl.com/4dnp3whv. Accessed on 4 January 2024.

24 'Ismat Chughtai: A Talk with One of Urdu's Most Outspoken Woman Writers', *Mahfil*, Vol. 8, No. 2–3, 1972, pp. 169–88, http://tinyurl.com/54mr3fwt. Accessed on 4 January 2024.

25 'Remembering Midnight's Magnificent Daughter Ismat Chughtai on Her Birth Anniversary', *The Wire*, 15 August 2017, http://tinyurl.com/yddeawpj. Accessed on 4 January 2024.

26 Jalil, Rakhshanda, *An Uncivil Woman: Writings on Ismat Chughtai*, OUP India, 2017.

27 Ibid.

28 Shah, Noor, 'Ismat Chughtai—Her Life and Ideals,' *The Milli Gazette*, 2005, http://tinyurl.com/4cydzn39. Accessed on 18 January 2024.

15

JANAKI AMMAL

STEEL MAGNOLIA

What connection does the sugar you add to your tea or coffee today have with a woman born way back in 1897, in the town of Tellicherry (now Thalassery) in Kerala? Quite a lot, even though you may not know it today. In fact, the sugar we use today wouldn't have been half as sweet had it not been for Edavalath Kakkat (E.K.) Janaki Ammal, widely regarded as India's first woman botanist.

Born on 4 November 1897, E.K. Janaki Ammal was the tenth child in a family of 19 siblings.[1] Hers was a very interesting family. Her father, Diwan Bahadur Edavalath Kakkat Krishnan, was a judge in a subordinate court system in Tellicherry. An educated man of refined tastes, he was an ornithologist of fair repute, an author and a hobby horticulturalist. He kept a fine garden in their home and wrote two books on birds from the North Malabar region of India. The love for plants and consequently the professional journey into botany that came to define Janaki's life, perhaps, came from this garden nurtured by her father.

Her mother, Devi Kuruvayi, was the daughter of John Child Hannyngton (the colonial administrator and resident at Travancore) and Kunhi Kurumbi Kuruvai. The liaison had resulted in two daughters. One was settled in Madras, while young Devi had refused to leave her mother. The famous entomologist, Frank Hannyngton, also an Indian civil servant, was a half-brother of Janaki Ammal's mother. It was a mixed family filled with interesting anecdotes. Janaki's father had six children by his first wife and had 13 children with Devi, his second wife. J.C. Hannygnton asked him in a letter whether he was having too much of a good thing by having so many children.[2]

The children born of such mixed heritage naturally faced some social ostracism. Add to this the fact that they were fair-skinned, tall and broad-boned. The children of Krishnan, by virtue of his position, received the best education possible back then. He set great store by education and books, and had made a well-stocked library in his home. As a man of diverse interests in ornithology, botany and natural sciences, he passed on his interests to his children. The family did not see themselves as socially ostracized even though they came from the Thiyya community which was considered backward. In fact, they regarded themselves as part of the respected Edathil family.[3]

Janaki studied at Sacred Heart Convent in Tellicherry for her primary education. As a child, she saw her older sisters being married off through arranged marriages. She was determined not to be married off and confined to a life of domesticity and childbearing like her sisters. She told her parents that she was keen to study further. It was an unconventional choice, but, to the credit of her parents, she went ahead to get her bachelor's degree from Queen Mary's College, Madras (now Chennai), followed by an honours degree in botany from the Presidency College. It was a rare subject that she chose to major in, and it was rarer still that she was a woman doing so. She had moved out of home and gone to Madras to pursue her education. At that time, in 1913, literacy among women in India was less than 1 per cent, and less than a thousand women across the country had studied above the tenth grade, according to science historian Vinita Damodaran.[4]

Janaki then taught for three years at the Women's Christian

College in Madras. It was at this point in 1924 that she received the opportunity that completely changed the trajectory of her life. She was awarded the Barbour Scholarship, established at the University of Michigan by Levi Barbour in 1917 to encourage women from Asia to study in the United States (US). There is a story about Janaki waiting, along with other passengers from the East, for immigration clearance into New York on Ellis Island. To quote her, 'I think my long hair and attire in traditional Indian silks allowed me in straight away. They asked me whether I was an Indian Princess. I did not deny it.'[5]

She joined the botany department in the University of Michigan as the Barbour Scholar in 1924. At the University of Michigan her focus area was plant cytology, the study of the genetic composition and patterns of gene expression in plants. She specialized in the breeding of inter-specific hybrids (created from plants of different species) as well as inter-generic hybrids (created from plants of a different genera within the same family).

In 1925, Janaki earned a Master of Science degree. She stayed in the Martha Cook Building, an all-female residence hall, working with Harley Harris Bartlett, who was a professor at the department of botany. Creditably, she created a cross known as 'Janaki Brengal' ('brengal' being the Indian name for eggplant).[6] After finishing her degree, Janaki moved back to India to teach for a few years, but returned to Ann Arbor as the first Indian Oriental Barbour Fellow, completing her doctorate in botany in 1931.

With her doctorate, she became the first Indian woman to receive a doctorate in botany in the US. In a letter from Michigan, she wrote:

> I was very happy to get Brother-in-law's letter and to find that he is interested in my projects for North Malabar. I shall be writing to him in detail about my plans. [...] Having met many Chinese and Japanese girls out here, I

> realize what a lot Asia has in common. You know, I have started an organization that is going to link the University Women of Asia—we are still in an embryonic state—but I am getting new members for all quarters. It is my dream to send some Indian girls to study in China and Japan and have girls from these countries to come to our country. I have just had an invitation from a college in China to teach botany.[7]

Her doctoral thesis was titled *Chromosome Studies in Nicandra Physaloides* and was published in 1932.[8] On her return to India, she became professor of botany at the Maharaja's College of Science in Trivandrum (now University College, Thiruvananthapuram) and served there as assistant professor for two years between 1932 and 1934.

She was keenly interested in ethno-botany, and plants of medicinal and economic value from the rainforests of Kerala. Her expertise in cytogenetics led her to join the Sugarcane Breeding Station at Coimbatore to work on sugarcane biology. At the time, India would import sugarcane from Southeast Asia, and the *Saccharum officinarum* variety from Papua New Guinea was considered the sweetest in the world.

There was a concerted effort to improve India's indigenous sugarcane varieties, and the Coimbatore-based Sugarcane Breeding Station had been set up in the early 1920s for precisely this purpose. Janaki's research into hybrids helped identify native plant varieties that could be cross-bred with *Saccharum officinarum* to create a high-yielding strain of the sugarcane that could thrive across the diverse climatic conditions in India. She did this by manipulating polyploid cells through cross-breeding of hybrids in the laboratory. Her research also established the fact that the *Saccharum spontaneum* variety of sugarcane had originated in India. Thanks to her pioneering work, India could reduce its dependence on sugarcane imports.[9]

However, she came up against different hurdles during her

stint at Coimbatore. As she was a single woman, her male peers looked down on her. Her mixed ancestry created other issues. As mentioned earlier, she belonged to the Thiyya community which was considered to be backward, but had risen due to education and opportunities that the colonial system had provided. It is said that there was a 'double whammy' of caste and gender discrimination that led her to look for other opportunities, though those who knew her strongly dispute this. She was too fiercely independent to let such things bog her down. In a letter, dated August 1938, she wrote about the visit of the biologist Reginald Ruggles Gates to Coimbatore. She wrote:

> It has taken seven long months to undo the harm that Gates did in the course of a simple day spent in Coimbatore. Mr Venkatraman was completely taken in by the 'Professor's keen interest in the work done at Coimbatore'-his fund of information and his gracious manner-hence the doubt expressed not to me but to Venkatraman about the validity of the Saccharum-Zea cross stuck in the expert's brain and my note to *Nature* was not sent up to the Director of Agriculture for the necessary permission to publish it outside India - I very nearly decided to leave this station as a result of all this-and life became very complicated-however I refused to be defeated and I am glad to report that Venkatraman is at last convinced that the cross is genuine.[10]

Opportunity for change came in 1940 and she moved to Norfolk, England, and began working at the John Innes Centre. She began working with geneticist and eugenicist Cyril Dean Darlington, with whom she had struck up a correspondence earlier as well. They had worked together for a year before Janaki returned to India. He was at the time researching chromosomes influencing heredity, and then the role of race in intelligence. She worked with him on plants, collaborating and co-authoring the *Chromosome Atlas of Cultivated Plants* after five years of working together, which to this date is an important research resource for plant scientists.[11] This Atlas not only had botanical classification but also recorded the chromosome number of over 100,000 plants, with details about the breeding and the evolutionary patterns of botanical groups.

In the John Innes staff file there's a statement by Ellis Marks that Janaki Ammal 'smuggled a palm squirrel into the country and it was kept at J.I.I. for many years. Its name was "Kapok"'.[12] She was in London just around the time the Second World War broke out, and lived there through the bombings. She later told her friends about how she would dive under her bed when the air raid sirens went off in the night, and clean the broken glass the next morning before getting back to her research work at the institute.[13]

In 1946, she got an offer from the Royal Horticultural Society, Wisley, to join as a cytologist. It was a paid position.[14] She then quit the John Innes Centre to become the first salaried woman staff member of the Society. At Wisley, she also investigated the effects of colchicine on woody plants, including magnolias. This involved making a stock solution in water and applying it to the growing tip of the young seedlings, once the cotyledons or the seed leaves had fully expanded. The doubling of chromosomes then occurs, giving the cells twice the usual number. The resulting plants have heavier leaves and variable flowers with thicker tepals, which let the flowers stay in bloom for longer.

A number of these seedlings treated by her were planted on Battleston Hill at Wisley. To this date, at the Wisley campus of the Horticultural Society, there are magnolia shrubs that she planted—and one among them is a variety of a small white flower with purple stamens, named *Magnolia kobus Janaki Ammal* by the Royal Horticultural Society, Wisley, in honour of the work she did in plant breeding.[15]

She lived close to the gardens at Kew during her stint in

London and would take guests from her family to the banks of the River Thames for picnics if the weather was sunny. A young relative recounts that Janaki was rather strict about bedtime for children, like the English. They were expected to be tucked in and asleep by 7.00 p.m. She would sometimes read to them from the books of Beatrix Potter, or from illustrated books about tree fairies and elves. She would cook simple meals of dal, rice and vegetables for herself and her guests.[16]

She returned to India in 1950 at the personal invitation of then Prime Minister (PM) Jawaharlal Nehru. At the time, India was recovering from many years of successive famines, including the horrific Bengal Famine of 1943 which had taken a toll on millions of lives. To quote Vinita Damodaran from an interview to the *Smithsonian*, 'Nehru was very keen to get [Ammal] back [to India] to improve the botanical base of Indian agriculture.'[17]

She was appointed as the supervisor in charge of the Central Botanical Laboratory in Lucknow. She was also in charge of reorganizing the Botanical Survey of India (BSI), which had originally been established in 1890 under the oversight of Britain's Kew Gardens to collect and survey India's flora. She was then appointed as officer on special duty (OSD) to the BSI, and was instrumental in reorganizing the Calcutta (now Kolkata) office in 1954. There are anecdotes of how she would unhesitatingly take the broom herself to clean the streets outside the BSI office on the famous Chowringhee Lane in Calcutta.[18]

She was soon disillusioned with the initiatives taken by the government to boost food production in India. The Grow More Food Campaign of the 1940s saw the government reclaim over 25 million acres of land to cultivate grains and other cereals. However, the resources had not been utilized judiciously. In a letter to Darlington, she writes, 'I went 37 miles from Shillong in search of the only tree of *Magnolia griffithii* in that part of

Assam and found that it had been burnt down.'[19]

At this point, she saw the need to preserve indigenous plants which were threatened by deforestation and other factors. She planned to create a herbarium that contained the specimens collected from across the continent. She felt the BSI should be conducted by Indian scientists for India, but she was stymied when the government superseded her and appointed a European as the director and her superior.

She wrote about it to Darlington, saying, 'I bring you news of a major defeat for botanical science in India. The Govt. of India has appointed as the chief botanist of India—a man with the Kew tradition and I—the director of the Central Botanical Laboratory must now take orders from him ... Kew has won ... and we have lost.'[20]

She wrote scathingly about this in a memorandum on the survey, saying, 'The plants collected in India during the last thirty years have been chiefly by foreign botanists and often sponsored by institutions outside India. They are now found in various gardens and herbaria in Europe, so that modern research on the flora of India can be conducted more intensely outside India than within this country.'[21]

She was a strong advocate of learning and preserving indigenous knowledge of Indian plants to preserve the country's biodiverse heritage. In 1955, she attended an international symposium in Chicago, titled *Man's Role in Changing the Face of the Earth* as the only woman there. She was a forerunner of sorts; back then she fiercely advocated for tribal cultures and their knowledge of native plants, and talked about how India's matrilineal traditions that valued plants and flora of the property were threatened by the mass-production of cereals.

She also worked on the genera *Solanum, Datura, Mentha, Cymbopogon* and *Dioscorea* apart from medicinal plants and other varieties of plants. She pinpointed that the higher rate of plant speciation in the cold and humid northeast Himalayas, when compared with the cold and dry northwest Himalayas, was due to polyploidy. The confluence of Chinese and Malayan elements in the flora of the northeast, according to Janaki, was what had contributed to this natural hybridization between them and the native flora of the region, leading to enhanced plant diversification. She published the original findings of her research post her retirement, and focussed on medicinal plants and ethno-botany.

She developed a garden of medicinal plants in the Madras Field Laboratory where she lived and worked. According to her niece Geeta Doctor, she was fiercely independent and did not care about the bureaucracy that often sought to bog her down. She would travel across the country to the most remote regions to find and study the indigenous lore surrounding the plants of the region. She went to Northeast India; to the borders of India and what is now Myanmar; to Ladakh and to Wayanad in Kerala in search of medicinal plants, and to explore the possibility of high-altitude sustainable agriculture.[22]

She was awarded an honorary LLD (Legum Doctor or Doctor of Laws) in 1956 by the University of Michigan in recognition of her work.[23] In 1962, she was the OSD at the Regional Research Laboratory in Jammu & Kashmir. She also briefly worked at the Bhabha Atomic Research Centre at Trombay before finally settling down in Madras in 1970, as the emeritus scientist at the Centre for Advanced Study in Botany, University of Madras. Until she passed away in February 1984, she lived and worked in the Centre's field laboratory at Maduravoyal.[24]

She was, in her twilight years, one of the most prominent voices in a citizen's campaign to stop a hydro-electric project. In 1973, the Kerala State Electricity Board announced a plan to dam the River Kunthipuzha, resulting in a reservoir that would flood 8.3 sq. km of virgin evergreen tropical forest to build a hydro-electric power plant. The power plant was planned in order to provide electricity and jobs to the people of the state. The plan would not just threaten the flora of the region, but also the wildlife of the region, including the lion-tailed macaque. She, along with Romulus Whitaker, the founder of the Madras Snake Park and the Madras Crocodile Bank, protested vociferously against the plan, along with other environmentally-conscious citizens. She wrote to Darlington at this time, saying, 'I am about to start a daring feat. I have made up my mind to take a chromosome survey of the forest trees of the Silent Valley which is about to be made into a lake by letting in the waters of the river Kunthi.'[25]

She led the chromosomal survey of the plants of the Silent Valley. The larger environmental movement to protest the hydro-electric power plant emerged as one of the most prominent environmental movements of the 1970s. The government was compelled to abandon the project and the forest was declared as a national park by the government in November 1984. She unfortunately passed away before she could see this happening. She had died nine months before, at the age of 87, on 7 February 1984, while working in her research lab at Maduravoyal.

Today, the Silent Valley Forest is a repository for over 1,000 species of endemic flowering plants, endangered orchids and wildlife, including lion-tailed macaques. Interestingly, in her twilight years, her attention had been focussed on the rearing of a large family of cats and kittens. To this she brought her expertise as a geneticist, to track down subtle differentiations in the characteristics of her kittens.

She never got married, and there are some speculations, never confirmed, though, that perhaps she had developed an attachment to Darlington. A family member recounts an occasion when Darlington came to a relative's home in Delhi in the early 1960s to meet Janaki. The family member recounted, 'There was a tension in the air when he entered. He was a tall, very distinguished looking man. He hesitated a moment and then went straight ahead and kissed Aunt Janaki on her cheek. She blushed a deep pink but said nothing.' In one of her letters to Darlington, she wrote in 1939, 'I am a born wanderer. There is a great restlessness in me.'[26]

She lived out her life in a spartan, austere manner, influenced by Gandhian precepts. She wrote in a letter to her brother, Raghavan, about her meeting with Gandhi ji when she was barely 19, saying that she was greatly moved by his words on social reform and was inspired to give up everything and devote herself to the service of the Mother Country, but knew she must first pass her BA and then think of her next steps.[27]

However, in her later years, when she visited his ashram in Wardha, she was sad to find no plants being grown there and nothing to make the environment beautiful. She had gone there in the expectation of an ashram like the hermitages of the ancient *rishis*, but found no beauty there.[28] She was always focussed on simple beauty in her surroundings: a beautiful print on the wall, or a simple bowl with orange and white parijat flowers.

Her niece, Geeta Doctor wrote of her, saying:

> Janaki was a tall and commanding presence in her prime. She tied her lustrous long hair into a loose bun at the nape of her neck. In her later years, she took to wearing brilliant yellow silk sarees with a long loose blouse or jacket in the same colour. Her statuesque presence reminded people of a Buddhist lady monk. Like certain Buddhist orders, she took a vow of chastity, austerity and silence for herself, limiting her needs to the barest minimum.[29]

She was elected Fellow of the Indian Academy of Sciences in 1935, and to the Indian National Science Academy in 1957. In 1977, she was awarded the Padma Shri by the then PM of India. In 2000, the Ministry of Environment and Forestry of the Government of India instituted the National Award of Taxonomy in her name, as the E.K. Janaki Ammal National Award on Animal Taxonomy.[30] There is a herbarium with 25,000 species of plants in Jammutawi named after her. The John Innes Centre instituted a scholarship for PhD students from developing countries in her name.

In 2018, rose breeders Girija and Viru Viraraghavan bred a new yellow-petalled rose variety, which they named 'E.K. Janaki Ammal.'[31] These are not the only things named after her. The name *Janakia arayalpathra,* given to a rare and endemic plant species found in the Southern forests of the Western Ghat region of Kerala, is also a tribute to her. A species of plant in the family Melastomataceae, *Sonerila janakiana,* is named after her. There is also *Dravidogecko janakiae,* a species of geckos found in India that is named after her.

Her greatest contribution is towards identifying and conserving the biodiversity of India. In a 2015 article, Geeta Doctor said that Janaki Ammal rarely spoke about her work, believing instead that 'my work is what will survive.'[32] Her work is everywhere, in the spoonful of sugar we put into our cups of tea or coffee; in the verdant, rich green stretches of the Silent Valley; and in all the plants she chronicled and catalogued. Her work was her life, and it is a life lived to the fullest in the devotion of a passion. The earth, and we as a country, are richer and sweeter for the work she did. Yet, her legacy remains wreathed in oblivion, despite her immense contribution to the field of cytology.

Perhaps, we should end her story with these lines from her obituary, 'The sun receives thine eye, the wind thy spirit; go as thy merit is, to earth or heaven. Go, if it be thy lot, unto water; go make thine house in plants with all thy members.'[33]

NOTES

1 'Edavaleth Kakkat Janaki Ammal - An Introduction,' *Janaki Ammal Herbarium,* http://tinyurl.com/5b8amj53. Accessed on 5 January 2024.

2 Doctor, Geeta, 'Celebrating Janaki Ammal, Botanist and a Passionate Wanderer of Many Worlds,' *The Wire,* 6 November 2016, http://tinyurl.com/ys9ewvu2. Accessed on 5 January 2024.

3 Ibid.

4 Damodaran, Vinita, 'Gender, Race and Science in Twentieth-Century India: E. K. Janaki Ammal and the History of Science', *History of Science*, Vol. 51, No. 3, 2013, http://tinyurl.com/5n7v6mm6. Accessed on 5 January 2024; McNeill, Leila, 'The Pioneering Female Botanist Who Sweetened a Nation and Saved a Valley', *Smithsonian Magazine*, 31 July 2019, http://tinyurl.com/mtwbwpnw. Accessed on 5 January 2024.

5 Doctor, Geeta, 'Celebrating Janaki Ammal, Botanist and a Passionate Wanderer of Many Worlds', *The Wire*, 6 November 2016, http://tinyurl.com/ys9ewvu2. Accessed on 5 January 2024.

6 'Janaki Ammal', *History of Scientific Women*, http://tinyurl.com/3kked8s6. Accessed on 5 January 2024.

7 Doctor, Geeta, 'Celebrating Janaki Ammal, Botanist and a Passionate Wanderer of Many Worlds', *The Wire*, 6 November 2016, http://tinyurl.com/ys9ewvu2. Accessed on 5 January 2024.

8 Edavaleth Kakkat Janaki, *Chromosome Studies in Nicandra Physaloides*, A. Uystpruyst, 1932.

9 McNeill, Leila, 'The Pioneering Female Botanist Who Sweetened a Nation and Saved a Valley', *Smithsonian Magazine*, 31 July 2019, http://tinyurl.com/mtwbwpnw. Accessed on 5 January 2024.

10 'Jankai Ammal', *Science Gallery*, http://tinyurl.com/4tt4s8vm. Accessed on 17 January 2024.

11 McNeill, Leila, 'The Pioneering Female Botanist Who Sweetened a Nation and Saved a Valley', *Smithsonian Magazine*, 31 July 2019, http://tinyurl.com/mtwbwpnw. Accessed on 5 January 2024.

12 'Janaki Ammal', *History of Scientific Women*, http://tinyurl.com/3kked8s6. Accessed on 5 January 2024.

13 Bhatia, Neha, '"It's Important to Normalise That Women Don't Have to Compromise on Their Dreams"', *MPG*, http://tinyurl.com/37y4vtz2. Accessed on 17 January 2024.

14 McNeill, Leila, 'The Pioneering Female Botanist Who Sweetened a Nation and Saved a Valley,' *Smithsonian Magazine,* 31 July 2019, http://tinyurl.com/mtwbwpnw. Accessed on 5 January 2024.

15 Doctor, Geeta, 'Celebrating Janaki Ammal, Botanist and a Passionate Wanderer of Many Worlds,' *The Wire,* 6 November 2016, http://tinyurl.com/ys9ewvu2. Accessed on 5 January 2024.

16 Doctor, Geeta, 'Remembering Dr Janaki Ammal, Pioneering Botanist, Cytogeneticist and Passionate Gandhian,' *Scroll.in,* 23 June 2015, http://tinyurl.com/4x2yr3ht. Accessed on 5 January 2024.

17 McNeill, Leila, 'The Pioneering Female Botanist Who Sweetened a Nation and Saved a Valley,' *Smithsonian Magazine,* 31 July 2019, http://tinyurl.com/mtwbwpnw. Accessed on 5 January 2024.

18 'India's First Woman PhD in Botany, Her Research Added a Extra Bit of Sweetness in Your Sugar,' *The Logical Indian,* 20 January 2017, http://tinyurl.com/2t289w4n. Accessed on 17 January 2024.

19 McNeill, Leila, 'The Pioneering Female Botanist Who Sweetened a Nation and Saved a Valley,' *Smithsonian Magazine,* 31 July 2019, http://tinyurl.com/mtwbwpnw. Accessed on 5 January 2024.

20 Damodaran, Vinita, 'Gender, Race and Science in Twentieth-Century India: E. K. Janaki Ammal and the History of Science,' *History of Science,* Vol. 51, No. 3, 2013, http://tinyurl.com/5n7v6mm6. Accessed on 5 January 2024

21 McNeill, Leila, 'The Pioneering Female Botanist Who Sweetened a Nation and Saved a Valley,' *Smithsonian Magazine,* 31 July 2019, http://tinyurl.com/mtwbwpnw. Accessed on 5 January 2024.

22 Doctor, Geeta, 'Celebrating Janaki Ammal, Botanist and a Passionate Wanderer of Many Worlds,' *The Wire,* 6 November

2016, http://tinyurl.com/ys9ewvu2. Accessed on 5 January 2024.

23 C.V. Subramanian, 'Edavaleth Kakkat Janaki Ammal,' *Resonance*, 2007, http://tinyurl.com/y6wwnvkd. Accessed on 12 January 2024.

24 'Janaki Ammal,' *History of Scientific Women*, http://tinyurl.com/3kked8s6. Accessed on 5 January 2024.

25 C.V. Subramanian, 'Edavaleth Kakkat Janaki Ammal,' *RESONANCE*, June 2007, http://tinyurl.com/mvf3p7mv. Accessed on 17 January 2024.

26 Doctor, Geeta, 'Celebrating Janaki Ammal, Botanist and a Passionate Wanderer of Many Worlds,' *The Wire*, 6 November 2016, http://tinyurl.com/ys9ewvu2. Accessed on 5 January 2024.

27 Ibid.

28 Doctor, Geeta, 'Remembering Dr Janaki Ammal, Pioneering Botanist, Cytogeneticist and Passionate Gandhian,' *Scroll.in*, 23 June 2015, http://tinyurl.com/4x2yr3ht. Accessed on 5 January 2024.

29 Pal, Sanchari, 'Meet India's First Woman PhD in Botany – She Is the Reason Your Sugar Tastes Sweeter!,' *Kractivism*, http://tinyurl.com/36t8h2e6. Accessed on 17 January 2024.

30 'Dr Janaki Ammal: India's First Woman Botanist,' *Indian Liberals*, 11 February 2022, http://tinyurl.com/2w5pk6pk. Accessed on 5 January 2024.

31 Shaji, K.A., 'A Rose Named E.K. Janaki Ammal,' *The Telegraph Online*, 6 June 2019, http://tinyurl.com/2s925w72. Accessed on 5 January 2024.

32 Bhatia, Neha, '"It's Important to Normalise That Women Don't Have to Compromise on Their Dreams",' *MPG*, http://tinyurl.com/37y4vtz2. Accessed on 17 January 2024.

33 'Janaki Ammal,' *History of Scientific Women*, http://tinyurl.com/3kked8s6. Accessed on 5 January 2024.

16

KAMALADEVI CHATTOPADHYAY

REVIVALIST OF OUR HERITAGE

She is a towering personality whom we barely acknowledge these days. We owe more than we realize to Kamaladevi Chattopadhyay. As an Indian social reformer and freedom activist, she was instrumental in the revival of Indian handicrafts, handlooms and theatre in post-Independence India, creating a renaissance of pride in our traditional textiles and handlooms.

There's another lesser known first to her credit. She was the first Indian woman to contest elections, but unfortunately, she lost. More on that later, though. Right now, let's go back to 3 April 1903 when Kamaladevi was born in Mangalore (now Mangaluru). She was born into a Saraswat Brahmin family, and was the fourth and youngest daughter of her parents, Ananthaya Dhareshwar (a district collector in South Kanara district of the then Madras Presidency) and his wife Girijabai.[1] The family was well-respected in society. Her father was a civil servant, and her mother came from a land-owning family from coastal Karnataka. Her paternal grandmother and her mother were both well-read and educated in ancient epics, although homeschooled and not formally educated. The two of them ensured that the children got a firm grounding in ancient culture and history. Young

Kamaladevi was a bright student, and did well in her studies.

She saw tragedy young when she lost her older sister, Suguna, whom she was very close to. Suguna was barely in her teens and had died after an early marriage. Kamaladevi was barely seven years old when her father died. He hadn't made a will, so her mother did not receive any of his property. It all went to her stepson, in keeping with the property laws at the time. Girija and her children were entitled to a monthly allowance, which she refused, choosing to manage her expenses with the income from her own property. Kamaladevi and her mother then moved to her maternal uncle's home. Kamaladevi's maternal uncle was a noted social reformer and was well-acquainted with prominent freedom fighters and intellectuals of the time, like Mahadev Govind Ranade, Gopal Krishna Gokhale and women leaders of the freedom movement like Ramabai Ranade and Annie Besant, who often visited his home.[2] In such a fertile cultural environment, it is no wonder that Kamaladevi became an ardent espouser of the nationalist movement at an early age.

As a young child, she studied the ancient Sanskrit drama tradition *Kutiyattam* from Natyacharya Padma Shri Mani Madhava Chakyar, who was widely considered as the greatest expert of the tradition. In true *guru-shishya parampara,* she stayed and learnt at the guru's home in Killikkurussimangalam. [3]

Even as a child, Kamaladevi refused to adhere to the divisions of hierarchy within the home, and defiantly played with the children of the staff of the house, much to the despair of the elders. This sense of defiance carried on into her adulthood. When she was 14, her mother got her married, in keeping with the customs of the time. But unfortunately, barely a couple of years later, her husband passed away. It was yet another early loss she had to deal with, after the deaths of her sister and father. It could not have been easy, being a widow in those conservative times when widows were shunned and ostracized by society. Luckily, her mother and father-in-law were both very supportive of her continuing her education. So, after she finished her schooling from St Anne's School in Mangalore, she went to Queen Mary's College in Madras (now Chennai) to complete her graduation. It was here that she got acquainted with Suhasini Chattopadhyay (later Nambiar), who was her classmate and the younger sister of Sarojini Naidu. Through Suhasini, she got acquainted with her brother, Harindranath. He was a talented young man, already gathering fame as a poet, actor and playwright. Their mutual interest in the performing arts brought them together.[4]

When Harindranath moved to London, Kamaladevi followed him and joined the Bedford College in the University of London for a diploma in sociology. The course in sociology, combined with practical training, needed Kamaladevi to visit slums in London for on-ground work. Anecdotally, it is believed that Miss Luke, the principal of Bedford College, tried to dissuade her from the course because it needed field work in the east-end of London. Miss Luke is believed to have said that moving around might be difficult for her because of the 'weird garb' Kamaladevi wore. However, Kamaladevi was persistent and did the course.[5]

She married Harindranath when she was 20 years old. This shocked society because she was a widow, and, at the time, widow remarriage was unheard of, even though social reformists had started to advocate for it. They had a son, Rama, who was born a year after.[6] In London, Kamaladevi heard of Mahatma Gandhi's Non-Cooperation Movement gathering momentum, and, in 1923, she decided to return to India and joined the Seva Dal, a Gandhian organization which had been set up to promote social upliftment.[7] She was given charge of the women's section, which had her recruiting, training and organizing corps of women across the country to volunteer with the Seva Dal.

A few years later, in 1926, she met Margaret E. Cousins, who was the founder of the All India Women's Conference (AIWC).[8] She, along with other activists like Sarojini Naidu, the Maharani of Baroda and other prominent women, campaigned for legislations such as the Child Marriage Restraint and the Age of Consent Bill to be passed in the Legislative Assembly. Cousins urged her to stand for elections to the Madras Provincial Legislative Assembly in 1926.[9] She did so, and campaigned for a few days, but lost with a slim margin of 55 votes. As mentioned before, this made her the first woman in India to throw her hat into electoral politics. At that time, even women back in England didn't have the right to vote. She formally joined Indian National Congress (INC) in 1927 and was elected to the All India Congress Committee (AICC) within a year.

Kamaladevi also became the first organizing secretary of the AIWC in 1927.[10] In the years to come, AIWC grew to become a national organization, with voluntary programmes run in centres across India working towards legislative reforms for women. In her position as organizing secretary, Kamaladevi travelled to many European countries to study how they implemented women's reforms. She then sought to replicate and initiate several similar models here in India. She did this in the space of social reform and community welfare programmes, as well as by setting up educational institutions run for women and by women.

A prime example of this was the setting up of the Lady Irwin College for Home Sciences in Delhi, which was, at the time, the first of its kind. At the AIWC, she took up advocacy of breastfeeding and family planning, both immensely controversial at the time. As part of the AIWC, she also advocated for the recognition of women's work within the home and on the field, demanding equal wage with equal opportunities. She also spoke about women's right to property and guardianship of children in case of dissolution of a marriage. Some of these issues, like equal wage, are still being debated a century down the line. She was a firm advocate for equal rights for women, but found the term 'feminist' too limiting. To quote her from her autobiography, 'Obviously women were not the only victims of social and economic disabilities and discriminations...the women's struggle had, therefore, to be an indivisible part of the larger political, social and economic struggle.'[11] She felt that home science institutions, like the Lady Irwin College in Delhi, should not be bound to a single gender.[12]

Kamaladevi was an active participant in the freedom movement. She was instrumental in getting Gandhi ji to allow women to participate in the marches of the freedom movement. During the 1930 Dandi March, led by Gandhi, she made salt on the beach in Bombay (now Mumbai). The other woman on the team was Avantikabai Gokhale.[13] On 26 January 1930, during a street protest, she clung to the tricolour and shot into the limelight.[14] She was sentenced to a prison term for violation of the salt laws. In prison, she shared a cell with Sarojini Naidu. It was around this time that her marriage to Harindranath began souring. They eventually separated and had an amicable divorce. In fact, hers was the first legal divorce granted by an Indian court of law.[15]

She was in England when the Second World War started, and decided to tour the countries of the world in order to gather support for India's struggle for independence. In the course of this journey, she travelled to the United States in 1941. In the southern state of Louisiana, where colour segregation was still in place at the time, a train conductor tried to remove her from a car which was reserved for white passengers. He was however confused as to 'what' she was, because she did not look like a black American. He asked her where she came from. 'New York,' she replied. It was not the answer he was looking for, so he asked her which land she had come from. She was unperturbed and replied, 'It makes no difference. I am a coloured woman obviously and it is unnecessary for you to disturb me for I have no intention of moving from here.' The conductor could not remove her, and let her sit in the train car for the rest of the journey.[16]

She also went on to act in movies when she returned to India. It was another bold move for her. Women from 'respectable families' did not act in movies then. Her first outing on celluloid was through two silent movies, including *Mricchakatika*, which was the first silent film of the Kannada film industry. The film was based on the famous play written by Shudraka. It also featured Yenakshi Rama Rao, and was directed by the Kannada director Mohan Dayaram Bhavnani. She came back to acting over a decade later with the Hindi movie *Tansen*, which had K.L. Saigal and Khursheed in the leading roles, following it up with *Shankar Parvati* and *Dhanna Bhagat*.[17]

The independence of India brought about a new phase in her career path. Post Partition, she became fully involved in the rehabilitation of refugees. She set up the Indian Cooperative Union to help with rehabilitation, and planned a township along the lines of the cooperative movement. She received grudging permission from then Prime Minister Jawaharlal Nehru, on the condition that she did not ask for the state to help out. She managed to set up the township of Faridabad on the outskirts of Delhi, rehabilitating over 50,000 refugees from the Northwest Frontier. She worked on-ground relentlessly to build homes and set up businesses, helping to train the refugees in new skills so that they could earn their livelihood. She also set up health facilities in the new town for the refugees.[18]

Along with the rehabilitation of the dispossessed, she began what eventually emerged as her life's mission—the revival of Indian handicrafts and handlooms post-Independence. She realized, at this time, that the Western methods of factory-based production could adversely impact traditional artisans. The mass-production model, as espoused by Nehru for India's development, while ambitious, would have ruined traditional artisans, and impacted the lives of all the women in the unorganized sector who relied on traditional handicrafts and handlooms for their sustenance. She then set up a series of craft museums dedicated towards the preservation and chronicling of the indigenous arts and crafts of India for future generations to learn from. This included the Theatre Crafts Museum in Delhi.

She could rightly be termed as the doyenne of the cultural renaissance in post-Independence India. The Central Cottage Industries Emporium set up by the government with the aim of popularizing traditional arts and crafts was doing badly at the time, and the government decided to hand it over to the Indian Cooperative Union headed by Kamaladevi.[19] She reached out to artists practising traditional art forms across the country, even in the most remote areas. By doing so, she became instrumental in the survival and revival of traditional weaves and art forms like Srikalahasti kalamkari, Pochampalli sarees, Jaipur blue pottery, Nandra Buti in Indigo, Toda embroidery, stone sculptures of Mahabalipuram and much more. In 1956, she went to the last practitioner of kalamkari, Jonnalagadda Lakshamajah, to request him to train students in the dying art.[20] Because of her efforts, we have kalamkari thriving today. She reached out to Pochampalli and Nalgonda artists to get them to stay with their traditional practice of weaving, making ikat sarees in silk which are much sought after now.

She also instituted the National Awards for Master Craftsmen, and all these factors came together to help expand the Central Cottage Industries Emporia across India to bring traditional textiles and handicrafts to the people. She started the Natya Institute of Kathak and Choreography (NIKC) in Bangalore (now Bengaluru) in 1964, under the aegis of the Bharatiya Natya Sangh, affiliated to the UNESCO. She was instrumental in setting up the All India Handicrafts and Handlooms Board with Pupul Jayakar and was its first chairperson.[21] She was also, while representing India, elected vice president of the World Crafts Council in 1964. She was the chairperson of the National Centre for Cultural Resources and Training, the Children's Book Trust and the Dolls Museum.

It is because of her that we have some of our most prominent cultural organizations, like the National School of Drama, Sangeet Natak Akademi, Central Cottage Industries Emporium and the Crafts Council of India. The Indian National Theatre that she set up in 1944 was the forerunner for the National School of Drama.[22] The Indian National Theatre sought to celebrate traditional performing arts, including dance, folk performances and poetry to support the freedom movement.

She was a firm advocate of the role handicrafts and cooperative movements at the grassroots level played in uplifting people, both socially and economically. To push through with her vision, she withstood great opposition and criticism from those in power. Her work in the space of handicrafts and handlooms got her the title *'Hatkargha Maa.'* As an author, she wrote over 20 books, with her first writings on the rights of women in India dating back to 1929. One of her last books, *Indian Women's Battle for Freedom*, was published in 1982. She had the opportunity to enter politics and was offered the charge of ministries, which she consistently turned down. She had no interest in politics—her real interest lay in renewing the pride for our traditional art forms and culture.

To quote author Raja Rao in his introduction to her memoir, *Inner Recesses, Outer Spaces*, 1986, 'Perhaps the most august woman on the Indian scene today. Firmly, Indian and therefore universal, highly sophisticated both in sensibility and intelligence, she walks with everyone, in city and country with utter simplicity.'[23]

To quote Gloria Steinem on Kamaladevi, 'There are some people who guide our lives, even though they enter them very briefly. For me, Kamaladevi Chattopadhyay has played that role for a long time.' Steinem provided the foreword to the book, *A Passionate Life: Writings by and on Kamaladevi Chattopadhyay*.[24]

In an article titled *Remembering Kamaladevi*, Jasleen Dhamija, Indian textile art historian and a colleague of Kamaladevi writes:

> She was a real adventurer traveling throughout the world and learning at every step. She met all the great leaders of her time and attracted them by her charismatic personality. [...] She talked of meeting Haile Selassie and having coffee with a rebel Eritrean. She described walking down the large hall to shake hands with the King of Morocco while her Chamba sandal squeaked all the way, to discuss their strategies of resistance and encourage them in their struggle against the French colonists. She was very supportive of the Tunisian freedom struggle office in exile, which functioned from Delhi.[25]

Devaki Jain wrote about Kamaladevi Chattopadhyay, saying:

> Kamaladevi Chattopadhyay was perhaps the most effective, exemplary, constructive worker that was 'thrown up' by the pre-independence decades. It is conventional to suggest that she was influenced by Gandhi. The Gandhian touch or Gandhian political economy was certainly the model of the era; but she was not one of those who directly took the mantra or initiation from Gandhi. Hers was the strength of personal struggle and of course the 'inheritance' of spirit of revolution and rebellion that her mother inculcated into her.[26]

Chattopadhyay was awarded the Padma Bhushan in 1955, the Padma Vibhushan in 1987, the Ramon Magsaysay Award in 1966 and the Sangeet Natak Akademi Fellowship and the Ratna Sadasya in 1974.[27] The Ramon Magsaysay Award Foundation (RMAF) stated, 'The RMAF Board of Trustees recognizes her enduring creativity with handicrafts and cooperatives, as in politics, art and the theater.'[28] In 1977, she was honoured by the UNESCO, and Santiniketan gave her the 'Desikottama,' its most prestigious award. She was also awarded the Charles Eames' Award for contributing to the Quality of Life in India. On her 115th birth anniversary, 3 April 2018, Google honoured her with a Google Doodle dedicated to her on its homepage.[29]

She passed away at the age of 85, on 29 October 1988, in Bombay. With her passing ended an era, an era which saw the resurgence of national pride and the emergence of a nation. She came with a fierce determination that a move towards a modern economy should not leave behind our craftsmen and our traditional weavers, a consideration that has enriched us as a nation. This is the marvellous legacy she has left behind.

NOTES

1 Pal, Sanchari, 'A Freedom Fighter with a Feminist Soul, This Woman's Contributions to Modern India Are Staggering!,' *The Better India*, 3 April 2017, http://tinyurl.com/4tevdjcf. Accessed on 9 January 2024.

2 'Who Was Kamaladevi Chattopadhyay?,' *The Indian Express*, 3 April 2018, http://tinyurl.com/2794zz9d. Accessed on 9 January 2024.

3 '25 Facts about Kamaladevi Chattopadhyay,' *FactSnippet*, 26 May 2023, http://tinyurl.com/bdz5rymn. Accessed on 9 January 2024.

4 Jyothi, 'Kamaladevi: How Could We Forget!,' *Deccan Herald*, 29 October 2020, http://tinyurl.com/4ur92nbf. Accessed on 9 January 2024.

5 Thakur, Richa, 'Kamaladevi Chattopadhyay: The Feminist Who Revived Indian Handicrafts | #IndianWomenInHistory,' *Feminism in India*, 21 March 2017, http://tinyurl.com/57nh6a8w. Accessed on 9 January 2024.

6 Pal, Sanchari, 'A Freedom Fighter with a Feminist Soul, This Woman's Contributions to Modern India Are Staggering!,' *The Better India*, 3 April 2017, http://tinyurl.com/4tevdjcf. Accessed on 9 January 2024.

7 'Kamaladevi Chattopadhyay,' *Azadi ka Amrit Mahotsav*, http://tinyurl.com/2ptsnfj4. Accessed on 17 January 2024.

8 Abrol, Somya, 'Who Was Kamladevi Chattopadhyay, India's Original Feminist?,' *India Today*, 3 April 2018, http://tinyurl.com/dc8yhfks. Accessed on 9 January 2024.

9 Thakur, Richa, 'Kamaladevi Chattopadhyay: The Feminist Who Revived Indian Handicrafts | #IndianWomenInHistory,' *Feminism in India*, 21 March 2017, http://tinyurl.com/57nh6a8w. Accessed on 9 January 2024.

10 '337. Kamaladevi Chattopadhyay- Founder and First Organizing Secretary of AIWC,' *Civil Aspirant*, 1 June 2021, http://tinyurl.com/5cfxphvx. Accessed on 9 January 2024.

11 Chopra, Yauvanika, 'Kamaladevi Dismissed Govt Awards, High Offices but Left India Its Best Art Institutions,' *ThePrint*, 5 April 2022, http://tinyurl.com/4y72rrxw. Accessed on 9 January 2024.

12 Bhargava, G.S., 'Kamaladevi Chattopadhyay: The Many-Splendoured Figure,' *Mainstream Weekly*, Vol. XLV, No. 43, 16 October 2007, http://tinyurl.com/26r75w5y. Accessed on 9 January 2024.

13 '337. Kamaladevi Chattopadhyay-Founder and First Organizing Secretary of AIWC,' *Civil Aspirant*, 1 June 2021, http://tinyurl.com/5cfxphvx. Accessed on 9 January 2024.

14 Nayak, Mayadhar, 'Saluting August 15,1947,' *Orissa Review*, August 2010, http://tinyurl.com/2s49tksx. Accessed on 17 January 2024.

15 Jyothi, 'Kamaladevi: How Could We Forget!,' *Deccan Herald*, 29 October 2020, http://tinyurl.com/4ur92nbf. Accessed on 9 January 2024.

16 Slate, Nico, *Colored Cosmopolitanism: The Shared Struggle for Freedom in the United States and India*, Harvard University Press, 2012.

17 'Kamaladevi Chattopadhyay,' *UPSC with Nikhil*, 27 September 2022, http://tinyurl.com/ppp66bue. Accessed on 9 January 2024.

18 'Who Was Kamaladevi Chattopadhyay?,' *The Indian Express*,

3 April 2018, http://tinyurl.com/2794zz9d. Accessed on 9 January 2024.

19 'Kamaladevi Chattopadhyay,' *Azadi Ka Amrit Mahotsav*, http://tinyurl.com/yc69wxsr. Accessed on 9 January 2024.

20 Thakur, Richa, 'Kamaladevi Chattopadhyay: The Feminist Who Revived Indian Handicrafts | #IndianWomenInHistory,' *Feminism in India*, 21 March 2017, http://tinyurl.com/57nh6a8w. Accessed on 9 January 2024.

21 'All India Handloom Board,' *MAP Academy*, 21 April 2022, http://tinyurl.com/2n8xff42. Accessed on 9 January 2024.

22 'Who Was Kamaladevi Chattopadhyay?,' *The Indian Express*, 3 April 2018, http://tinyurl.com/2794zz9d. Accessed on 9 January 2024.

23 Priya, Mallika, 'Kamaladevi Chattopadhyay—the Torchbearer of Indian Crafts,' *Sarangi*, 8 March 2018, http://tinyurl.com/mwdpukkr. Accessed on 9 January 2024.

24 Dubois, Ellen Carol, and Vinay Lal (eds), *A Passionate Life: Writings by and on Kamaladevi Chattopadhyay*, Zubaan Books, 2017.

25 Priya, Mallika, 'Kamaladevi Chattopadhyay—the Torchbearer of Indian Crafts,' *Sarangi*, 8 March 2018, http://tinyurl.com/mwdpukkr. Accessed on 9 January 2024.

26 Dhamija, Jasleen, 'Remembering Kamaladevi', *India Seminar*, http://tinyurl.com/2j664ptn. Accessed on 9 January 2024.

27 'Sangeet Natak Akademi Ratna Puraskar (Akademi Fellow)', *Wayback Machine Internet Archive*, http://tinyurl.com/2s3d8yaw. Accessed on 9 January 2024.

28 'Chattopadhyay, Kamaladevi,' *Ramon Magsaysay Award Foundation*, http://tinyurl.com/46fcmzry. Accessed on 9 January 2024.

29 'Kamaladevi Chattopadhyay's 115th Birthday Doodle,' *Google Doodles*, 3 April 2018, http://tinyurl.com/3ztnsn2c. Accessed on 9 January 2024.

17

KAMALA DAS

HER STORY

The literary world knows her by many names. At first as Madhavikutty, then Kamala Das and finally, in the later years of her life, as Kamala Surayya. All the names together don't quite encompass the complexity of the woman with the full features, curly hair and the steady gaze. They tell us nothing of the iconoclast she was. Kamala Das—poet, artist, writer and rebel—remains, years after her passing, a woman who refuses to be boxed into any compartments.

She was born in Punnayurkulam, in the Malabar district of British India (present-day Thrissur district in Kerala) on 31 March 1934. She came from the illustrious noble Nalapat family, considered to be the literary royalty of Kerala. Her father, V.M. Nair, was an automobile company executive, and her mother, Nalapat Balamani Amma, was a renowned Malayali poet who published over 20 anthologies of poetry. In fact, some still consider her mother to be a better poet than Kamala Das.[1] Her uncle, Nalapat Narayana Menon, was a poet and translator.[2] Also within the external family was C.V. Subramanya Iyer, the founder-editor of the first English-language journal published in the Malabar district, the *Malabar Quarterly Review*. Aubrey Menen, the controversial writer of *Rama Retold*, was also related to Kamala Das.[3]

Perhaps, words were always meant to be in her destiny,

given her parentage. She was a headstrong child. Her son, M.D. Nalapat, writes, 'From the start, Amma must have been a handful to bring up, as the only mind she felt compelled to obey was her own.'[4] She grew up in Calcutta (now Kolkata). Her father worked with the Walford Transport Company that dealt in Bentley and Rolls-Royce cars. She grew up in Calcutta, and also at the Nalapat ancestral home back in Punnayurkulam in Kerala. Shifting between Calcutta and Kerala caused a sense of dislocation. As Shahnaz Habib writes of her in *The Guardian*, 'This early lesson in dislocation may have inspired many of her literary themes—the vulnerable child-woman trying to create meaning in an inconstant world; nostalgia for a serene, rural past; the unfair privileges of caste and wealth; and the contradictions of motherhood.'[5]

She began writing early, observing the elders of her family immersed in their writing. She would see her uncle writing from morning to night, and her mother writing as she pleased, with the household responsibilities and the care of the children handed over to trusted house-help. When she was barely six, she started a magazine where she would write 'sad poems about dolls who had lost their heads and had to remain headless for eternity'. Her brother would illustrate the pages for her. As they grew older, she would stage plays with her brother, performing classics like Victor Hugo's *Les Misérables* and Kalidas' *Sakuntalam*. The patio of their ancestral home in Kerala was their stage and all the villagers were their audience. Kamala was never formally educated. She was educated at home till she was 15 and was then married to Madhav Das, a bank officer almost two decades older than her. At 16, she had her first son, but in her own words, she 'was mature enough to be a mother only when my third child was born.'[6]

She was a prosaic and an unconventional mother. Her son, M.D. Nalapat, recounts an incident when he didn't fare too well in school, saying, 'One day, when this columnist returned home from school with awful grades, Amma showed him dozens of rejection slips from editors, each safely stowed away. She showed the lot and smiled, for by then Kamala Das was already among the more famous of poets in English and novelists in Malayalam.'[7]

Kamala's husband, aware of the age difference between the two, encouraged her to spend time with people her own age. Kamala has often mentioned that he was always very understanding and supportive of her, and the strongest advocate of her writing, even though at times her controversial writings put a strain on their marriage. To quote her, there 'shall not be another person so proud of me and my achievements.'[8] This is in contrast with the account of their marriage in Merrily Weisbord's biographical work published after Das' death.[9]

To quote Rosemary Marangoly George, an associate professor of literature at the University of California, San Diego, 'She's always consistently being inconsistent. She had many poems and many interviews where she talked about the oppression of the marriage, and then others where she talked about her husband and how much she loved him and how much he loved her and how much she missed him when he died.'[10]

Nalapat wrote of his parents' marriage, saying:

> At a very young age she decided to marry my father, who cherished her to the close of his life in 1992, and who stood by her no matter how many the controversies her writings and on occasion her lifestyle created. Father had begun to love my mother about a year before they married, and this flame never faltered in him, nor the reciprocal feelings in her. They quarrelled with each other, each sometimes exasperated the other, but the shock absorber preventing serious damage to their 43-year relationship was their devotion to each other, a feeling that weathered all storms.[11]

Her husband was encouraging of her efforts and she was soon being published in both English and Malayalam publications. She was very young, and had to balance her passion for writing with the pressures of being a mother and housewife. She spoke about being a woman writer in an interview, saying:

> A woman had to prove herself to be a good wife, a good mother, before she could become anything else. And that meant years and years of waiting. That meant waiting till the graying years. [...]I was impatient. So, I started writing quite early in my life. And perhaps I was lucky. My husband appreciated the fact that I was trying to supplement the family income. So, he allowed me to write at night. [...][12]

She spoke about the writer who didn't even have a writing table to herself, the middle-class woman with a dream to write. She only had the kitchen table where she also cut her vegetables. After clearing everything from the table, she would sit and write there. In the same interview she said about her mother:

> Mother was given the chance to write, to be a full-time writer. It was easy for her because my father was a very old-fashioned gentleman, so he gave her plenty of servants to look after the children, servants to look after the kitchen. She did not have to do anything other than write. And I think she must have enjoyed it. She brought out several books when she was young.[13]

Kamala was published in cult anthologies with the new emerging voices in English poetry in India. She eventually published six poetry collections in English. Her writing was done, as she wrote in *My Story*, in the dead of the night at the dining table, after her husband and sons had gone to sleep, 'until it was 5 and the milkman clanked at the gate, with his cycle and his pails.'[14]

She gained acclaim for her short stories in Malayalam as well as her poems in English. She also wrote columns for many publications. While her poems reached a limited audience, her columns were very well-received and popular. She wrote on a plethora of subjects, from women's issues and child care to politics. Her first book of poems, *Summer in Calcutta*, was well-received. She wrote of love, betrayal and despair. She was uncaring of the niceties of social propriety, writing of bold themes when poets in India were still writing on genteel topics, in keeping with a bygone Romanticism. 'Poetry does not sell in India,' she would say. She would, with her poems, become 'The Mother of Modern Indian Poetry'—a title she never took very seriously.[15]

In her second book of poetry, titled *The Descendants*, she wrote:

> *Gift him what makes you woman, the scent of*
> *Long hair, the musk of sweat between the breasts,*
> *The warm shock of menstrual blood, and all your*
> *Endless female hungers ...*[16]

Her voice, direct as it was, led to it being compared with renowned writers like Marguerite Duras and Sylvia Plath. To quote Jeet Thayil about her, 'It's only when we see her entire body of work that we realise how brave she was. She was writing poems in the 60s and 70s that poets today would think twice about.'[17]

When she was 42, she published her autobiography, titled, rather prosaically, *My Story*. Originally in Malayalam, titled *Ente Katha*, she translated it into English herself. This book brought her both fame and notoriety for the no-holds-barred confessional style it was in. An excerpt from the book is as such:

> Some people told me that writing an autobiography like this, with absolute honesty, keeping nothing to oneself, is like doing a striptease. True, maybe. I, will, firstly, strip

> myself of clothes and ornaments. Then I intend to peel off this light brown skin and shatter my bones. At last, I hope you will be able to see my homeless, orphan, intensely beautiful soul, deep within the bone, deep down under, beneath even the marrow, in a fourth dimension...[18]

My Story, published in 1976, speaks of Kamala's awakening as a woman as well as a writer. It speaks with painful honesty of the difficulties in her marriage. Through her autobiography, she put forth a new form of confessional writing, which resonated with women across India. Termed an autobiography with the subtitle, 'The Compelling Autobiography of The Most Controversial Indian Writer', she later stated that there were quite a few fictional elements in the book.

With her autobiography, Kamala Das became one of the earliest women writers from India to write about sex, the lack of sexual fulfilment in a marriage, her husband's lack of desire for her and her trysts outside the marriage. M.D. Nalapat writes about *My Story*, saying, 'My mother—Amma—wrote about relationships that she had had, being among the very few women to do so at that time. Her premise was that the body of a woman belonged only to herself, and hence she alone had the right to decide on relationships, no matter what her marital or maternal status.'[19]

Naturally, it created an uproar when it was released, with critics deriding it as obscene. However, literary reviewers saw her writing—deeply personal, emotional and confessional—as it was, comparable to the writings of Sylvia Plath and Anne Sexton, who also wrote about the same issues. K. Sachithananthan said about *My Story* in his foreword to an edition, 'I cannot think of any other Indian autobiography that so honestly captures a woman's inner life in all its sad solitude, its desperate longing for real love and its desire for transcendence, its tumult of colours and its turbulent poetry.'[20]

She and Madhav Das had three sons—M.D. Nalapat, Chinen

Das and Jaisurya Das. Her husband passed away in 1992. She wrote over 20 books, with several collections of short stories and poems as well as six novels and three memoirs. She also wrote a newspaper column which dealt with a diverse range of topics, ranging from religion to politics and more. She brought the emotional honesty of her poems and books to her columns, which were often controversial. She was not the only controversial writer in the family, as mentioned earlier—the Nehru government had banned *Rama Retold*, a satirical novel written by Aubrey Menen.

Kamala was also the vice chairperson of the Kerala Sahitya Akademi, chairperson of the Kerala Forestry Board, president of the Kerala Children's Film Society, editor of the *Poet* magazine and poetry editor of the *Illustrated Weekly of India*. The shock value of her early years as a poet and writer, when she was perceived as 'attention-seeking,' had by then changed to her being perceived as a radical, iconoclastic influence on formative post-colonial Indian English poetry. She was called 'The Mother of Modern Indian English Poetry' by *The Times* in 2009.

In the course of her lifetime, she travelled to various universities and festivals around the world to read her poetry, and her works have been translated extensively into international languages. She launched a national party called the Lok Seva Party, to promote secularism and to help women. She also contested the elections for the Indian Parliament in 1984, but her political career went nowhere. She turned to painting, and scandalized many by the nudes she painted.

She converted to Islam when she was 65. Her interest in Islam might have been piqued years earlier, according to M.D. Nalapat. He writes that his parents brought two Muslim boys into their home to live with them, and it was perhaps from them that she first grew interested in Islam.[21]

She said in an interview at the time, in 1999, 'I have given up my freedom, it has made me feel so shabby. Islam is not a lenient husband. Islam is rigid, very stern, I think of Allah as my master. I am his subservient handmaiden. I delight in being subservient.'[22]

It was a decision that shocked everyone, but then, Kamala Das had lived her life uncaring of what people thought about her. She would do exactly as she felt like doing, regardless of societal expectations. In an interview with *rediff.com* she said, '[It is] probably because I have some courage to be what I am, and I don't see my faults as faults—I see them as characteristics; strengths too. Why not, if you realise that you are only a human being.'[23]

She passed away in 2009 at the age of 75 in Pune's Jehangir Hospital, after a prolonged bout of pneumonia.[24] Her body was flown back to Kerala, where she was interred with full state honours at the Palayam Juma Masjid at Thiruvananthapuram, where she had taken her vows of conversion to Islam.

Her writing journey was peppered with awards and recognition. She was awarded the PEN Asian Poetry Prize in 1963, the Kerala Sahitya Akademi Award in 1968, the Kendra Sahitya Academy Award in 1985, the Asian World Prize for Literature in 1985, the Kerala State Film Award in 1988 and the Asian Poetry Prize in 1998, among others. In 2006, the University of Calicut awarded her an honorary D.Litt. On 1 February 2018, Google Doodle honoured her with a doodle to celebrate 42 years of *My Story*. The doodle had an illustration of Kamala with a pen and notebook in hand, with flowers and a row of houses as the backdrop.[25] A movie on her life, *Aami*, was released in 2018. Her last book, *The Kept Woman and Other Stories*, which was a translation of her short stories, was published after she passed away.

Who was Kamala Das? It is an answer that perhaps she herself wanted to keep elusive. Was she Madhavikutty, as she called herself in her writing in Malayalam? Was she just Kamala, as she signed her work before she got married? Was she Aami, the name she called herself in her memoirs? Was she Kamala

Das, the name she took on when she got married? Or was she Kamala Surayya, the name she adopted after converting to Islam in 1999?

Perhaps, the answer lies here, in the opening stanza of her poem 'Someone Else's Song':

I am a million, million people
Talking all at once, with voices
Raised in clamour, like maids
At village-wells.[26]

NOTES

1 Doctor, Geeta, 'Not a Well-Behaved Woman', *The Indian Express*, 5 June 2009, http://tinyurl.com/4xkhfhdr. Accessed on 10 January 2024.

2 Sirur, Simrin, 'Remembering Kamala Das, Feminist Indian Writer Who Chose a "Stern Husband" in Islam', *The Print*, 31 March 2019, http://tinyurl.com/3dvytava. Accessed on 10 January 2024.

3 Nalapat, M. D., 'Thank You, Google, for Remembering Kamala Das', *The Sunday Guardian*, 4 February 2018, http://tinyurl.com/3em77etm. Accessed on 10 January 2024.

4 Ibid.

5 Habib, Shahnaz, 'Kamala Das', *The Guardian*, 18 June 2009, http://tinyurl.com/285b8cfp. Accessed on 10 January 2024.

6 'Woman Who Wrote of Passion and Created a Stir Poet, Painter and Politician', *The Telegraph Online*, 1 June 2009, http://tinyurl.com/v7fwmcyc. Accessed on 17 January 2024.

7 Nalapat, M. D., 'Thank You, Google, for Remembering Kamala Das', *The Sunday Guardian*, 3 February 2018, http://tinyurl.com/3em77etm. Accessed on 10 January 2024.

8 Warrier, Shobha, 'Rediff on the NeT: An Interview with Controversial Poet Kamala Das', *Rediff on the Net*, http://

tinyurl.com/5cvbhdrc. Accessed on 10 January 2024.

9 Roy, Piali, 'The Love Queen of Malabar: Memoir of a Friendship with Kamala Das, by Merrily Weisbord,' *The Globe and Mail*, 19 November 2010, http://tinyurl.com/26bv6s2d. Accessed on 10 January 2024.

10 Fox, Margalit, 'Kamala Das, Indian Poet and Daring Memoirist, Dies at 75,' *The New York Times*, 9 June 2009, http://tinyurl.com/2cb8rn2d. Accessed on 10 January 2024.

11 Nalapat, M. D., 'Thank You, Google, for Remembering Kamala Das,' *The Sunday Guardian*, 3 February 2018, http://tinyurl.com/3em77etm. Accessed on 10 January 2024.

12 Warrier, Shobha, 'Rediff on the NeT: An Interview with Controversial Poet Kamala Das,' *Rediff on the Net*, http://tinyurl.com/5cvbhdrc. Accessed on 10 January 2024.

13 Ibid.

14 Fox, Margalit, 'Kamala Das, Indian Poet and Daring Memoirist, Dies at 75,' *The New York Times*, 9 June 2009, http://tinyurl.com/2cb8rn2d. Accessed on 10 January 2024.

15 Nair, Devika, 'Kamala Das: Many Selves, Many Tongues,' *The Hindu*, 2 April 2015, http://tinyurl.com/52w496cj. Accessed on 10 January 2024.

16 Nair, Vijay, 'Kamala Das: A Life in Verse,' *mint*, 4 June 2009, http://tinyurl.com/47z69yy2. Accessed on 10 January 2024.

17 Mollan, Cherylann, 'Vikram Seth to Kamala Das: The Dark, Brooding World of Indian Poets,' *BBC*, 15 September 2022, http://tinyurl.com/4t9s8r29. Accessed on 10 January 2024.

18 Das, Kamala, *My Story*, HarperCollins, 2009.

19 Nalapat, M. D., 'Thank You, Google, for Remembering Kamala Das,' *The Sunday Guardian*, 3 February 2018, http://tinyurl.com/3em77etm. Accessed on 10 January 2024.

20 Sebastian, Sheryl, 'Kamala Das - The Mother of Modern Indian English Poetry | #IndianWomenInHistory,' *Feminism in India*, 31 March 2017, http://tinyurl.com/yvwwf7w2. Accessed on 10 January 2024.

21 Nalapat, M. D., 'Thank You, Google, for Remembering Kamala Das,' *The Sunday Guardian*, 4 February 2018, http://tinyurl.com/3em77etm. Accessed on 10 January 2024.

22 '"I Am Allah's Handmaiden"', *Outlook*, 5 February 2022, http://tinyurl.com/yz5zt6vu. Accessed on 10 January 2024.

23 Warrier, Shobha, 'Rediff on the NeT: An Interview with Controversial Poet Kamala Das,' *Rediff on the Net*, http://tinyurl.com/5cvbhdrc. Accessed on 10 January 2024.

24 PTI, 'Society | Author Kamala Das, 75, Dies in Pune Hospital,' *mint*, 31 May 2009, http://tinyurl.com/bdepp92v. Accessed on 10 January 2024.

25 'Celebrating Kamala Das,' *Google Doodles*, 1 February 2018, http://tinyurl.com/5y6nuezw. Accessed on 10 January 2024.

26 Sirur, Simrin, 'Remembering Kamala Das, Feminist Indian Writer Who Chose a "Stern Husband" in Islam,' *ThePrint*, 31 March 2019, http://tinyurl.com/3dvytava. Accessed on 10 January 2024.

> My dad has been most influential in my career as a chef. He was the first to teach me how to cook, instilling a love for cooking since I was a child. He also supported my decision to become a chef and helped me understand business. With him, I was able to be strong and face the difficulties over the last two years as I had to think clearly and make decisions that affected not just my life, but the 40 other lives of my team. Yes, my father is the most influential in my life as a person and a chef.[3]

In 2008, she left for France to study at Le Cordon Bleu, graduating with the Grand Diplôme from the institute in 2010. After graduating, she worked briefly at Gordon Ramsay's restaurant, and, in 2013, she applied for an internship at Noma, Copenhagen, where she worked under the legendary Danish chef René Redzepi.

A major breakthrough in her career happened in 2016. She went to Bangkok to work at Gaggan, the eponymous restaurant by Gaggan Anand, which had been at the No. 1 position on the 'Asia's 50 Best Restaurants' list for four consecutive years then. Bangkok had actually not been on her agenda; she had been looking to come back to India. She connected with Anand on the possibility of her coming back to India to manage his restaurant in Mumbai. That, however, didn't work out, which is how she landed up in Bangkok at Gaggan. Garima went on to open a restaurant of her own, and Anand, along with the same team of investors, gave her space right opposite Gaggan in the heart of Bangkok. This is where she opened Restaurant Gaa in April 2017. Gaa received no external funding. The restaurant has five partners, with Garima owning a 20 per cent stake in the company.

As a three-storey restaurant that celebrated a modern tasting menu, using traditional Indian techniques, Gaa received a Michelin star in November 2018. The dining experience at Gaa has been said to be innovative, modern, playful and unpredictable. With it, Garima became the first female Indian chef to have a Michelin star to her credit. To quote *World's 50 Best Restaurants* deputy editor, Laura Price, on Restaurant Gaa,

> [While] the chef is from Mumbai, the location is in Bangkok and the ingredients are local-- yet Arora defines her debut solo restaurant as neither Thai nor Indian. Nevertheless, behind every dish there are cooking techniques based on centuries of Indian history; techniques that have crossed into Thailand and, over time, influenced much of Asia. It is these Indian techniques that are very much at the heart of Gaa and its success, and which Arora wants to show to the world.[4]

Naturally, the first person she called when she was awarded the Michelin star was her father—the person who first infused the love for food and cooking in her, and then supported her dreams to be a chef. Barely a few months after receiving a Michelin star, in March 2019, Restaurant Gaa debuted at No. 16 on *Asia's 50 Best Restaurants*' list, with it also getting the 'Highest New Entry' Award. A month earlier, in February 2019, she was named 'Asia's Best Female Chef' for the year by *World's 50 Best Restaurants*. In June 2019, Restaurant Gaa debuted on the *World's 50 Best Restaurants*' list at No. 95.

Restaurant Gaa has a team of 18 people from seven nationalities, and the menu reflects that. The cooking techniques are traditional Indian, with locally-sourced ingredients. Gaa offers its patrons a 10–14 course tasting menu which keeps changing according to the season and available ingredients. It is famous for its duck doughnut, and a signature unripe jackfruit, served with roti and pickles. Garima brings her experience from across the many countries she has worked in—France, United Arab Emirates, Denmark and Thailand—and this is reflected in the eclectic menu she has created.

In August 2019, Garima launched Food Forward India (FFI), which is an initiative prioritizing the future of Indian food. She had the inaugural event of the initiative on 17 October 2019. Her mission is to take Indian food to the rest of the world, beyond butter chicken and curry. With the Covid-19 pandemic and the lockdown, Gaa had to be closed. But there was no keeping Garima Arora down. She returned with HERE, an Indian all-day breakfast canteen concept, again in Bangkok. The pandemic led to a lot of plans going on hold, and with her expecting a baby, plans went on hold yet again. The food world is waiting to see what lies in store for them from Garima Arora.

Excerpts from a conversation with her:

The first female chef to be a judge on Masterchef India, how did that come about?

I've never done TV or camera before so my first instinct was to say 'no, not me' but I think Vikas (Chef Vikas Khanna) had a big role to play in it. He was adamant to make it all happen. And I'm glad he did; all in all it was a very good experience.

From mass media and journalism to Cordon Bleu, was there a specific moment or an incident that made you switch career paths? I believe there was a Singapore trip and a hot pot that was instrumental in the decision. Could you tell us more about it?

Cooking, eating was always a big part of growing up. My dad was always the cook at home, to be honest, so I spent a lot of time in the kitchen watching him cook and enjoy it, [and] somewhere it stuck with me. In those days, it was not a very popular profession for people to choose. I just went the journalism way because I loved to read and write, but I thought that this possibly was a profession I could pursue and enjoy. For me, journalism was interesting because it made you think and enquire and think about things in a different way. But somewhere along the line, I realized that if I wanted to do something with food and become a chef, it was best to start young because it is a physically demanding job.

It was a very straightforward course. Cordon Bleu is not difficult to get into. You apply and that's pretty much it. It was not very difficult to get into Cordon Bleu, the difficult part started after. I had to learn the basics of French, I had to. I don't have a flair for languages, so I had to struggle with that. But I got by.

What was moving to Paris like when you were so young?

I was all of 20–21, and it was my first time away from home. I remember it was the middle of December when I moved to Paris. It was very cold, it was snowing. I am a Mumbai girl so I hadn't seen temperatures so low. So, for me, moving by myself was quite a daunting task. I moved into a hostel when I got there, then started searching for an apartment. These were things that at 21 I had never done before, so it was a stepping out of my comfort zone, where your parents do everything for you and then trying to learn how to do things for yourself. That was probably the best part of moving away from home. I think it is essential that everyone does this at least once in their lives. That was quite a learning experience for me. The language part, getting Internet set up at home, dealing with the landlord, all of those things, it was interesting.

Would you still hold that you need to get into food when you are young because it is a very demanding job?

Well, yes and no. The profession has been changing for a while now. For the longest time, it was considered a blue-collar job, so to speak. The profession and the technology are changing. I think it is now attracting people from different backgrounds, different educational backgrounds. When I started off in the kitchen so many decades ago, you would have culinary school drop outs and culinary school graduates but today you will find Harvard graduates, people with microbiology degrees working in the kitchen and doing R&D, so the whole profession has changed, so to speak. Food is beyond simply cooking it and being a chef. I think it is a cerebral profession now. It has changed; it is different now and for the better.

What would you say are your strongest memories of your time in Paris; mentors you are grateful for from your stint at Le Cordon Bleu; and the lessons you took away from the institute, apart from the curriculum, which have stood you in good stead till date?

This was around 2008–09, we didn't have a lot of international cuisine in India back then, and, for me, it was the first time tasting foie gras and oysters and frog legs. I used to be a vegetarian before that. So, for someone like me who enjoyed food, Paris was like a wonderland, a child's playground. To me, being a student in Paris, at that time and that age, coming from India, meeting all these different people coming from all over the world—I've had a Polish friend, I've had an Italian friend, American, Canadian friends. I think making friends from different parts of the world, who are all into food, you get exposed to their kind of cuisine. It was a great eye opener to me, so it was fun, all in all.

There's no better place to start out as a chef or a cook than in one of the greatest food cities of the world. I think Noma for me was the most pivotal point of my career; it changed me not just as a cook but also a person. It made me think about where I came from, my food heritage, my culinary heritage and what I wanted to do with it. It was very easy to leave India and go abroad and study French cuisine, but the more you stay abroad you see what other cuisines have to offer and you start appreciating your own. I think my time at Noma was a big, big, part of that. When you see how much they do with so little produce, you think of everything you have at home; I think it drew me back to Indian cooking in a big way.

You've worked with some of the most influential and respected names in food and restaurants—Gordon Ramsay, René Redzepi and Gaggan Anand—before setting out on your own. How have each of them contributed to your understanding of food? You've said that the chef who has inspired you the most in your career is Redzepi. Could you elaborate?

From Noma, I was fascinated with how they created an entire new cuisine from what you have around you; we compare it back to the multiple seasons, ingredients and techniques we have back home and think about what we can do with all of that. That's probably the most interesting thing I took away from there. I worked at Gordon Ramsay's restaurant, that was my first job, even before Noma, but never had the opportunity of working with him. It was a very tough kitchen, what you see on TV is exactly what those kitchens are like. They're hardcore like that. For me, it was a very humbling experience going into those kitchens and realizing that you don't know everything. You think you've come out of culinary school and you know everything but that's a young person's folly. I'm glad I realized I had so much to learn, and I'm glad for my head chefs there who taught me humility, which was very essential at that point. Just learning how to work with people and learn as you go along.

You're running a team, right, so most chefs have to learn to appreciate what everyone brings to the table. Not everyone is a great cook or a great chef. What they bring to the team, sometimes it is stability, sometimes it is good humour, sometimes it is a different approach. It is not as simple as 'everyone is the best cook at Gaa today.' They're good cooks, yes, but everyone has a role to play in a team and that is what you realize as you go along.

You were supposed to move to Mumbai to a restaurant being set up by Gaggan Anand, but eventually moved to Bangkok to work with him, and eventually set up your own restaurant there. You were very young when you did so. What made you feel this was the right time to strike out on your own? Did you face any scepticism from any quarters?

Gaggan Anand was looking for a head chef for his restaurant

that he planned to open in Mumbai; I was looking to move back to India from Copenhagen at that point. So, he offered me the position of a head chef in his restaurant which he was planning to open, but that restaurant never opened. That never happened. Part of that process was that I was supposed to come to Bangkok, spend a couple of months here, and then move to India and run that restaurant for him. But that restaurant never happened. I met the same investors who were the investors for his restaurant. I was then there at Gaggan for maybe two or three months, not long. And we realized that if India was not happening then we would do something in Bangkok itself. So, I got to know them, they got to know me, we were happy to get into business together and that's how Gaa happened. So, instead of me going to India to become the head chef for Gaggan, I ended up opening my own restaurant here with them.

There's a very strong cultural connection between India and Thailand. I don't think it is spoken about enough so people [don't] know that. I mean, the religion is so similar, the language is so similar, the gods are so similar. Thailand is a very interesting backdrop through which one can explore Indian cuisine and that's what I discovered when I moved here. I also realized that this could be a very interesting place to live in and explore this a little more.

You were very young when you set up Gaa. Did you face scepticism from any quarters, did you feel people were wondering how were you going to pull this off?

I was 29 when I set up Gaa. I don't think it was about me being a girl or anything. For me, I don't think about why things don't happen. I mean, so many times things don't go my way. I have the tendency to take stock of a situation and move on to the next thing. So, I'm not the kind of person who thinks too much about why—is it because I'm a woman or is it because I'm too young? I'm lucky that my profession is such that it does not matter what gender you are, what age you are—it is experience that matters. The way somebody holds a knife, you know how much experience they are bringing to the table. I was lucky enough that my experience spoke for itself. We opened and within two years we had so many accolades, and so many things going for us. So, I didn't really have to worry too much about proving myself after that, I guess.

Restaurant Gaa debuted on the 'Asia Best 50' list as the highest new entry. Did you feel the pressure with that recognition, that you've already set the bar so high in your first year, so how do you keep up?

No, not at all. Being recognized is great, it is great to get recognition from your peers, it is great for the team morale, obviously, not taking anything away from it. But I'll be honest, it is not something we work for or work towards. It is a by-product of all the hard work that the team puts in. We get it, it is great; we don't get it, we don't spend too much time thinking about it. Our principle is very simple, we got into this profession not for the accolades but for the joy of cooking, and that's what we continue to do.

What was your vision for Restaurant Gaa and how has this vision evolved since its inception?

It was always to explore Indian cooking. I have always believed that Indian cuisine can do for Asia what French cuisine did for Europe. We have a history and tradition of thousands of years, [which] when actually broken down and examined, it can give you the resources to explore Asian cuisine in a big way. You can talk about Nordic cuisine being based in French techniques to such a large extent. With India and Asia, the way Asia eats, the spices, the food, the ingredients, that can all be explored more. That was what Gaa was about, to explore these techniques in Indian culinary history.

I think we're one of the very few Michelin restaurants in the world, or fine dining restaurants in the world, where our main course has always been vegetarian. We do a tasting menu, and we have always had a vegetarian main course. I've almost never ever had anyone complain about this, and I think this is a testament to Indian techniques and drawing *umami* from vegetables so you don't miss meat. I guess, in the West, people are just starting to pick up on this, on vegetarian food. But I feel this is such an important part of our food history and it is important to highlight it. Actually, our entire menu is around 80 per cent vegetarian as well, and honest to God no one has ever noticed or mentioned or commented because it is so satisfying. That's something I'm very proud of—that we can pull this off without people even realizing. It's interesting that Indian food has the capability to do that.

You were the first Indian woman to head a restaurant that was awarded a Michelin star. Tell us about the moment you heard that you had been awarded it, the emotions you felt and the kind of responsibility and pressures that being a Michelin-starred chef brings for you, as well as the joys.

It was such a perfect moment. It happened with the two most important people in my core team. We were going through the menu doing the wine pairing when we got the call. I was happy, I was excited, no doubt, but what gave me the biggest joy was seeing the reaction on the staff's face when I hung up. I took the call, and I don't know how they knew, and when I turned around they were already in tears and hugging. They just knew. That moment, the victory was not mine, it was theirs, it was the team's. That moment was a very precious moment. To be able to share that moment with them. I don't think anything came close to that afterwards.

I don't feel it, the pressure. It's a good validation to have, we are very happy and proud to have it. But that is not going to stop us from doing what we want to, or we are not going to change our plans just because the Michelin happened. Honestly, what would you rather have: a hundred accolades and an empty restaurant or a restaurant full of guests who are happy and no accolades. I would take the latter. There are so many restaurants around who don't have these stars, but they're full and the guests are happy and the chefs are happy and what else would you rather want? So, I think, happy guests are what I want.

After Gaa, which was 'modern eclectic cuisine' with modern Indian flavours and interpretation with Thai ingredients, you came up with HERE, which had an Indian breakfast concept. Both are completely unique in their concepts. Why did you feel that this concept would work at this point? How do you fuse an Indian canteen breakfast concept with Thai sensibilities, setting and local produce?

It started out as a breakfast concept and it evolved into an all-day dining restaurant. We started it during the lockdown because Gaa was kind of slow and things weren't moving. So, we used the kitchen space. I was missing home. So, it was kind of taking genuine Indian flavours and giving that centre stage; people really loved it and enjoyed it, and it kind of snowballed into something bigger and we decided that we would take it and open it at a new location.

What is your regular day like?

I'm always at the restaurant, 24x7. I live right next door. My day normally begins—the first thing in the morning, I work out. I'm very particular about nutrition and working out, that's something I pay a lot of attention to. So, I work out six days a week, my day starts with that. Then into office work. You know, being a chef is not about creativity anymore, it is all about managing numbers. I start my day by spending time in the office, with my manager and with accounts. Then I get into the kitchen, do some R&D sometimes and then get ready for service. So, during service, there is a team that manages everything but it is important that I go around [to] manage the guests, explain the food. I think it makes a lot of difference when it comes from the source directly. I try to spend as much time as I can with the guests on the floor and in the kitchen. It is a very important part of what makes Gaa what it is. We're always looking for feedback; it is very important to accept criticism and to sieve through it and know what is genuine and what we can use and what we cannot.

It's a constantly evolving thing. Especially when we put out a new dish, we never put out one dish for everybody, we do it in phases. We'll give it to a few tables, get the feedback, understand how they feel about it, make tweaks and changes and then go full on. It is a restaurant where the guests have to enjoy their food. I am not the kind of chef who says that 'this is what you get' and 'this is what you eat'. Of course, that is the format when you have a tasting menu, but at the end of the day if you don't enjoy your meal it is all for nothing. Which is why we always recommend that, not only for our restaurant, but for any restaurant, if you're unhappy with something let the team know. Nobody wants anyone to have a bad time but if you do not communicate and let your server know or your chef know what is it that is going to make you happy, you're not going to be happy. Don't hesitate to let them know, give them a chance to fix it. Because once you have left the restaurant there is nothing they can do.

Tell us more about FFI. What motivated you to set it up and what are the goals you hope to achieve through it?

So, FFI started right after we got the Michelin and the 50 Best of Asia, so we were getting so much media attention and we thought 'what do we do with all of this' and we decided to throw back at India and all the food there. So, we started this nomadic initiative where the idea was to go to every state and explore the culinary history of that state, but six months down we went into lockdown and had to stop the whole thing. But now that I was able to go back to India for *Masterchef*, it is spurring that again. Again, by the end of the year or early next year we should be able to see some movement [...]. Maybe not in the same avatar but it will definitely be picked up again. When it started, it went off really well, we went to Telangana, we had a sort of a think-tank session in Mumbai and we straight went into a lockdown and I went back only three years later.

The professional kitchen is still perceived to be male-dominated, while kitchens are still considered a woman's domain. You were the only woman in the kitchen at a point while at Noma. As a woman entering this arena, the professional kitchen, what were the challenges you expected, the unexpected challenges you encountered and did you face any sexism consciously or unconsciously? Are professional kitchens more accommodating of women and the demands of family and home now?

It is not an easy job; it is simply not an easy job. You're working 14, 15, 16 hours a day. A job like this asks for much more from a woman than it does from a man. When I did it, I did it because sometimes I think I have a death wish. Today, the industry has evolved so much you have so many options within the industry to pursue food and your love for food. It is the same reason why you have more female nurses than male nurses, and why you have more male construction workers than female workers. It's a physically very demanding job. People see it from the outside and assume it is all glitz and glamour, but it is not. It is standing in a hot kitchen for 12–14 hours a day with no rest, and most days no food. So, it is not a job I would recommend women to take up.

It's just so simple, there is no conspiracy to keep women out, if people think that is what is happening. As a business owner and a chef myself, I don't care what gender my employees belong to, I just need good people to show up. That's all I care about. So, nobody is keeping women out, it's just a profession that's not easy. It is physically very, very demanding. It's definitely not easy for women. You definitely 100 per cent cannot have a family in your 20s if you want to be a chef. Is that a sacrifice that women want to make or be asked to make? It's not fair. It is a decision that women have to make for themselves and to each their own.

If this is something you want, the doors are wide open, you can work hard and you'll get to places. This is a profession, to be honest, where there is a dearth of hardworking chefs today, man or woman. If that's what you want, you can really, really, excel. But you're going to have to make that sacrifice, that you're not going to have any family life in your 20s. Hopefully in your 30s, when you have your own business you can think about settling down and having the other side of it. The cost of a profession like this is higher on women than on men. It's not going to be easy, I'm not saying it can't be done, but I do think it is unfair to put the onus of all of this on the girls and what they have to do to get into this job.

It is also a big responsibility of the family around the girls. You can't create legends without an ecosystem that helps propel them. I think it is a give and take, it is very important to surround yourself with the right kind of people. I'm lucky enough to have a very supportive husband who was with me through my 20s. We've been together for 15 years, married for five, and, having him in my life, I don't see many other men who would support the kind of crazy decisions I've taken in my life. I have him supporting me, I have my father who has been supporting me throughout, my mom who has always been so proud of all I've done. So, these things help you take those tough decisions.

But if you don't have that support from the people around you, the society around you and from your family, then taking those tough decisions is not easy. It is not easy to leave everything and to move to Copenhagen one day and then not come back for 10 years. I think the change is not something that women need to make. I think women are capable, they are born with all the capability in them. But it is people around them who put limitations on what is acceptable and what is not. It's changing, it is getting easier. You cannot take it away whether it is cooking or any profession. If you want to excel at any career, you have to make sacrifices, and women generally will make more sacrifices than men to excel at their career. That's a given. There is no way around it no matter what your job is. So, I think, coming together and supporting a woman's career choices and goals, I think it is the people around her who need to do that.

What is Garima Arora's favourite food?

Most days I'm like a dog, a puppy. I eat the same thing every day. For breakfast, lunch, dinner. As I said, I'm very particular about my nutrition and when I lock onto something I don't want to experiment a lot myself. I am a simple, plain eater. My comfort food is always chaat. There's always a version of chaat on my menu.

And finally, after being the first woman from India to helm a Michelin-starred restaurant, what would you want your legacy to food to be?

If we can leave a working framework for the next generation of chefs to explore Indian food, I think we would have done our job. Every time we get stuck, because we don't know how to break it down and understand it. I think if we come up with a system where we can start digging into the history of our food culture and start making it relevant for today's diners and restaurants and food systems, that would really be something. I know that one lifetime is not even close to being enough, but if we could begin somewhere and lay the groundwork, that would make me very happy.

NOTES

1 '"Cook with Honesty": The Inspiration for Chef Garima Arora, Winner of Michelin Guide Young Chef Award', *Michelin Guide*, 25 January 2022, http://tinyurl.com/45ebsx4b. Accessed on 5 January 2024.

2 Jaychander, Neeti, 'Garima Arora Is India's First Michelin Star Woman Chef', *Femina*, 11 November 2019, http://tinyurl.com/5n8fam6z. Accessed on 5 January 2024.

3 '"Cook with Honesty": The Inspiration for Chef Garima Arora, Winner of Michelin Guide Young Chef Award', *Michelin Guide*, 25 January 2022, http://tinyurl.com/45ebsx4b. Accessed on 5 January 2024.

4 Tiu, Cheryl, 'Garima Arora, the First Indian Woman to Receive a Michelin Star, Is Now Asia's Best Female Chef 2019', *Forbes*, 28 February 2019, http://tinyurl.com/4539tkxm. Accessed on 5 January 2024.

19

KAVITA DEVI BUNDELKHANDI

REVOLUTIONIZING STORIES FROM THE HINTERLAND

She is an unlikely hero. Born in the hinterlands of rural India, to an underprivileged family of farmers, denied an education when she was a child, Kavita Devi, also known as Kavita Bundelkhandi, is today the editor-in-chief and co-founder of the grassroots feminist news network *Khabar Lahariya.* She was also the first Dalit woman to become a member of the Editor's Guild of India, a momentous achievement in and of itself.

Born in the remote village of Kunjan Purwa, in Chitrakoot district, Kavita Devi is the eldest of six surviving children of her parents. The family is from the Dalit community, and farming is the hereditary profession. No one in the family had received any education, not even the adults, and neither did they expect to. The children grew up without any education. The girls learnt housework and the boys worked on the farm. As was the norm, she was married off when she was barely 12. She stayed with her parents till she was 15, and once she came of age, she was sent off to live with her in-laws. At the time, she didn't even understand what marriage meant. For her, it was just a fun experience.

It was around then that she defied her parents and went to an NGO which was teaching the women of the village to read and write. A Government of India programme launched in 1989, called Mahila Samakhya, had opened a learning centre in her village, called the Mahila Shiksha Kendra, to help girls and adult women gain basic functional literacy. The young Kavita had heard about it when she was filling water at the communal tap, and was determined to go. Her family scoffed at her ambitions when she told them. But she was determined. She would make sure she finished all her chores and then go to the centre, and study for an hour or so every day. Her greatest joy came from learning to write her name.

There was a camp for the girls who were promising students. She convinced two other girls from the village to attend with her. Their parents came to take them back. While the other two girls returned, she remained defiant. She refused to go back with her father. Eventually, the NGO workers took her home and spoke with her parents and in-laws, making them understand the need for Kavita to get an education. The family relented in the face of Kavita's continued defiance and she went back to the centre, where she studied for six months.

This defiance made her the first woman in her village to get an education. She went on to complete her graduation and get a master's degree in journalism, but still considers those initial six months of studying with the Mahila Samakhya her most fulfilling learning moments. The NGO in her village began a newsletter, called *Mahila Dakiya*, which sent out a printed newsletter with women-related news of the region. *Mahila Dakiya* was a handwritten newsletter, with hand-drawn sketches, in the Bundeli dialect. It was very popular but ran into some problems, and had to be shut down. Kavita was involved with this newsletter until it was shut down. This was her first tryst with journalism.

In 2002, she co-founded *Khabar Lahariya* with seven other women. She also drew from her experience with *Mahila Dakiya* while ideating *Khabar Lahariya*. Kavita felt that the need for the newsletter still existed, and, therefore, began the conversation with the NGO Nirantar to start a newspaper, which then became *Khabar Lahariya*. From the outset, *Khabar Lahariya* was meant to be a platform for marginalized women to tell their stories, and they recruited and trained their journalists accordingly. It wasn't easy for Kavita. She worked at a brick kiln to pay off a debt while she was in her intermediary year. She gave her exams, and joined the team that later produced *Khabar Lahariya*. She learnt on the job, so to speak. They did get basic training—clicking photos, writing reports—but she had to find her footing before getting the show running. Newspapers were alien to her; she had never had newspapers come home as a child. Women never read them, only a few men in the village did. She actually read a newspaper for the first time ever when she joined *Khabar Lahariya*.

The initial years were tough. Her reporting has always been on-ground, going into the villages and getting first-hand accounts of the stories. The very first story she covered was the '*Muh nochwa*' rumour that had gained traction at the time, about some beast that would eat away a person's face or arm while they were asleep. She investigated and wrote about how it was a geological phenomenon caused by hot, dry weather. Nonetheless, it took a while for her to be accepted as a journalist. Being a woman, and a Dalit at that, she found doors being closed in her face and often had to encounter open hostility and threats to her safety.

The team also had to get around the objections their families had to what they were doing. In the first few years, their families imposed strict codes. Kavita initially wore a saree even when out on field for her reporting. She's chased dacoits in dacoit-infested Bundelkhand, reported from towns and villages across the region and gone every month to Delhi for editorial meetings. She and the team are daredevils of sorts, going across treacherous territory, navigating social censure and more to bring us stories which otherwise would never get reported in mainstream media.

Barely two years later, the team received the Chameli Devi Jain Award for 'Outstanding Women Mediapersons'. The team grew to have six editions by 2014, with a staff of around 40. While it was initially started as a Bundeli newspaper, *Khabar Lahariya* has on its staff Dalit, Muslim, Adivasi and other backward-caste women as well as urban, upper-caste women. Since the beginning, the team composition has been a healthy mix of diverse identities. While the paper had eight editions, and was sold in eight districts of Uttar Pradesh, it was reinvented as a digital news platform when the rising costs of newsprint made it difficult to sustain. Technology and the Internet were an opportunity for them, which they capitalized upon swiftly. Now, with everyone in the villages having smartphones and Internet access, their stories reach the remotest corners of the hinterland, becoming the backbone of Bundelkhand and Awadh.

Of all the stories she has done, she feels a special affinity with crime stories. She dispels perceptions that women cannot cover crime. Kavita also has a fortnightly news commentary show called *The Kavita Show*, and has been the editor-in-chief of the publication since 2019. Her moment of fame came when she was a speaker at the TED conference hosted by Shah Rukh Khan. She now gives back by training young women and girls as a mentor and trainer with the Chambal Academy, the digital learning vertical of the company. She is a mentor on the Academy's hybrid course on rural mobile journalism, and an expert for the Academy's toolkits on digital safety and security and rural reporting. She hopes her journey, against all odds as it has been, inspires many girls from the region to aspire to get into news, to tell the stories only they can tell, as they come from the land.

Excerpts from a conversation with her:

In your childhood, growing up in the village, there was absolutely no indication that you would grow up to be a journalist, and such an important journalist at that. Can you remember any incidents which perhaps sowed the seeds of wanting to speak out against injustice in you back in your growing years?

No, I don't think there was any background as such. Often, questions would be raised in my mind about caste discrimination. Sometimes, when people would call my father in a derogatory way, I would ask my father why do these people speak to you like this or call you in this manner. So, I was slowly learning about caste and discrimination at this point, in a sense. Although, where we lived, the gram panchayat did not have too much of a population but mostly Dalits lived there. In a way, I began to learn about the politics of caste back then. And then there was the issue of how women are treated. There was domestic violence in my home when I was growing up, my father would beat up my mother regularly; my mother had 12 children, of which six passed away as infants, and six of us survived. Many of my mother's children were born in front of me—I helped with some of the deliveries, being the eldest child. I remember when one of my sisters was born, my father was very annoyed that a girl had been born again, and he wouldn't speak to my mother.

We come from a farming family, and my father would go to the fields to do the ploughing, and I took the morning meal to him, boiled wheat and chana, which we then [ate] with a green chutney. So, I asked my father then, 'Why are you angry with my mother? Is it because a girl has been born?' And my father replied very angrily, and it was then that I began to understand that girls are not wanted. Another incident I remember, my father was beating my mother. I was small at the time, and I was beating him with my small fists trying to get him to stop beating my mother. I couldn't do much else at the time, I was very young. But as I grew and I joined the organization and I learnt about things, I got a little more confident.

One day, my father was shouting at my mother, and I stood at the doorway and told him very sternly that you say what you say, but you will not raise your hand on her or there will be no one worse than me. My mother would tell me that my father would beat her so much and stuff a cloth in her mouth while beating her so she would not scream aloud. No one has ever asked me this question before about how my childhood has influenced my activism, and perhaps that is why I have never spoken about this before. I was very small at the time, I don't even remember exactly how old I was, probably seven or eight years, but now that you ask me, these memories are coming to mind.

You were very young when you were married off, and perhaps you were not even educated at the time. How did you get yourself educated?

Back in the village no one would study, everyone would work on the farms. There was one son of my grandfather's who would go to school, then there was my father, who then would educate me. I was married off when I was 12 years old. I didn't even understand marriage and what it actually meant back then. I began studying only after I was married.

Did your father or your husband and in-laws support you in your education? What challenges did you have to overcome in order to get educated?

My father was staunchly against me getting an education, although now his thinking has completely changed and he's become a staunch supporter of women's rights. Initially, of course, it was why should I get educated, what will I do by getting educated. I will get married, I will have to manage the household, do the housework; it would be better for me to focus on learning how to do housework rather than getting an education. So, the thought was that we will get her married off and her husband and her in-laws will be responsible for her.

When I used to go to the Mahila Centre to attend the classes they conducted, my father wouldn't even allow me to go there. It was in the village itself, and I would go there for an hour after doing the household chores. There was always a lot of work to be done in the house. We were a farming family, and there was farm work and house work to be done. We had animals—we had to cut grass and feed them, clean their stables. I was the eldest of the children and the maximum quota of work came to me, as well as taking care of the younger children. We had a very big house and all the cleaning, etc., all this needed to be done. So, the *didi* would come at around 2.00–3.00 p.m. at the Centre, and I would ensure I had finished with all the work that needed to be done and run off to the Centre for an hour. I enjoyed studying.

I would hear my name being called, and not know how to write it. I learnt how to write my name at the Centre itself. The others there were grown women, I was very young and the teacher told me 'you are very young, but if you want to study with the older women it is okay'. I wore a saree and had tied my hair in two plaits, and slipped into the crowd. Two other girls from the village also came with me, but their family members came and took them away saying, 'We don't want them to get educated, they're girls and they should be in the house, doing housework, what good will education be for them?' So then my father came to take me back home, too. Those two girls were also related to me.

Pappa said, 'Both of them have gone, now you come too.' I began crying, saying that I wouldn't go, I wanted to study. So, the people from the Centre did some counselling, and my father said that while he was okay with me studying, he wouldn't take responsibility for it now that I was married, and that they should go to my in-laws' home and take permission from my in-laws. They went to my in-laws home to ask for permission. My husband was not educated, as were all my in-laws. They were counselled by the people from the Mahila Centre and they agreed to allow me to attend the Centre and study.

Did your in-laws, your husband, have any apprehensions or misconceptions about you getting educated, given none of them were educated?

Of course, there were apprehensions, and there's a whole long story about it. I had to eventually leave my in-laws home but that is another story.

The first newsletter that you worked with at the Mahila Centre was the Mahila Dakiya, *which was a printed newsletter. From* Mahila Dakiya *to* Khabar Lahariya, *what was the journey like?*

I had a long history with *Mahila Dakiya*. When I studied from the Mahila Centre, they thought that the girls who have studied from the Mahila Centre should somehow stay connected with the Mahila Centre, so I used to be involved in the production of *Mahila Dakiya*. It was like a broadsheet newspaper, and we used to do quite a bit of marketing for it, going to villages whenever there were fairs, etc., and talk[ing] about the newspaper. I had built up quite a good network in the villages because of *Mahila Dakiya* and people were very fond of it because it was in the local language. When *Mahila Dakiya* shut down, people would keep telling us, 'Why did you shut it down? At least through it we would get some local news.' So, we felt that there was really a need for a newspaper in the rural area, because the real issues of the villages were not coming out in the national media.

We realized also that there are so many issues at the national level that villagers would not be aware of—schemes, laws, issues that were relevant for them. What was happening with women and girls in the rural areas, the water issues, other such issues, they weren't getting spoken about and we felt that there was a need to have a medium where these issues could be highlighted and brought to the attention of the government and the relevant authorities. As a democracy, it is their right to receive information. Whatever media did reach was in a language removed from what the villagers spoke and the issues were not issues relevant to them. We then started *Khabar Lahariya*, with the aim that if we start a newspaper or a channel we will only hire women journalists because journalism is not seen as a space for women to enter, especially in the villages, and that too women from across communities to ensure a diverse representation. We decided to use language that was familiar to people in the villages, write our reports in a certain way so that everyone could read them, including those who aren't used to reading. We had very detailed discussions on all this, including the name, the layout, the style, and then we began.

Apart from the fact that you were looking for women journalists and women from across caste and minority segments—because you need a different mindset in order to be a journalist, there needs to be fearlessness, tenacity and more—how did you narrow down on your team?

When we started we were determined to make only women journalists. First, there were women who had been with me at the Mahila Centre, who could read and write and had been involved with the work of the Centre. Then we went into the villages, searching for women who could probably become journalists, and we couldn't find any such women far and wide. Most women had studied to around the fifth [grade], the Adivasi and Dalit women were not educated. And there were some women from the Mahila Centre who had done perhaps six months of studying. When we interviewed them and started training them (they are still with the team today) we used to ask them what are the issues facing the village, and they would tell us about the issues in great detail. We thought, this is what we want. They might not be able to write, but they were able to narrate very well and tell us in great detail. We trained them across education levels, we sent them into the field, getting us news from the villages of how some villages, even after so many years of Independence, have seen no officials visit; how there are no roads, no water, no electricity; how the forests are being cut down and there had been no action taken; the issues women and the girl child were facing in the villages, violence against women, as well as anecdotes which were most amusing. So, we would get them to write the drafts in their basic language, then we had a team that sat with them and worked further on the drafts with them to get the details of what they were trying to share and got the final draft into place. Then, slowly, *Khabar Lahariya* picked up and I could see the change happening around me. In my village itself, when I was young, no girl was educated; but now, all the girls are getting an education, many are working. Some are teachers, some are in the police, in the *anganwadi*; there is so much change. Those in my village who told my parents that 'she will run away, what are you thinking sending a young girl to study and get educated,' the young girls from their family now are all educated, some with jobs in the police force.

How does this make you feel?

I feel very happy seeing this, to be honest. I see the greatest change in my own village where they decried me so much. My friends who had left at the time tell me they regret their decision and say that had they only stood their ground at the time, they would have been able to do a job now, or, if nothing, they would be able to speak out against the violence and domestic abuse they face. But now they are ensuring they are educating all their daughters. I've seen a lot of progress in this space in my village. All the girls are getting educated.

What was the first story that you did or that you remember which was very impactful, and brought about perceptible change?

I remember two stories. This rumour about Muh nochwa, about a creature or person who comes into the villages and scratches the face. The rumours were that it flew in the skies, and it was very hot at the time, but people who would normally sleep out of their homes to beat the heat would sleep inside their homes for fear of this Muh Nochwa. There was no cooler, [or] fans in the village, of course, so people would sleep inside in the sweltering heat. And those who slept outside, there were strange incidents of them waking up with their face scratched out or blisters on their face. I wrote an article on this creature and at the production meeting everyone quite liked this article. And afterwards, I researched about this and found that something in the air, a phenomenon due to the extreme heat, was causing this. And I was pleased because what people were putting down to superstition, I could find a scientific explanation for and present[ed] it to people.

Another story is that of a temple to a *Devi* which is very well regarded among the community. I went there with my in-laws and my husband and saw there how the *pandas* keep telling you put money here and there, and I wrote an article on how if you go to a temple believing in a god, why should you be pressurized to put money here and there. So, these stories were really appreciated and got a wide readership, at that time, there was nothing like viewership and numbers to know exactly, but I got a good response from those who had read it. But this was right in the beginning and I did so many stories after those.

The kind of stories that you do, mainstream media doesn't touch. There is no interest unless it is a big incident that catches national headlines. You must have faced many instances where you faced physical danger, threats or more because of the reporting you've done?

There has always been pressure of different kinds. First, it was that women can't be journalists, that we were bringing disrepute to the village. Then, it was going against the powerful people in the village who knew our families and our life situation. Raising issues, asking questions—that would make them very angry. 'The famous journalists of the region aren't asking us any questions,' they thought, 'who is this girl to be asking us questions?' This was how it was in the beginning. Then there were the stories on caste-related issues, on dowry, against certain higher castes or the panchayat, so there were threats of getting the newspaper shut down; of getting us raped, killed. We've always been receiving threats, back then, and even now. Or, we get trolled. The threats keep coming. Earlier, they would come to our face, now they come to us via trolls on Internet.

Then there is also the emotional stress of doing the kind of stories that we do. For instance, we go to report a story of a six-year-old who has been raped and it disturbs us, and we keep thinking about why such things happen, the trauma of the child who has been raped. On-ground reporting of dacoits, for instance—the crimes they commit also disturbs you. So, it is not just the threats, it is also the mental stress one goes through when reporting on crime. I think why we are able to do this is that at *Khabar Lahariya* we are from the community, we have reporters from farmer's homes, bonded labourer's daughters, women who have educated themselves against all odds, women who have seen these things happening around them and understand the issues and can write about them. Those who have experienced these things are the ones who can write about them because they identify with these experiences and understand the context and the nuances that perhaps reporters from the cities would not. I think it is the background of *Khabar Lahariya* reporters that gives us an advantage. When we have lived it we can write about it, whether caste-based issues, religious issues, rural concerns, forest issues.

What made you start The Kavita Show?

I started *The Kavita Show* because there was no such show that focussed on the women in the villages, the Dalit women. There were many shows, but none that spoke about the issues that mattered to these women. I thought that I should also do a show that spoke about these issues, under the banner of *Khabar Lahariya.*

When the world shifted to digital, it was an opportunity for Khabar Lahariya *to move beyond the boundaries of print, one that you took advantage of. Can you tell us about the decision to move to digital?*

Everything was going digital. People we would go to in the villages would say that the newspaper reached them much later, [but] the news reached them immediately via social media. Another reason for moving to digital was that print was proving to be very expensive to produce. We didn't take advertising, and that made production and distribution very difficult. So, we thought that now that phones have reached the villages and villagers are accessing news through the phone, we would be able to reach more people immediately.

We did a survey asking our readers what they would like. What we found was that people preferred to get their news on their phones, so we also decided to shift completely to digital. We've had many advantages in going digital. Our reach has increased substantially. We could reach potential readers in states we didn't have a physical presence in, not just in India, but we could reach the expatriate community as well around the world. We realized how wide a reach digital had. During the lockdown, people from Uttar Pradesh, who had moved to different states in India, turned to us [for] help when they were stranded and without food and resources.

You have been covering various issues from the grassroots level for years now. Have you seen any perceptible change in attitudes or do things continue to be the same?

We had kept an entire page in *Khabar Lahariya* dedicated to women's issues but sometimes we found it difficult to get enough content to fill an entire page. Now, there is so much violence against women—sexual harassment, rapes, abduction, murder—over the past 15 years, I've only seen it increasing. If I have seen any changes, for instance, we've done stories in the past about how women in the panchayat were just figureheads for their husbands but that has changed now. Women are coming forward now to do actual work in the panchayats, even though the percentage might be limited, even if it is just 2–4 per cent, but that in itself is a big change for us. With issues regarding caste discrimination, people are becoming more aware and that is also a good thing. We've seen positive change in the issue of bonded labourers. That has also substantially reduced. Where we haven't seen any positive change, it is regarding women's issues and violence against women. Crime and corruption have also not lessened, they keep rising.

If a young girl from the rural area wants to get into journalism like you have, what advice would you give her?

We've seen how women are kept away from the world at large and now denying them access to the phone is another way of limiting their circumference, when it is the era of the Internet right now. We realized that if young girls and women want to get into journalism, they will not only gain financial freedom, but also become agents of change. To this end, we began the Chambal Academy to train young girls and women from rural and underprivileged backgrounds to get into media. We launched it last year and we have two-three batches of students who have completed the course. Our students come from a wide section of society, from underprivileged castes and communities, Dalits and more. We've started a fellowship called the Rizwana Fellowship where girls come and study to be journalists. We want young girls from the rural areas to come and study to be journalists; not just journalists, if they want to be producers or Youtubers, make films. We want them to learn what they want to learn. We want the girls to come learn and become reporters, producers or whatever, and tell their stories and the stories of their villages and their people.

20

SINDHUTAI SAPKAL

MOTHER OF ORPHANS

Mai. This is what all her children called her. Mother. The mother of orphans, as Sindhutai Sapkal was called, was born on 14 November 1948, a year after India attained independence. She was born into a cow-herding family in Pimpri Meghe village in the Wardha district in what was then known as the Central Provinces and Berar. She was an unwanted child to her parents. They made no bones about the fact that she was unwanted; they gave her the unfortunate nickname of *Chindhi* or a rag in Marathi.

Interestingly, though, while as a norm the girls of the community were not educated, Sindhutai's father, Abhimanji Sathe, was keen to see his daughter educated, and managed to get her educated up to the fourth grade, even though her mother was dead set against the idea. Her father would send her to school under the pretext of sending her out to graze the cattle. She would use the leaves of the bharadi tree as a slate, as she could not afford a real slate. However, her education was destined to be short-lived. When she had barely passed the fourth grade, her family got her married off. She was only 12.

Her husband was much older than her, Shrihari Sapkal from Nawargaon village, Seloo, in Wardha. Her life, after marriage, was confined to domesticity, housework and the rigours of childbearing and rearing. Her husband did not like her reading and would beat her if he saw her reading. She would swallow pages of books and newspapers to avoid being caught reading and to escape a beating. By the time she was 20, she had given birth to three sons and was pregnant with her fourth child. At the time, the cow dung of the village was being collected by the strongmen of the village and being sold in cahoots with the forest department. The village women who made these dung cakes with their hard labour earned absolutely nothing from it.

Sindhutai was the only one from the village who protested against this practice, angry at the injustice of it all. To get back at her, rumours were spread about her infidelity, even while she was carrying a baby. To quote from an interview:

> My agitation brought the district collector to the village and on realizing I was right, he passed an order in our favor. This insulted the strongman of the village who managed to convince my husband to abandon me when I was beyond nine months of pregnancy. He thrashed me and kicked me on my full-term belly and threw me in a cowshed. I was in immense pain and lost my senses. When I woke up I found a baby girl next to me guarded by a cow. With much effort, I cut my umbilical cord with a stone, and then I passed out again.[1]

She took her newborn to her parents' home, but was turned away from there as well. She contemplated ending her life. She was left all alone in the world with her little daughter to look after. She was hungry and so was her daughter. She felt broken and was almost on the brink of death, but she had the responsibility of her child.

To quote her much later in life, 'Because I spoke for women's rights, the zamindar spread rumours about my character. So, my in-laws abandoned me and my mother too refused to stand by me. The sound of crushing my umbilical chord and the cry of my newborn child echo in my ears even after so many years.'[2]

She then went to a railway station, and stayed there, singing and begging from the passengers in order to feed herself and her child. To quote her:

> I was in my twenties with a child. Although I managed to fare in the day, I was afraid to sleep in the station at night. I feared the men so I took shelter in a crematory. No man would enter the place and so I chose it. This continued for many days and one day I saw a pyre. The last rites were over and the relatives of the departed had left. They had left some flour as an offering which I took kneaded and prepared a *bhakari* (roti) and baked it on the fire which was still consuming the dead body. There came scavengers to feed on the remains, and there was also a dead cow beside me being devoured by vultures. At that point, I had to leave and find the courage to carry on no matter what.[3]

She has also said that she contemplated suicide, but something would happen at that point and make her change her mind. To quote her, 'Yes, I wanted to die many times. But every time I tried, I failed. Once I was attempting suicide and there was a man in need of food. I gave him some roti and water and suddenly has an urge to live.'[4]

She then began visiting temples, travelling by train, begging and singing to survive. Thus, she wandered for many years, begging and feeding her child, and, in the process, feeding other children who had also been abandoned by their parents or were orphaned.

In the course of her wanderings, she reached Chikhaldara. According to a report in the weekly publication, *Optimist Citizen*, dated May 2016, she found that 84 tribal villages in Chikhaldara were evacuated because of a tiger conservation project. A project officer had impounded 132 cows of the Adivasi villagers and one of the cows had died in the process. She was very disturbed by the injustice of it all, and so began her journey as an activist.

She began an agitation to call attention to the situation the tribals faced. She met Chhedilal Gupta, the then minister of forests, and spoke to him about why the villagers should not be displaced before alternate arrangements to resettle them had been made. When then Prime Minister Indira Gandhi arrived for the inauguration of the conservation project, Sindhutai showed her the photograph of a man who had been brutally injured by a wild animal. Sindhutai argued that if a cow or a hen was lost to wild animals, their owners got compensation, so why were humans not given compensation for being displaced from their ancestral lands. Indira Gandhi immediately ordered that compensation be paid.[5]

She once found a young orphan begging for alms, and took him to the police station. No one paid heed to her or took down her complaint. She took him under her wing, and so began her mission of caring for abandoned and orphaned children. Her first adopted son, Deepak, now carries her legacy forward. It was at Chikhaldara that she opened her first orphanage. She later set up orphanages in Manjiri, Saswad and Wardha.[6] People who donated money asked her for a receipt, and so she realized that she needed to form an NGO. She registered her first NGO, the Savitribai Phule Girls' Hostel under the foundation Vanvasi Gopalkrushna Shikshan Evam Kreeda Prasarak Mandal, in Chikhaldara in Amravati.[7] The second one is named Mamta Bal Bhawan, after her biological daughter, Mamta. She also built a cow shelter, Gopika Gai Rakshan Kendra, to save old cows that were being sent to slaughter houses.

From needing support from others and finding none, to becoming the support for many, it was a long and ardous journey for Sindhutai. In her lifetime, she received over 700 awards for her work and ploughed back all the award money to buy land in order to build a home for orphans. She raised over 2,500 orphans and abandoned children. She built over six orphanages and shelter homes for abandoned women in her lifetime. She had the gift of being a fine raconteur. She could share her story with songs and humour, without watering down the tragedy she had faced in her life. She quoted effortlessly from the poet saints from Maharashtra—Tukaram, Namdeo, Bahinabai, Gadgebaba and Tukdoji Maharaj. She would also quote from Urdu poets, switching her discourse between Hindi and Marathi easily.

She would give inspiring talks on her life story and then ask the audience to contribute to her orphanages by spreading the loose end of her saree pallu. To quote her:

> I am still a beggar. Hunger is bigger than humans or humanity. Humans are not bad; it is hunger that turns people into baddies. Even today, I have so many children, who need to be fed every day. Therefore, I continue to beg, seek help from people like you. [...] I have no regrets. When I started these orphanages, I often requested my mother to come and stay with me, since there was no one to look after her. She, however, continuously refused, saying, 'When you needed my shelter, I threw you out, and now how can I seek shelter from you?' Today, I think, this journey would not have been possible, if my mother had not thrown me out.[8]

She took upon herself the onus of mothering all the abandoned children she came across. In a strange decision, she gave away her own daughter to the Shreemant Dagdusheth Halwai Trust to be cared for, in order to do away with the feeling that perhaps she wasn't impartial towards all the children.[9] To quote her on that decision, 'I used to think that my daughter will start getting possessive about me and I was also worried about her well-being and upbringing. That is when I entrusted my little Mamata to Shrimant Dagaduseth Halwai Trust so that she could be looked after properly. I told them you look after my child and I will look after other children.'[10]

She often said that she understands what it means to have no one to turn to, no shelter, no food, and the work she does is to help her heal her own wounds.[11] She went from being an unwanted child, disparagingly called Chindi by her parents, to a woman who took on the responsibility to raise over a thousand orphans in her lifetime, earning the title of Mai. From being cast away by her husband, with no home and no family to turn to, she came to have a large family of over 380 sons-in-law, nearly 50 daughters-in-law and over 1,000 grandchildren. Many of the children she raised are well-educated lawyers and doctors, and some, including her biological daughter, run their independent orphanages. All the children she raised have her name as their middle and last name. The boys use Sapkal as their surname and the girls use Sathe, her maiden surname as their last name.[12]

She especially cared for abandoned and orphaned girls, because she had grown up being an uncared child. At her orphanage, run on donations, she would feed, clothe and educate the children, and even get them married into good homes. She was soon called '*anathanchee aai*' or 'the mother of orphans'. She used to disagree with that title. To quote her, 'They are not orphans. I am their mother. *Aaj maze pora doctor zalet, vakil zaleet ani sahib sudha zalet* (Today my children have become doctors, lawyers and even big officers).' Most orphanages keep children till they turn 18. Sindhutai would keep her wards with her till they were married or had found jobs and were settled in life.[13]

She faced challenges in her work. In June 2016, the Department of Women and Child Development (WCD) of the state of Maharashtra wanted to take the orphans residing in her Sanmati Bal Niketan and place them in government orphanages, as the orphanage Sindhutai had founded was not registered with WCD.[14] It took an online petition that led to then Chief Minister Devendra Fadnavis granting special permission to Mai's orphanage.[15] Her work has all been funded by private donations. She didn't receive any governmental support for her work financially, except for the money from the awards she won.

When he was around 80, her husband came back to her, apologizing for his behaviour and how he had treated her. She was forgiving of him. To quote her: 'He continues to live in the jungle but he visits me sometimes. He's like one of my children now, *maine usse maaf kar diya hai* (I've forgiven him).'[16]

She passed away from a heart attack on 4 January 2022 in Pune. She was 74 at the time.[17] She was honoured with a state funeral at Pune's Thosar Paga crematorium. Upon her demise, PM Narendra Modi said, 'Dr Sindhutai Sapkal will be remembered for her noble service to society. Due to her efforts, many children could lead a better quality of life. She also did a lot of work among marginalised communities. Pained by her demise. Condolences to her family and admirers. Om Shanti.'[18] Her biological daughter and her son Deepak now carry forward their mother's life's work.

She was awarded multiple awards, including the Nari Shakti Puraskar from the President of India in 2017 and the Padma Shri in social work in 2021. She was also awarded an honorary doctorate by the Dr D.Y. Patil College of Engineering, Pune, in 2016.

Filmmaker Anant Mahadevan made a biopic on her life titled *Mee Sindhutai Sapkal* in 2010. The film was premiered at the 54th London Film Festival.

Her life could, perhaps, be encapsulated with these words, said by her: 'I have no complaints with the life I have led. It has only made me strong and helped me learn about the world. The world needs love, and can't exist without it.'[19]

NOTES

1 Tanima, 'Sindhutai Sapkal: A Mother to 1400+ Orphans and Her Incredible Legacy', *Life Beyond Numbers*, 8 May 2022, http://tinyurl.com/mtjf3u5e. Accessed on 10 January 2024.

2 Jaipurkar, Anoop, 'Sindhutai Was Alone Yet She Gave New

Life to More than 2,500 Orphans', *The Federal*, 5 January 2022, http://tinyurl.com/mrp58cj5. Accessed on 17 January 2024.

3 Tanima, 'Sindhutai Sapkal: A Mother to 1400+ Orphans and Her Incredible Legacy', *Life Beyond Numbers*, 8 May 2022, http://tinyurl.com/mtjf3u5e. Accessed on 10 January 2024.

4 Ibid.

5 'Sindhutai Sapkal: The "Mother of Orphans" Who Fought for Empowerment of Downtrodden', *News9*, 5 January 2022, http://tinyurl.com/2drywdxn. Accessed on 5 January 2024.

6 Satyajit, Anita, 'Sindhutai Sapkal Was Begging at Train Stations When She Found Her Calling—Helping Street Children', *The Christian Science Monitor*, 10 December 2015, http://tinyurl.com/mshvfa96. Accessed on 5 January 2024.

7 Paharia, Raksha, 'The Story of Sindhutai Sapkal - A Mother to Orphaned Children', *eSamskriti*, September 2018, http://tinyurl.com/mrstkreu. Accessed on 17 January 2024.

8 Sapkale, Yogesh, 'Sindhutai Sapkal: A Life of Immense Courage and Determination', *Moneylife*, 5 January 2022, http://tinyurl.com/58rvhn7y. Accessed on 5 January 2024.

9 Majumdar, Swapna, 'Beyond Begging: Meet the Mother of a Thousand Orphans', *WOMEN'SeNews*, 21 May 2018, http://tinyurl.com/25jj4p6x. Accessed on 24 January 2024.

10 Tanima, 'Sindhutai Sapkal: A Mother to 1400+ Orphans and Her Incredible Legacy', *Life Beyond Numbers*, 8 May 2022, http://tinyurl.com/mtjf3u5e. Accessed on 10 January 2024.

11 Satyajit, Anita, 'Sindhutai Sapkal Was Begging at Train Stations When She Found Her Calling—Helping Street Children', *The Christian Science Monitor*, 10 December 2015, http://tinyurl.com/mshvfa96. Accessed on 5 January 2024.

12 Sapkale, Yogesh, 'Sindhutai Sapkal: A Life of Immense Courage and Determination', *Moneylife*, 5 January 2022, http://tinyurl.com/58rvhn7y. Accessed on 5 January 2024.

13 Jaipurkar, Anoop, 'Sindhutai Was Alone Yet She Gave New Life to More than 2,500 Orphans', *The Federal*, 5 January 2022, http://tinyurl.com/mrp58cj5. Accessed on 17 January 2024;

Sindhutai Sapkal.org, http://tinyurl.com/s9mjsc2v. Accessed on 17 January 2024.

14 Daga, Darshana, '"Mother of Orphans" Running Illegal Children's Home', *Pune Mirror*, 25 June 2016, http://tinyurl.com/yc5j935r. Accessed on 5 January 2024.

15 Sapkale, Yogesh, 'Sindhutai Sapkal: A Life of Immense Courage and Determination', *Moneylife*, 5 January 2022, http://tinyurl.com/58rvhn7y. Accessed on 5 January 2024; Deshmukh, Vinita, 'Moneylife Impact: CM Assures Sindhutai Sapkal of Special Permission for Her Orphanage', *Moneylife*, 5 July 2016, http://tinyurl.com/2cz4sejr. Accessed on 5 January 2024.

16 Bhattacharya, Roshmila, '"My Husband Still Refuses to Accept Our Daughter as His Own"', *Hindustan Times*, 10 November 2010, http://tinyurl.com/4cvyvdr3. Accessed on 5 January 2024.

17 PTI, 'Social Worker Sindhutai Sapkal, "Orphan Children's Mother", Dies', *India Today*, 5 January 2022, http://tinyurl.com/ym8998vu. Accessed on 17 January 2024.

18 PTI, 'Sindhutai Sapkal Will Be Remembered for Her Noble Service to Society: PM Modi', *Deccan Herald*, 5 January 2022, http://tinyurl.com/msr7mwch. Accessed on 5 January 2024.

19 Tanima, 'Sindhutai Sapkal: A Mother to 1400+ Orphans and Her Incredible Legacy', *Life Beyond Numbers*, 8 May 2022, http://tinyurl.com/mtjf3u5e. Accessed on 10 January 2024.

ACKNOWLEDGEMENTS

I owe the Rising series to Saswati Bora, who commissioned me to write the first one, and Nishtha Kapil, who believed there was a second book in the series.

To Rupa Publications who believed and supported it; to Geetu Martolia who has been fierce in getting the first book, *Rising*, the visibility it received, thank you. Gratitude to Sagareeka Pradhan for her eagle eye over the copy, given I am so not the 'devil is in the details' kind of person. To Suhail Mathur of The Book Bakers, thank you for all the support through the books you represent for me.

Gratitude to Seema Rao, Garima Arora and Kavita Devi Bundelkhandi for taking time out to speak with me.

For the lovely cover, gratitude to Amrita Chakravorty.

And, of course, I would be remiss if I didn't thank my family for putting up with me when I'm this unbearable creature constantly at her desk when I'm in the midst of writing a book.